RECEIVED **DATE DUE**

| APR | 2 5 2005 | | |
|---|---|---|---|
| | | | |
| | | | |
| | | | |
| | | | |
| | | | |
| | | | |
| | | | |
| | | | |
| | | | |
| | | | |
| | | | |
| | | | |
| | | | |
| | | | |
| | | | |
| | | | |

Demco, Inc. 38-293

# JUSTICE MATTERS

# JUSTICE
# MATTERS

*Legacies of the Holocaust
and World War II*

*Mona Sue Weissmark*

OXFORD
UNIVERSITY PRESS

2004

# OXFORD
UNIVERSITY PRESS

Oxford   New York
Auckland   Bangkok   Buenos Aires   Cape Town   Chennai
Dar es Salaam   Delhi   Hong Kong   Istanbul   Karachi   Kolkata
Kuala Lumpur   Madrid   Melbourne   Mexico City   Mumbai   Nairobi
São Paulo   Shanghai   Taipei   Tokyo   Toronto

Copyright © 2004 by Oxford University Press, Inc.

Published by Oxford University Press, Inc.
198 Madison Avenue, New York, New York 10016

www.oup.com

Oxford is a registered trademark of Oxford University Press

Library of Congress Cataloging-in-Publication Data
Weissmark, Mona Sue.
Justice matters : legacies of the Holocaust and World War II / Mona Sue Weissmark.
p.   cm.
ISBN 0-19-515757-5
1. Holocaust, Jewish (1939–1945)—Influence.   2. Holocaust, Jewish (1939–1945)—Germany—
Influence.   3. Holocaust, Jewish (1939–1945)—Germany—Public opinion.   4. Public opinion—
Germany.   5. Children of Holocaust survivors—Attitudes.   6. Children of Nazis—Germany—
Attitudes.   I. Title.
D804.44.W45 2003
940.53'18—dc21     2003048685

9 8 7 6 5 4 3 2 1

Printed in the United States of America
on acid-free paper

# DEDICATION

I dedicate this book to my unknown relatives who perished in obscurity: my aunts, my uncles, my cousins, my grandparents, my great-grandparents, all of whom were killed at concentration camps. The youngest died at about age four at Auschwitz, the oldest at eighty-seven at Dachau, the others apparently killed at Treblinka and Buchenwald. Because their names were never recorded, their bodies never buried, I offer this book as a memorial. May it convey my compassion for the injustices they suffered. And I dedicate this book to Pastor Seebasz's family—his wife, sons, and daughters—for saving my father's life. And finally to my little daughter, Brittany Weissmark Giacomo. So that you may realize your own legacy with a winged heart.

# ACKNOWLEDGMENTS

A program of research spanning more than ten years is possible only with much help. I am grateful to many people.

To my husband, Daniel Giacomo, whose love and care have kept me steady in the wind. He is my research partner, without whom this book would not be possible.

To my daughter, Brittany Weissmark Giacomo, whose birth and being have stretched my heart.

To my former teacher at the University of Pennsylvania, Aron Katsenelinboigen, whose instruction and wisdom have guided my thinking about justice matters.

To my former teacher at Harvard, Brendan Maher, whose methodological guidance and research have taught me how to test my thinking about matters of justice.

To my former colleagues at Harvard, Myron Belfer, Emily Cahan, Jill Hooley, and Robert Rosenthal, whose intellectual support and encouragement have enabled me to organize the first-ever meeting for the descendants of Nazis and of Holocaust survivors at the Harvard Education Medical Center.

To Gerald Posner, author of *Hitler's Children*, whose unselfish help and generosity made it possible for me to locate the children of Nazis.

To Ilona Kuphal, the daughter of a Waffen SS officer, whose kindness and hard work made it possible for me to invite other children of Nazis to participate in the meeting.

To my colleagues at Roosevelt University, Judith Dygdon, Stuart Fagan, Ted Gross, Jonathan Smith, Ronald Tallman and Lynn Weiner, whose support and encouragement have enabled me to organize the first-ever meeting for the descendants of slaves and of slave owners at Roosevelt University.

To my research participants, whose willingness and involvement have enabled me to examine the emotional impact of injustice.

To the students in my research methods courses at Harvard and Roosevelt, whose curiosity and enthusiasm have compelled me to learn more about justice matters.

To the Mansfield family foundation, whose commitment and generosity have provided me with the opportunity to set up an Institute for Social Justice at Roosevelt University.

To Joan Bossert, vice president and associate publisher of Oxford University Press, whose support and belief in the manuscript brought it out into the world.

To Kim Robinson, assistant editor of Oxford University Press, whose skill and patience helped ready the manuscript for the Press.

To Melita Garza, columnist for the *Chicago Tribune*, whose help and talent helped better the manuscript.

And to my childhood friends, Mara Lund and Beth Roth, whose support and tolerance have helped me bear the pains of injustice.

I am also grateful to Dieter Dettke, executive director of the Friedrich Ebert Foundation in Washington D.C.; Miles Lerman, chairman emeritus, United States Holocaust Museum; Bill Niven, Reader in German at the Nottingham Trent University in Great Britain; and Rudolf Klepfisz, my father's childhood best friend and fellow concentration camp survivor.

Finally, I am grateful to Michael Betzle and Ellen Fauser, both in Germany, for helping me find Pastor Julius Seebasz's daughter, Sister Renate of the Convent of the Holy Name, in Great Britain; and Pastor Seebasz's son, Pastor Johannes Seebasz, in Bad Harzburg, Germany.

Mere words are but empty expressions in thanking Sister Renate, Pastor Johannes Seebasz, and their family for saving my father's life. They not only saved his life but made my life possible. Their compassion for a stranger's anguish gives me faith. That faith lies in my heart. May it help my little daughter Brittany go forth without a wound in her spirit.

# CONTENTS

# JUSTICE MATTERS

# INTRODUCTION

My mother and father, survivors of Auschwitz, Dachau, and Buchenwald, had decided not to frighten me with their recollections about the death camps. They were determined to make my childhood happy. Not that the past was a forbidden topic with my parents. They spoke truthfully about their experiences in concentration camp, but only when asked.

I can't pinpoint exactly when I first learned that, apart from my parents, every family member (besides a few cousins) was killed by the Nazis. No one ever sat me down and told me such things had happened. I would learn about the past haphazardly, shocked by each new discovery.

My mother kept an old yellow faded photograph in an envelope, next to her bed. It was a picture of a man sitting next to a wide-eyed little boy. The man's shoulder rested against the little boy's. Both had dark hair and sad eyes. To the best of my recollection our conversation went like this:

"Mommy, who are they?" I asked when I was about eight or nine.

"That's my father," said my mother.

"Where is he?"

"He was killed."

"Why, did he do something bad?" I asked.

"No," said my mother. "The people who killed him were mean and very bad."

"Who's that boy sitting next to him?"

"That's my little brother."

"And where is he?"

"He was killed too."

"How, Mommy, how was the boy killed?"

My mother hesitated. She worried about answering me, yet she did not want to lie.

"One night my little brother was crying because he had a terrible pain on his side. We were living in the ghetto then. So it was impossible to get medical help. But my father managed to get my brother to a hospital. It was his appendix. They had to remove it. My father paid a doctor to do the surgery. A few days later the ghetto was liquidated. We were rounded up, put on the trains, and taken to the camps. My brother was taken to Treblinka. Someone who survived Treblinka told me the day they arrived at Treblinka they were told to run fast. My brother couldn't run; he was convalescing from the surgery. So a guard shot him. He was ten years old."

"Why would the guard do that?" I asked.

My mother looked startled. "The guard was German. The Germans were the bad people, very bad. They hated the Jews," my mother said. "Enough already with the questions. We have things to do now."

This and other stories of injustice had me trying to imagine the horrors that contained my mother's and father's history. I wanted to hear more, but as usual, my mother pushed aside the past for what was, for her, the far more important task of making sure it didn't intrude on my childhood. Still, try as she did, the past was always there—an abyss that cried out for an answer.

I never stopped asking my parents questions. One question after another: Who put those numbers on your arms? How did my aunts, uncles, and grandparents die? Did the guards ever hurt you? How did the Germans know you were Jewish? Findings about the atrocities greatly affected my young mind. What inquisitive child could simply accept the Nazi assault on humanity? What child could avoid wondering how those bad people could fairly be punished for the atrocities they committed? I could only guess about those bad people because my parents never described them directly.

## Eichmann's Trial

My earliest memory of actually seeing one of those bad people is when I saw my mother in front of the television watching the trial of Adolf Eichmann (1961). I was about seven then, and for the first time, I actually saw one of those bad people. "Who is that, Mommy?" "That's him. One of those bad German people," said my mother. "He killed my family."

To this day, I remember seeing Eichmann sitting within an armored glass booth. To a child, he looked like a monster, evil incarnate. Gideon Hausner, the attorney general who first saw Eichmann when the trial opened, wrote that Eichmann had "disconcerting eyes," which during the cross-examination "burned with bottomless hatred." A closer look, the attorney general wrote, revealed that he also had "hands like talons"—a photograph of his fingers was published in the press and was, Hausner said, "frightening" (cited in Segev, 2000, p. 345).

Settling accounts, I thought then, was a straightforward procedure. An evil monster with hands like talons killed my family, so punish the monster. We're the good people. They're the bad people. We're the source of all virtue, with a few defects. They are the personification of all that is bad. Getting even, for me, was a matter of simple justice. It was a view shared by many Holocaust survivors and their families. Hausner encapsulated this view in his opening statement at the Eichmann trial. His speech began:

> As I stand before you, judges of Israel, to lead the prosecution of Adolf Eichmann, I am not standing alone. With me are six million accusers. But they cannot rise to their feet to point an accusing finger toward the glass booth and cry out at the man sitting there, "I accuse." For their ashes are piled up on the hills of Auschwitz and the fields of Treblinka, washed by the rivers of Poland, and their graves are scattered the length and breadth of Europe. Their blood cries out, but their voices cannot be heard. I, therefore, will be their spokesman and will pronounce, in their names, this awesome indictment. (cited in Segev, 2000, p. 347)

Then came what Hausner called in his memoirs "the parade of the Holocaust witnesses." More than a hundred Holocaust survivors were called as "background witnesses." Hausner instructed the witnesses to recount every horrifying detail of the atrocities they had endured (cited in Segev, 2000, pp. 350–351). For instance, Rivka Joselewska testified how "SS soldiers had shot the people of her village after ordering them to undress and stand at the edge of a deep pit; her parents and sister were shot before her eyes by a single SS solider. Then it was her turn. She held her daughter in her arms. The German asked her which to shoot first, her or her daughter. She did not answer. He shot the girl. Then he shot her and she fell into the pit. 'I thought I was dead,' she related. She was under a pile of bodies; many of them were still dying. She began to suffocate: 'People were dragging, biting, scratching, pulling me down'" (cited in Segev, 2000, p. 351). Other witnesses spoke of the abuse of children, the elderly, the ill, and religious Jews in traditional dress. And still others spoke about the gas chambers with an insufficient quantity of gas, the brutal smashing of babies to save ammunition, and the burning of people alive.

As witness followed witness and horror was piled upon horror, to a child's eye the figure in the glass became more ghostlike. There, I thought, sits the monster responsible for killing my aunts, uncles, grandparents. He committed crimes against my family, humanity, and the Jewish people. Eichmann deserves to be killed. The judges agreed. After several months, the court pronounced judgment. Eichmann was convicted of crimes against humanity and the Jewish people and was sentenced to death. He was hanged in Israel in the evening of May 31, 1962. His body was burned, and the ashes scattered at sea, outside Israel's territorial waters.

As I grew older, I continued to think about principles of justice. Although legal justice was served, my feeling of indignation did not go away. I was indignant at the immoral, unjust, wrong, bad, heinous (I use these terms interchangeably) acts of the Nazis. My indignation was provoked by my parents' and the witnesses' accounts of how they were treated. They were abused, degraded, and humiliated. They were not just victims of some misfortune; they were subject to extreme disrespect. The degrading treatment they received at the hands of another broke all social rules under which people of a moral community are expected to live. All people are entitled by virtue of their humanity the right to be treated in a way that fosters positive self-regard (Rawls, 1971).

The violation of how my parents ought to have been treated was an insult to their integrity. And it provoked in me both indignation and the urge to punish the wrongdoers. The judicial proceedings did not satisfy that urge fully. Legal punishment gave me a brief satisfaction, but in the end my sense of injustice was not fully appeased. Legal justice could not wipe away the stain of injustice as I experienced it, because more than legal or material violations were involved. The injustices of the Holocaust were of such magnitude and scale that the agencies of law seemed inadequate to address the wrongdoing.

I mention this here not as a remark upon the law but to show how complex the notion of injustice is. Indeed, this book has no distinct bearing upon legal justice. My subject is personal injustice—that is to say, how we experience injustice and the ways in which we respond to it. My response to the injustices that my parents suffered was not just a call for legal procedures, but for revenge. I was outraged by the degrading treatment my parents suffered. And I felt the need to "get even." Getting even for my parents was a personal matter. It was between those evil anti-Semitic German people and me.

### Hannah Arendt's Conclusions

But who were those people, exactly? Did they feel accountable for the wrong that they had done? What were the perpetrators' responses to their unjust acts? I first encountered Hannah Arendt's answer to these questions as a high school student during the 1970s. Hannah Arendt's book on the Eichmann trial contended that most Germans were not evil anti-Semitic monsters. Arendt argued that the prosecution's effort to depict Eichmann as a sadistic monster was wrong. A monster was needed, she concluded, to make sense of the awful memories of the Holocaust survivors and to keep faith in the social order.

But for Arendt, Nazi Germany could not be understood as some monstrous outcome of a sick German psyche. For Arendt, Eichmann and the vast majority of Germans were not evil monsters. Rather, they were just bureaucrats, ordinary people who were "terribly and terrifyingly normal" (Arendt, 1964, p. 276). This, according to Arendt, was the essence of the Nazi ideological context: it was typified not by the sadistic perversions or anti-Semitic hostilities that were let loose under its influence but rather by its ability to corrupt a person's moral qualities. So encompassing was the context that not even the victims were immune (Arendt, 1964). According to Arendt, Jewish leaders and Jewish councils helped in the killing of Jews. They organized deportations and handed the people over to their killers. Arendt's point was that any person's moral behavior could be altered by placing it in a particular context.

In a January 1945 essay titled "Organized Guilt and Universal Responsibility," Arendt was already pursuing the thesis that would lead to the conclusion that Eichmann's "evil" grew out of the encompassing context. She wrote that Himmler

> consciously built up his newest terror organization, covering the whole country, on the assumption that most people are not Bohemians nor fanatics, nor adventurers, nor sex maniacs, nor sadists, but, first and foremost, job-holders and good family men. . . . It became clear that for the sake of his pension, his life insurance, the security of his wife and children, such a man was ready to sacrifice his beliefs, his honor, and his human dignity. . . . The only condition he put was that he should be fully exempted from responsibility for his acts. Thus that very person, the average German, whom the Nazis notwithstanding years of the most furious propaganda could not induce to kill Jews (not even when they made it quite clear that such a murder would go unpunished) now serves the machine of destruction without opposition. (Arendt, 1978, p. 232)

Many people, including me, found Arendt's conclusions disturbing, even infuriating. How could normal people commit such heinous, immoral acts? Somehow, it was felt that the horrific deeds carried out by Eichmann required a brutal, sadistic personality. It required irrational, anti-Semitic hatred. From a Jewish viewpoint, it felt like Arendt was belittling the horrific nature of the deed: the mass killings of innocent Jewish victims. The extraordinary nature of the deed, it was felt, required an extraordinary explanation. The conclusion that Eichmann's unjust acts were "banal," that they grew out of mundane causes, felt deficient. And Arendt's assertion that the victims were not immune to the moral collapse felt like she was "blaming the victims."

Arendt was widely attacked for her conclusions. She was vilified for her interpretation of Eichmann and the trial and her discussion of the Jewish leadership and of how the deportations were organized. "For asserting [her] views, Arendt became the object of considerable scorn, even calumny" (Milgram, 1974, p. 5). "There were those," according to Segev, "who said she wished to minimize Eichmann's guilt and that of all Nazis, and to accuse the Jews themselves" (Segev, 2002, p. 360). Some critics attacked Arendt personally, declaring that she herself was influenced by anti-Semitic thinking. Yet other critics said that she distorted the truth and sullied the "honor of the dead." The scholar Gershom Scholem denounced her for not having shown enough "love for the Jewish people" (cited in Segev, 2000, p. 360). One critic said Arendt was arrogant, devoid of compassion, to reach such a sweeping verdict of the Jewish leadership (Bondy, 1981). Another critic said, "Miss Arendt does not convey reliable information. She has misread many of the documents and books referred to in her text and bibliography. She has not equipped herself with the necessary background for an understanding and analysis of the trial" (Robinson, 1965, p. viii). "In all discussions that touch on legal problems, Miss. Arendt displays unfamiliarity with her subject. She knows neither the present status of international criminal law nor its history and development. . . . She misreads and misinterprets the Israel law under which Eichmann was tried, and she fails to comprehend the basis for, and factual history of, the war crimes trials in general" (Robinson, 1965, p. 100). And finally, some critics said her conclusions were liable to give aid and comfort to neo-Nazis (Novick, 1999; Segev, 2000).

However, the psychiatric reports on Eichmann lent support to Arendt's conclusions. The psychiatrists who examined Eichmann before the trial described him as "normal," a man whose life in exile made him seem a pillar of the community, even a model father and husband. And during the court proceedings Eichmann himself declared that he was just following orders and was not a monster: "I see that my hope for a just trial has been disappointed. . . . my guilt is only in my obedience, my dutiful service in time of war, my loyalty to the oath, to the flag. . . . I did not persecute Jews with eagerness and passion. That the government did. . . . I would now like to request the forgiveness of the Jewish people and to confess that I am ashamed at the memory of what was inflicted on them. . . . I am not the monster that was depicted here . . ." (cited in Segev, 2000. pp. 356–357).

Throughout the trial, Eichmann tried to clarify his plea of "not guilty in the sense of the indictment." The indictment implied that he acted in full knowledge of the criminal nature of his deeds, but Eichmann maintained that what he had done was a crime only in retrospect. He had always been a law-abiding citizen, because Hitler's orders, which he had executed to the best of his ability, had possessed the "force of the law" in the Third Reich. And for his motives, Eichmann said he was not what he called an *innerer Schwinehund*, a dirty bastard in the depths of his heart (Arendt, 1964, pp. 24–25).

Similarly, and perhaps, even more shocking was Auschwitz Camp

Commandant Rudolf Hoess' statement. While awaiting his war-crimes trial, Auschwitz Camp Commandant Rudolf Hoess declared that he was not a cruel sadist, just a loyal follower of a righteous cause. In his autobiography Hoess wrote:

> I regarded the National Socialist attitude to the world as the only one suited to the German people. I believed that the SS was the most energetic champion of this attitude and that the SS alone was capable of gradually bringing the German people back to its proper way of life. My second worship was my family. To them I was securely anchored. My thoughts were always with their future, and our farm was to become their permanent home. In our children both my wife and I saw our aim in life. To bring them up so that they could play their part in the world, and to give them all a steady home, was our one task in life. . . . Unknowingly I was a cog in the wheel of the great extermination machine created by the Third Reich. . . . Let the public continue to regard me as the blood-thirsty beast, the cruel sadist and the mass murderer; for the masses could never imagine the commandant of Auschwitz in any other light. They could never understand that he, too, had a heart and that he was not evil. (Hoess, 1959, pp. 180–181)

### Milgram's Experiments

But, it was Stanley Milgram's experimental evidence that lent the most convincing support to Arendt's thesis. Milgram carried out a series of experiments at Yale University from 1960 through 1963. Eleven years later, Milgram (1974) wrote a book describing the experiments. His book, *Obedience to Authority: An Experimental View*, supported Arendt's argument that ordinary people will hurt innocent victims when told to do so by a legitimate authority.

Milgram chose 80 ordinary people of various ages and occupational backgrounds and asked them to take part in what he said was an important scientific experiment on learning. The subjects were required to teach a list of word pairs to a "learner" (the experimenter's confederate) and to punish errors by delivering shock of increasing intensity. The subjects were urged by the experimenter to raise the amount of electricity higher and higher—and most did, even though the "learner" shouted that the shocks were painful and later began to groan and finally scream in pain. Moreover, like Eichmann and Hoess, Milgram's subjects claimed their immoral actions were justifiable, given the context. They shocked the victim out of a sense of obligation to the experimenter and not from any sadistic or hostile tendencies (Milgram, 1974, p. 6).

Arendt's and Milgram's books and Eichmann's and Hoess' testimony created a difficulty for me. Their assertions presented an opposing viewpoint. It challenged the commonly offered explanation that those who shock victims at the most severe level or partake in the mass killing and brutalizing of people were monsters, the sadistic fringe of society. It suggested the dismaying conclusion that good people can commit unjust, heinous acts. Arendt's and Milgram's work and the perpetrators' statements showed that shocking victims, the dehumanizing treatment of Jews, even the act of killing acquired a different meaning when it served an ideological cause: far from appearing as a heinous act, it was changed into a virtue. Thus, I was confronted with questioning my image of the perpetrators. If they were not evil monsters, then I could not assume that the perpetrators failed to share my values and morality. Settling accounts, I realized then, was not a straightforward procedure.

## Justice as Intergenerational

The debate about whether the injustices of the Holocaust were carried out by sadistic, anti-Semitic Nazis or by ordinary people whose moral qualities were corrupted by an all-encompassing context persists today. This book focuses, however, not on the debate per se, but rather on the opposing viewpoints to the children of both the perpetrators and victims. I was teaching a course at Harvard when the idea struck me: Injustice is an intergenerational matter. Viewpoints and feelings, including those about the "other side," are passed from one generation to the next. If the perpetrators did not perceive themselves as evil, then what about their children? How had these children perceived their fathers' unjust acts? Injustice is an interpersonal matter too. As Aristotle asserted, "For a man can give something away if he likes, but he cannot suffer injustice if he likes—there must be somebody else to do him the injustice" (Aristotle, 1955, p. 163).

With this hypothesis in mind, which derived from my experiences, my first task was to search the literature. I found many books had studied the psychological effects of the Holocaust on the descendants of the survivors. And several books had studied the psychological effects of the Holocaust on the descendants of Nazis, but at the time there were no attempts to study the two groups together. Moreover, the research was predominantly individuocentric, psychoanalytic, and pathological in focus, unconcerned with how historic injustices thread together the two sets of descendants as they adapt to an unjust historic event.

Previous psychological studies overlooked how stories about past injustices are transmitted from former Nazi parent or survivor parent to child, how the offspring of both sides make sense of the stories, the way the stories influence their identities and rebalance an injustice in their lives. There were no studies relating to the actual experiences of offspring whose parents inflicted injustice or of those whose parents suffered injustice. In short, there was no research on the quality of emotions or cognitive processes that follow perception of a past injustice. To advance the research in this area, during the fall of 1991 I undertook a study with my husband, Daniel Giacomo, then a Harvard psychiatrist, and a team of students at Harvard to learn more about the different ways in which thoughts, feelings, and behavior of injustice manifest themselves in the lives of descendants of Nazis and survivors.

How had these children of victims and of perpetrators dealt with their heritage, with the past injustices and their parents' involvement in those injustices? How had they found out about the past injustices? How had they made sense of the stories transmitted to them by their parents? What impact did it have on their identities? What coping responses did they use to deal with the past injustices? How had they tried to rebalance the past injustices in their present lives? Did the children of concentration camp survivors want to avenge the injustices their parents suffered? Did the children of Nazis feel their parents' roles in those injustices were justified? And how did they view the descendants of the other side?

## Justice as Interpersonal

Also I undertook, as a later aim, to organize the first meeting between children of Nazis and children of concentration camp survivors to examine how injustice influences interpersonal behavior. How would the offspring of survivors and Nazis react to the idea of participating in a joint meeting? Could children of survivors and Nazis talk to each other about the Holocaust and World II and understand the anxieties of each about the other as a gateway to establishing a relationship? Could they face the others' passions and viewpoints? How would children of survivors respond to hearing children of Nazis tell stories about how their parents suffered during the war? And how would children of Nazis respond to hearing children of survivors tell stories about how their parents suffered during the Holocaust?

Could children of Nazis understand and acknowledge the roots of pain that for children of survivors go back to the Holocaust? On the other hand, could children of survivors understand and acknowledge the roots of fear that for children of Nazis go back to World War II? Or would resentment and indignation stand as fatal obstacles to restoring equal moral relations between Nazis' children and survivors' children?

I knew the answers could only be found by bringing the groups together and observing them interact. There was no published work in this area. So I undertook to study children of survivors and Nazis coming to terms with the past and each other to benefit our understanding of the interpersonal effects of injustice. It was an exciting moment for me. I realized that these simple questions were both humanly important and capable of being empirically studied. The study brought 22 Jews and Germans together for a four-day meeting at the Harvard Medical Education Center.

The idea to study the descendants of Holocaust survivors and Nazis together was an intuitive and simple one. But the idea was seen as breaking a taboo. Many people feared that my study would be interpreted as a justification of Nazism or as a challenge to the Holocaust's status as the symbol of absolute evil. Or as a voice of moral obtuseness. The implication was that the study would obfuscate the distinction between good and evil.

But there is a difference between "understand" and "condone." Hearing the other side, seeing another view, only means we use thinking in an open manner, in contrast to a closed, biased manner. It means we consider conflicting viewpoints advanced by individuals and by groups within a society. It does not mean we forgive or excuse or approve their viewpoints or that "anything goes." And since the purpose of research is to foster our reasoning powers, studying opposing viewpoints should lead to a more elevated level of critical thought.

The previously mentioned fears may have inhibited others from proposing such a study and may explain why my study struck a chord. Besides the magazine publications in which the study featured, including *Psychology Today, Ms.*, and *Harvard Magazine*, the study received coverage in the *New York Times*, the *Boston Herald*, and several other daily newspapers. The study was also featured on many radio and TV shows, including National Public Radio's *All Things Considered*, the BBC, the *CBS Sunday Morning News*, and on international TV and radio programs in Germany, Canada, and England.

*Justice Matters: Legacies of the Holocaust and World War II* is the first book to describe what takes place when children of survivors and Nazis try to come to terms with the past and each other. What the Germans call *Verganenheitsbewältigung*—mastering the past, coming to terms with their parents' experiences of the Holocaust and World War II—is a painful and difficult legacy. It is also the legacy of a shattered relationship. Unlike other books on the Holocaust and the Second World War, *Justice Matters* explores this shattered relationship.

Most existing books fall into three categories: (1) books by scholars giving historical information and analyses, (2) books by psychologists using a psychoanalytic, pathological framework, and (3) oral testimonies. On the oral testimonies list, most of these focus on the traumatic impact of the events of the Holocaust on its surviving victims and on the children of the victims. A few testimonial books study the Nazi perpetrators and the children of the perpetrators. These focus on understanding the evil crimes and how Nazis and their children dealt with the crimes. Both categories of testimonial books approach the subject from a single point of view.

## Justice Matters

*Justice Matters* is the first book to show how survivors' children and Nazis' children develop different points of view. The emphasis is on understanding the Holocaust and World War II from a subjective perspective. Two peoples, two staggeringly different truths. How do people's points of view develop? What decides a person's particular viewpoint? Drawing on interviews and the conference findings, the book uncovers a complex story and reveals how unjust, painful events of decades past continue to shape the legacies of survivors' children and Nazis' children. *Justice Matters* is unique because it is the only book to show what happens when children of Holocaust survivors come face to face with the children of Nazis in a first-of-its-kind study aimed at understanding the interpersonal effects of injustice (Weissmark, 1993, 2000; Weissmark, Giacomo, & Yaw, 1996).

Thinking and writing about the Harvard study went on long after it had been conducted. A year later, in 1993, I conducted a replication study in Germany. Like the Harvard study, it too struck a chord. The study was featured in international newspapers such as the *Frankfurter Allgemeine Zeitung* and on many radio and TV shows, including *Dateline NBC*. Then, in 1995, I joined the faculty at Roosevelt University in Chicago. At Roosevelt, I continued to explore the influence of injustice on people's lives. I organized the first-ever meeting for the descendants of slaves and slaveholders. PBS television depicted the study in a program called *Coming to the Table*. And the study received front-page coverage in several daily newspapers, among them the *Chicago Tribune* and the *Chicago Sun Times*, and in such publications as *Psychology Today* and *She* magazine.

In 1995, I wrote a proposal to establish an Institute for Social Justice at Roosevelt University to promote the research program I had developed (Weissmark, 1995). In 1999, through a generous gift from the Mansfield family foundation, the Mansfield Institute for Social Justice was established. The newly established Institute, which I founded and directed, has given me a unique opportunity to develop an integrated program of research, outreach, and curriculum focused on social justice matters.

Now it is time for me to write about the research that has played such an important part in my own personal and professional life. Unlike others who have written about the Holocaust and World War II, I do not bring to the project a lifetime of historical or political or holocaust study. Instead I bring a lifetime of psychological studies and practice coupled with a solid grounding in research methods. My research, as described earlier, has been informed by my personal experiences.

Employing one's own experiences to expand knowledge is, after all, a central feature of the scientific method. The researcher's experiences are the starting points for constructing hypotheses, by making a theoretical guess as to the significance or meaning of a given fact (Rosenthal & Rosnow, 1991). They are also the concluding points for interpreting the data, by underscoring certain aspects of the data. Throughout this book I use both voices: the personal voice and the researcher's voice. I try to use my personal experiences to raise new hypotheses about the effects of injustice on people's lives and to provide new conclusions and insights into how it influences interpersonal relationships.

I make no claim of being "right," of having the final truth. My goal is simply to stimulate discussion among readers who share my fascination with the influence of justice matters on people's lives. I can remember when I was a student of Professor Brendan Maher at Harvard. Maher taught me to cast a cold eye on the final truth. And he taught me to be wary of accepting other people's ideas about the truth, including leading intellectual authorities. His core course, *Conceptions of Human Nature*, focused on critically examining different viewpoints (Freud, Skinner, E. O. Wilson, Marx) of human nature.

By the end of the term, there were always many students who said "OK, Professor Maher, we know what's wrong with these viewpoints, now which one is right?" Maher's response to that kind of question was that "If you're convinced you've got the final truth, there is a great danger that you will close your mind to the possibility that you are in error." The moral of the course, Maher would say, is that "We must learn to live in doubt, yet act based on our critical judgment" (Maher, 2003).

I hope readers of this book enjoy the glimpses into my research, question its conclusions critically, and test the implication in their own lives. "Good" conclusions are good only as far as they inspire questions for beginnings. A key part of successful research is a mutual criticism that keeps those who are criticizing each other involved in further innovation. So I hope the work reported here will serve as a useful point of departure for future work, both empirical and theoretical.

### Can Good People Pursue Heinous Acts?

Chapter 2 explores the critical question "Can good people pursue heinous acts?" The major point I make is that Eichmann and Milgram's subjects saw themselves as acting for a noble cause, truly thinking their heinous actions were right, moral, and just, because they served a higher legitimate purpose. Yet most people, and certainly the victims, saw them as nothing more than evil. The perceptions of victims and of those who, however remotely, might be victimizers tend to be different. And therein lies the complexity of justice. For as we know, something can be just—that is, legal—and still be evil, wrong, unethical, and immoral.

### Psychology of Injustice

Chapter 3 reviews research concerning the psychology of injustice. The chapter examines the link between revenge and people's sense of justice. It analyzes revenge and what it aims to do, as well as the forms that revenge can take. It examines the relationship between revenge and aggressive acts. In addition, it examines how, at a societal level, one act of revenge can result in another wrong to be righted. It discusses people's ethnic identities and notes that imbued in people's ethnic identities are the stored injustices of the past, handed down from generation to generation.

The chapter reviews psychological studies on the intergenerational effects of the Holocaust on victims' and perpetrators' offspring and concludes that none of these studies used a justice framework (research and theory about the psychology of injustice) for understanding how the perception of injustice plays an organizing role in the lives of descendants of victims and perpetrators. Next, the chapter reports on the interview study I undertook to examine the effects of injustice in the lives of survivors' and Nazis' offspring. A form letter, a one-page description of the study, and biographical information about the author were sent to thirty-one people. Each was told that an interview study of children of concentration camp survivors and children of Nazis was being conducted and that a four-day meeting with the children would be held later. Each was told that the discussions would be facilitated by my husband, a psychiatrist from Harvard Medical School, who is neither German nor Jewish. His role would be strictly facilitative. He would not offer solutions or therapeutic interventions. Each was told that the meeting would not be a therapy group or an encounter group; there was no goal other than to observe their behavior. Eventually ten children of Nazis and ten children of concentration camp survivors were interviewed and later attended the joint meeting.

Three criteria were used for choosing children of survivors: having at least one parent who was a survivor of either a Nazi concentration camp or slave labor camp, not having a parent who was a member of an organization that actively fought against the Nazis, and agreeing to participate in a meeting with children from the "other side" that would be televised on network television. Three criteria were used for choosing children of Nazis: having at least one parent who was an active member of the Nazi party during the Third Reich, not having a parent who was a member of an organization that actively fought against the Nazis, and agreeing to participate in the videotaped meeting.

Of the twenty interviewed, the average age was forty-three, ranging from thirty to forty-eight: Fourteen were female and six were male. Ten were born in Germany, one in Israel, and the remaining nine in the United States. Their parents' backgrounds varied. For survivors' children, some came from families where both parents were survivors of death camps and all other family members were killed. Others came from families where only one parent was a survivor of a labor camp and a limited part of the family was killed. Still others came from families that spent some time hiding in the forest before being transported to concentration camps. Similarly, Nazis' children came from varied backgrounds. Some were the children of high-ranking Nazis like the Gestapo chief, the deputy armaments minister, and lieutenants in the Third Reich's Waffen-SS. Others where the children of lowly Wehrmacht soldiers who served on the eastern front. Obviously, this is not a random group, but those who decided to speak on the record.

The interviews were conducted in English and German, tape-recorded, and transcribed. The interviews usually lasted about two hours. The interviews took place primarily in the Boston, New York, Hamburg, and Berlin areas. A semistructured interview was designed as the chief instrument of the study. The interview was designed to generate data by focusing on broad areas. I hypothesized that these areas would yield useful data for comparing (the similarities and differences) between the two groups of descendants. The areas also determined the sequence of inquiry followed during the interviews. The areas were: (1) subjects' developmental

Introduction 19

histories with special attention to the evolution of finding out about the war, the Holocaust, and their parents' involvement, (2) subjects' reports of their responses to information about the war and the Holocaust and of its influence on them, (3) subjects' perspectives on justice, and (4) subjects' views on descendants of the other side. Finally, the chapter analyses the interview data and discusses its significance for understanding justice as intergenerational.

*The Experience of Injustice*

Chapter 4 analyzes research concerning people's experience of injustice. The analysis focuses primarily on the link between the experience of injustice and degrading treatment. People's negative emotional responses to degrading treatment are reviewed. It is noted that people's responses fall into broad categories: withdrawal responses or attack responses. Both types of responses hinder or stop people's willingness to meet and discuss a past injustice. They stand as obstacles to restoring equal moral relationships between victims and wrongdoers. Indeed, the very notion of meeting the other side is an idea many Holocaust survivors and former Nazis feel should not even be mentioned, an impossibility that should never be proposed.

■ ■ ■

Although survivors' wounds can never heal, must their responses be passed on to the children of the wounded? And what about the children of Nazis? Must they inherit their parents' responses too? Do survivors' children and former Nazis' children want to meet the "other side"? Could they examine the injustices of the past from the perspective of the other? How would members of each side react to information that threatened or undermined their ethnic legacies? Would they be discomfited by opposing information or challenged to think more about their own legacies?

The chapter describes the first meeting between children of Nazis and children of survivors. For four days, the group met in discussion sessions under the auspices of the Harvard Medical Educational Center. The university has the advantage of providing an academic context, with its own set of norms to support an investigation of this kind. The facilitator's skills and knowledge and academic status served as a basis of credibility and evenhandedness. The facilitator tried to stay in the background as much as possible and was prepared to intercede only in order to keep the discussion moving forward. Thus, if the discussion went too far afield, became repetitive, or systematically avoided the topic, the facilitator would try to bring it back to the broad agenda of discussing the Holocaust, World War II, and their parents' involvement.

After data are collected, the researcher has the responsibility to assure that there are no undesirable consequences for the subjects, including, where relevant, long-term aftereffects. Previous social psychological research has suggested that working cooperatively has positive effects under conditions that lead people to define a new, inclusive group that dissolves their former subgroups. Old feelings of bias against another group diminish when members of two groups, for example, give their new group a name, and then work together on shared goals (Gaertner, Dovidio, Rus, Nier, Banker, Ward, Mottola & Houlette, 1999). So on the last day of the meeting, the facilitator and I suggested that the participants discuss forming an organization and work toward joint chosen superordinate goals.

All the discussion sessions were videotaped and later transcribed. In total about 32 hours of discussions were transcribed. The chapter analyzes the communicational patterns and reviews their significance for understanding justice as interpersonal.

### Changing the Legacy of Injustice

Chapter 5 explores a series of questions: What is involved in overcoming the responses to an injustice? Is it a matter of becoming fully aware of our own legacies? What happens when we have inherited a legacy (a worldview), a seemingly useful view, and then we are confronted with new information suggesting that our view needs to be changed? What stops us from changing our view? What enables us to change our view? Is it a matter of switching from close-minded, biased thinking to open-minded, hypothetical thinking? How can the prescription "hear the other side" help us switch from a single-minded understanding of an unjust, painful event to a two-sided understanding?

*Compassion*

Chapter 6 focuses on situations when people are most likely to "hear the other side." During the conference, some participants were able to consider the other side's views and responses. Are there unique aspects to these people that make them able to choose a different path? Does it require certain special abilities? The chapter explores the degree to which compassion is rooted in people's sense of justice. It examines the link between compassion and the ability to assume another individual's perspective. It analyzes compassion and what it aims to do, as well as the forms that compassion can take. It examines the relationship between compassion and helping acts and compares them to revenge and aggressive acts. The concluding section is devoted to discussing forgiveness. Can we expect people to forgive what has come before? Can we expect reconciliation between the descendants of Nazis and Holocaust survivors? The book ends with a discussion that draws upon the lessons derived from the study of children of Nazis and survivors. It proposes that the nature of overcoming past injustices be reconsidered, and it suggests some features of such a revised understanding.

# 2

## BACKGROUND

Can good people pursue heinous acts? With global terrorism, continued conflict in the Middle East, and upheaval in virtually every pocket of the globe, it would seem a modern question. But 2,000 years ago, before Hitler or his "final solution" were conceived, Aristotle concluded that, in fact, good people could do bad things.

Adolf Eichmann, the designer of Hitler's plan to exterminate the Jews, is widely viewed as evil personified. Still, psychiatrists who examined him prior to his trial described him as "normal," a man whose life in exile made him seem a pillar of the community, even a model father and husband.

Eichmann symbolizes the slippery nature of morality. Inspired by Hitler's sortie against communism, he went to his death arguing that he had not been anti-Semitic, but merely faithful to his flag.

Eichmann and other supporters of the Third Reich saw themselves acting for a noble cause, truly thinking their immoral behavior was right because it was legal and served a higher purpose. Yet the world saw them as nothing more than murderers.

On both sides of ongoing conflicts, each side thinks their perception of morality is the right one. And therein lies the complexity of justice. For, as we know, something can be just—that is, legal—and still be wrong, unethical, and immoral.

My interest in the Holocaust and the Second World War is personal. As mentioned before, both my parents were survivors of concentration camps. Apart from my parents, every family member on both sides was exterminated by the Nazis. All that was left of our family tree were three yellow faded photographs that my mother kept in a drawer and two that my father kept in a shoebox.

As a girl, I never could make sense of why our family tree was burnt to a stump, let alone conceive what happened. When I asked my parents about it, they'd say, "There was a war," and change the subject. When I asked about the blue number branded on their arms, they'd say, "It's our phone number." Many years later, when I asked why they evaded telling me about the Holocaust, they'd say, "We didn't want it intruding on your childhood." But try as they did, the past was always there—an inexplicable abyss that cried out for an answer.

Just as I can't place an exact date on the moment I learned to talk or to read, I can't pinpoint exactly when I learned about death camps and Nazis. But I have been aware for as long as I can remember that my parents had experienced cruel, unjust things in an earlier life.

I learned about the past haphazardly, shocked by each new discovery. Findings about the atrocities had a powerful effect on my young mind. It left me in a quandary, in a state of bewildered uncertainty. Why? How? What inquisitive child could simply accept the Nazi assault on humanity? What child could avoid wondering how Nazis would be punished for the atrocities they committed?

I first thought about justice and injustice when, as a seven-year-old child, I saw my mother watching the televised trial of Nazi Adolf Eichmann (1961). To this day, I remember seeing Adolf Eichmann, the man in the famous glass booth built for his protection: middle-aged, medium sized, thin, with receding hair. Eichmann looked ghostlike but human, despicable but ordinary.

Adolf Eichmann, the Nazi bureaucrat who came to symbolize the "banality of evil." He was an architect of Hitler's Final Solution and supervised the deportation and murder of six million Jews and others during World War II. He commissioned the design of the first gas chambers and founded the tactics of deceit to foster the victims' compliance.

Eichmann was the number-one war criminal hunted down in the postwar era. The last anyone had seen of him was April 1945, as he made his way down an Austrian mountain trail. For years afterward, he might as well have vanished from earth. Then, in the spring of 1960, the Israeli government verified what had seemed an unlikely tip from a blind German-Jewish refugee in rural Argentina: Eichmann was living under the name of Klement in a suburb of Buenos Aires.

Under orders from Ben-Gurion, then Prime Minister of Israel, a team of Israeli intelligence agents kidnapped Eichmann near his home and brought him back to Jerusalem to face justice. He was brought to the District Court of Jerusalem to stand trial for his role in the "final solution of the Jewish question." Eichmann stood accused of crimes against the Jewish people, crimes against humanity, and war crimes and, thus, liable to the death penalty.

As I watched his trial on television, I heard the words "Beth Hamishpath" (the House of Justice) shouted by the court escort, which made everyone jump to their feet, as the judges came in the courtroom. The courtroom was filled with Holocaust survivors, like my parents, who endured horrible sufferings in concentration camps. They were called upon as witnesses and as they recounted their stories, horror was piled upon horror, and to a child's eye the figure in the glass booth became paler and more ghostlike.

There, I thought, sits the monster responsible for murdering my extended family: my grandparents, my uncles, my aunts, my little cousins. Eichmann deserves to be killed. He committed crimes against my family, crimes against the Jewish people, crimes against humanity. As a child, justice was a simple matter; it was a matter of truth and fiction, of right and wrong, and of getting even for the wrongs committed.

On December 11, 1961, about nine months after the opening of the trial, the court pronounced judgment. My wish came true. They convicted Eichmann on all counts, and on May 31, 1962, Eichmann was hanged; his body was then cremated and the ashes scattered in the Mediterranean outside Israeli waters. The death sentence had been expected.

To watch this trial, even as a seven-year-old, was to question the idea of justice and punishment. What child could avoid wondering how Eichmann could be aptly punished for his crimes? But my curiosity was more deeply felt than the average child's; my desire to see Eichmann punished was a personal matter. It stemmed from overwhelming anger, from hatred, from resentment, from a need to seek vengeance.

Some survivors, who were witnesses, declared that Eichmann's deeds deserved an even harsher punishment. They said the death sentence was "unimaginative," and imaginative options were proposed. Some said Eichmann should be tortured and then killed. Others suggested he should spend the rest of his life at hard labor in the desert, helping with his sweat to reclaim the Jewish homeland (Arendt, 1964). Still, despite disagreements about which punishment Eichmann should receive, most survivors agreed that for justice to be served, Adolf Eichmann should suffer for what he did.

## Lessons from the Eichmann Trial

As I grew older, I continued to ponder principles of justice. The Eichmann trial raised problems that went beyond legal and punitive matters considered in the Jerusalem courthouse. Closely connected with deciding Eichmann's punishment was the task of understanding the person whom the court had come to judge. As Arendt says, the focus of most trials is upon the person, the defendant, "a man of flesh and blood with an individual history" (Arendt, 1964, p. 285). What lessons in psychology, in human nature, are we to learn from the Eichmann trial? What type of human being supervises the deportation and murder of six million Jews and others, commissions the design of carbon-monoxide gas chambers, and organizes a campaign of deceit to encourage the victims' compliance? What kind of mind organizes a conference to set out guidelines about whether a quarter Jew should live longer than a three-eighths Jew and by how long?

Many writers have addressed these questions. They needed addressing. The most famous explanation, and one many people had difficulty accepting, was Hannah Arendt's explanation that Adolf Eichmann was simply a bureaucrat who sat at his desk, followed orders, and did his job. Arendt used the phrase "banality of evil" as a general description of the entire Nazi project. According to Arendt, the trouble with Eichmann was that so many were like him, that they were neither perverted nor sadistic, they were just obedient agents (Arendt, 1964, p. 276).

For asserting this view and the view that Jewish leadership also was responsible for the crimes because they collaborated with the Nazis, that kidnapping Eichmann was illegal, and that the trial was unlawful because the court would not admit witnesses for the defense, Arendt became the object of abundant criticism. Some critics even claimed that Arendt told such implausible lies out of "self-hatred" (Bondy, 1981; Robinson, 1965; Novick 1999; Segev, 2000).

Like Arendt's work, Raul Hilberg's classic work *The Destruction of the*

*European Jews* (1985) placed part of the responsibility for the genocide on the Jews themselves, asserting that the Jewish leadership helped in the extermination program. And like Arendt, Hilberg became the object of abundant scorn. No mainstream publishing company would publish his manuscript. And when it was finally published, it received mostly critical reviews.

For many people, it was more comforting to think that Eichmann received a fair trial, that the kidnapping was legal, that Jewish leadership was blameless, and that Eichmann was a sadistic monster, not just a bureaucratic agent. Somehow, it was felt that the heinous deeds carried out by Eichmann required a brutal, twisted personality. Yet, during the trial, half a dozen psychiatrists examined Eichmann and certified him as "normal." One of them was said to have exclaimed, "More normal, at any rate, than I am after having examined him." Another found that his whole psychological outlook, his attitude toward his wife and children, mother and father, brothers, sisters, and friends, was "not only normal but most desirable" (cited in Arendt, 1964, pp. 25–26). Thus, by the measures usually applied, Eichmann was not an obviously cruel or thoughtless man. Were he living among us today, he would probably be regarded with quiet respect, a steady worker, husband, and father.

This is precisely what makes Eichmann's story continually unsettling. For it was not just about the crimes perpetrated by agents of Nazism where we are able to identify with the victims, but about the astonishing capacity of those not unlike ourselves for reasons of ideology, ambition—seemingly normal souls—to escape their better selves. This capacity to become an agent in a destructive process without any particular aggressive tendency suggested something many people did not want to hear. It is easier to think of a destructive process in terms of "them and us." And most of us would like to think we are incapable of acting like them—those agents of Nazism.

The Nazi extermination of Jews and others is an extreme example of destructive, unjust acts carried out by thousands of people in the name of obedience. Although people during the Nazi era may have had different motivations such as ambition or ideology or anti-Semitism, which Goldhagen (1997) so thoroughly describes, still they willingly obeyed orders that involved hurting innocent people. But how far will an ordinary individual go in carrying out orders that involve hurting another person? At what point will one refuse to carry out actions that conflict with one's conscience?

## The Psychology of Unjust Acts

Many psychologists have addressed these problems. The studies of Adorno, Asch, Fromm, Lewin, Frank, Cartwright, among others, are concerned with the psychological aspects of unjust acts, their human basis. But the most famous study is social psychologist Stanley Milgram's (1974) study conducted in 1960–63 in a laboratory at Yale University. Milgram's study testing what happens when the demands of authority clash with the demands of conscience has become social psychology's most famous study. "Perhaps more than any other empirical contributions in the history of social science," says Lee Ross, "they have become part of our society's shared intellectual legacy—that small body of historical incidents, biblical parables, and classic literature that serious thinkers feel free to draw on when they debate about human nature or contemplate human history" (cited in Myers, 2002, p. 211).

### Milgram's Experiments

Milgram recruited subjects by placing an ad in local paper. The ad invited men to participate in a study of memory and learning at Yale University. When a subject arrived at the selected time, he found two others waiting. One, in an impressive white labcoat, introduced himself as the experimenter (the legitimate authority figure). The other was introduced as another subject in the experiment (the learner). The experimenter explained that the study was about the effects of punishment on learning. The experimenter said one of the two subjects would be the teacher and the other, the learner. The two subjects drew lots (the drawing was rigged) to decide which would play each part. The real focus of the experiment was the teacher-subject.

Then, all three people went into a nearby room where the learner was strapped into a chair ("to prevent excessive movement"), and electrodes were taped onto his wrist. The experimenter explained that the learner's task would be to learn a list of word pairs that would be read to him by the teacher. Whenever the learner made a mistake, the teacher would be told by the experimenter to administer an electric shock of increasing intensity.

Then the teacher was led to the main experimental room, where he was seated in front of an impressive-looking shock generator. The generator had a horizontal line of 30 switches, each marked with a voltage. The first switch delivered 15 volts and the highest 450 volts. The generator was also marked from "Slight shock" at 15 volts to "DANGER: Severe Shock" at about 400 volts.

The teacher was directed by the experimenter to present a list of word pairs to the learner by means of an intercom. Whenever the learner made a mistake, the teacher was directed by the experimenter to give him a shock. He was to start at the lowest switch, 15 volts, and then go on to the next higher switch every time the learner made a mistake. The learner, or victim, you recall, was really a confederate receiving no shocks at all. The drawing was rigged so that the subject who responded to the ad always became the teacher, and the confederate always became the learner.

The learner had been trained to make many mistakes and to voice increasingly strong objections to being shocked. When the teacher had reached the 300-volt level, the learner shouted that he would no longer provide answers to the memory test. The experimenter told the teacher to treat the absences of a response as an error. After 330 volts the learner made no further response to the shocks or the memory tests.

If the teacher asked the experimenter's advice about what to do, or said that he wanted to stop administering shocks, the experimenter would tell him to continue. If the teacher asked whether the shocks were dangerous, the experimenter would say only something like they might be painful but would do no permanent damage. Only if the teacher refused to obey after he had been told to administer the shock four times was the experiment finished.

How far do you think the teacher would go in this situation? How far would you go? If you are like other people who have been asked this question, you probably think you would refuse to deliver the shocks, or you would stop somewhere between 120 and 150 volts. As a psychology professor, I have always used Milgram's experiment on obedience in classes as a source of discussion, since most students find the results of the experiment interesting. Most students, like other people who have been asked, say they would refuse to deliver the shocks or would stop somewhere between 120 and 150 volts. So they are surprised that Milgram's subjects so willingly submitted to orders to shock an innocent victim to the highest shock level on the generator.

However, despite these optimistic predictions, 62 percent of the subjects in Milgram's experiment continued administering shocks until they reached 450 volts, the last shock on the generator. Most obeyed the experimenter's instructions no matter how fervent the pleading of the person being shocked, no matter how painful the shocks seemed to be, and no matter how much the victim pleaded to be let out. It is the extreme willingness of adults to go to almost any lengths on the orders of an authority that was the chief finding of Milgram's study. This was seen time and again in Milgram's studies and observed in several universities where the experiment was repeated

Milgram's study became widely known within and outside the field of psychology. The notoriety is probably due to the intensity of the experience endured by Milgram's research subjects and the fact that his results, like Arendt's, suggested something that most people didn't want to hear. Milgram's results confirmed Arendt's assertion: an ordinary person will carry out orders to act against another person when told to do by a legitimate authority. Moreover, an ordinary person who becomes an agent in a destructive process does so out of a sense of obligation—a conception of his duties—and not from any aggressive, immoral tendencies.

Milgram's study clearly showed that individuals acting under authority will perform actions that violate standards of conscience. However, it would be untrue to say they lose their moral sense. According to Milgram this moral sense gets a radically different focus. Instead of focusing on their unjust actions, it shifts to how well they are doing their duties. The key to their behavior, according to Milgram, lies not in pent-up anger or aggression but in the nature of their relationship to authority. Once they have given themselves to the authority, they see themselves as instruments for carrying out orders; once so defined, they are unable to break free.

Some psychologists referred to Milgrams' study as the "Eichmann Experiment" because the study focused on something similar to the position occupied by Eichmann who, while "performing his duties," contributed to the destruction of human beings. But, according to Milgram, the term "Eichmann Experiment" was misleading because the point of Milgram's study was with the ordinary and routine destruction carried out by everyday people following orders. To refer to the problem as if it were a matter of history was to give it an illusory distance. Milgram maintained that the dilemma posed by the conflict between conscience and authority inheres in the very nature of society and would be with us even if Nazi Germany had never existed. Thus, the point of the experiment was to see whether everyday people living in a democratic society are likely to carry out orders to inflict harm on a helpless victim.

How can this disturbing phenomenon be understood? Why should adult men agree to administer painful and possibly lethal shocks to a person whose only crime was making errors on a memory task? Initially, my students suppose the men are aggressive types. But then I remind them, if we consider that these men responded to a newspaper ad and represented ordinary people drawn from working, managerial, and professional classes, the argument that they are unusually aggressive or sadistic becomes very shaky.

Why then did these men, who are usually decent, act with such severity against another person? Perhaps, my students say, the men were unconcerned with the fate of the learner. But, then I suggest, if we carefully observe the men's behavior on film, we can see the men give signs of being under emotional stress. For instance, while they are administering the shocks, we can notice signs of stress like sweating, trembling, and sometimes anxious laughter. Moreover, sometimes the men verbally express their concerns about the fate of the learner. Consider the following exchange between subject and experimenter. In this example the subject, under considerable stress, has gone on to 450 volts (Milgram, 1974, p. 160).

TEACHER: I think something's happened to that fellow in there. I don't get no answer. He was hollering at less voltage. Can't you check in and see if he's all right, please?

EXPERIMENTER: (*same detached calm*): Not once we've started. Please continue, Teacher.

TEACHER: (*sits down, sighs deeply*): "Cool-day, shade, water, paint." Answer, please. Are you all right in there? Are you all right?

EXPERIMENTER: Please continue, teacher. Continue, please.
(*Teacher pushes lever.*)
TEACHER: You accept all responsibility?
EXPERIMENTER: The responsibility is mine. Correct. Please go on.
(*Teacher returns to his list, starts running through words as rapidly as
he can read them, works through to 450 volts.*)
TEACHER: That's that.

Here we see that the fate of the learner strongly influences the subject,
whose distress is immediate and spontaneous. Many other subjects in the
study had similar reactions. And even Eichmann was distressed when he
saw the preparations for the future carbon monoxide chambers at Treblinka:

> For me, too, this was monstrous. I am not so tough as to be able to endure
> something of this sort without any reaction. . . . If today I am shown a gap-
> ing wound, I can't possibly look at it. I am that type of person, so that very
> often I was told that I couldn't have become a doctor. I still remember how
> I picture the thing to myself, and then I became physically weak, as though
> I had lived through some great agitation. Such things happen to everybody,
> and it left behind a certain inner trembling. (Arendt, 1964, pp. 87–88)

And, later, when Eichmann was sent to look at a concentration camp
where instead of gas chambers, mobile gas vans were used, Eichmann describes his reaction: "The Jews were in a large room, they were told to strip;
a truck arrived, and the naked Jews were told to enter, the doors closed and
the truck started off. I cannot tell [how many Jews entered], I hardly
looked. I could not; I could not; I had had enough. The shrieking, and . . .
I was much too upset. . . . I saw the most horrible sight I had thus far seen
in my life" (Arendt, 1964, p. 87).

Milgram acknowledged the important differences between the obedience in the laboratory and in Nazi Germany. "Consider the disparity in
time scale. The laboratory experiment takes an hour; the Nazi calamity
unfolded over more than a decade. Is the obedience observed in the laboratory in any way comparable to that seen in Nazi Germany? (Is a match
flame comparable to the Chicago fire of 1898?) The answer must be that,
while there are enormous differences of circumstances and scope, a com-

mon psychological process is centrally involved in both events" (Milgram, 1974, p. 175). (For a further discussion of the differences and similarities the reader may want to see Blass, 2000).

If one agrees with Milgram that both his laboratory studies and the Holocaust reveal a common psychological process—the process by which people cede personal autonomy in favor of obeying authority, even if this entails violating their own moral beliefs—then a close look at how Eichmann and Milgram's subjects explain their actions should have much to tell us about this process. So, to further define this process, let us now look more closely at Eichmann's statements and the subjects' statements and see how they explain their actions.

Eichmann's and the subjects' statements above more or less speak for themselves, but we may emphasize a few points. First, the statements show that Milgram's subjects and Eichmann recognize the wrongness of what is being done. They felt disturbed at seeing the victim suffer. Yet, despite their acknowledgment about the wrongness, they continue to partake in a destructive process. There is a split between what these men think and say and what they actually do. Their subjective feelings about the wrongness of what is being done do not translate into action.

If we admit, as I have tried to show here, that these men are ordinary people (not aggressive or sadistic or bad types) and are aware of the wrongness of what is being done, the question then remains: How do they explain their behavior? In what sense do they think they are accountable? Or do they?

In the postexperimental interviews, when subjects were asked why they had gone on with the shocks, a typical reply was, "I wouldn't have done it by myself. I was just doing what I was told" (Milgram, 1974, p. 8). "If it were up to me, I would not have administered shocks to the learner" (Milgram, 1974, p. 148). Another typical reply was, "I believe I conducted myself behaving obediently, and carried on instructions as I always do. . . . And I think I did a good job. So he's dead, I did my job! But it didn't even bother me to find that he was dead. I did a job" (Milgram, 1974, p. 88).

These statements show that these men view themselves as unaccountable for their actions. They see themselves as agents of an external authority, not as individuals acting autonomously. They explain their actions by attributing all motivation to the experimenter. "I was just obeying orders." They assume the experimenter has good, scientifically based reasons for directing them to shock the learner, so they comply.

Although the subjects are aware of the wrongness of their actions, they do not respond with a moral feeling to the actions they perform. Rather, their moral feeling now shifts to a consideration of how well they carried out their "scientific" duties.

Thus, the subjects see their actions in a different context—carrying out orders for an important "scientific experiment." What a subject actually does, then, depends more on how they define the context than on their personal feelings. The action of shocking a victim, which in isolation appears cruel and unjust, gets a different meaning when placed in the larger context of carrying out instructions for the "pursuit of scientific truth." In this respect, the men commit unjust actions under a context that makes it difficult for them to think they are doing wrong (Kelman & Hamilton, 1989).

### Unjust Action for a "Noble Cause"

If we look closely at Eichmann's account of his actions, we see a similar mode of thought. Consider the following exchange between Eichmann and the Israeli agent who captured him (cited by Malkin, 1990, pp. 203–214 and reported in an interview).

"How did it happen?" asked the Israeli agent. "How do you come to do what you did?"

"Es war den Auftrag den ich hatte," Eichmann said. "Ich hatte den Auftrag zu erfülen." (It was a job I had. I had a job to do.)

"Just a job?"

Eichmann hesitated. "You must believe me, it wasn't something I planned, nor anything I'd have chosen."

"But why you? Tell me exactly how it happened," asked the Israeli agent.

So Eichmann went on to relate the story of his early rise within the SS, describing how at first he was assigned boring clerical tasks, and so he jumped at the chance, in 1935, for a position at the new "Jewish Museum" being set up at headquarters. Yes, he acknowledged, matters had gotten out of control. But that hadn't been the intention at the beginning, not his immediate superiors' and certainly not his. Working from within, he had always argued for moderation. But he was a soldier, and a soldier is never entirely his own man. When decisions were made by those above, and orders issued, they had to be obeyed. This was duty. For him, this was a matter of moral responsibility.

"You must believe me," Eichmann added suddenly. "I had nothing against the Jews."

"Then what were you doing in the SS in the first place? The ideology was not exactly a secret," said the Israeli agent.

"But it wasn't only me. Everyone knew a change was necessary in Germany; it was only a question of what form it would take. Times were terrible. I had a job myself, selling gasoline products in Upper Austria, and for me things were not so bad. It was one of the most beautiful places on earth. I was moved and inspired every day by its glorious mountain forests. But a man does not live only for himself. Hitler was the only one who could rally the people against the Communists. He brought hope of jobs and bread. I freely admit it; I was inspired as much as anyone."

Eichmann argued his position—that he would have personally preferred to resettle Jews rather than exterminate them. "The idea," as he explained it to the Israeli agent, "was judenrein, a Jew-free Reich. . . . In fact, before the war it was policy to encourage Jews to leave. But there was no country that would take them at all." He paused, "I ask you, who was at fault, Germany or the rest of the world?"

Eichmann continued, "Perhaps you will not believe it, but I read Theodore Herzl's book *Der Judenstaat*, about the dream of Jewish homeland. In connection with my work, I read a wide variety of Jewish newspapers and periodicals. I fully understood the aspirations of the Jews, I can't tell you how much I loved studying Zionism."

In fact, Eichmann continued, "Ich war den Juden immer zugeneigt." (I have always been fond of Jews.) "You must believe, I was always an idealist. Had I been born Jewish, I'd have been the most fervent Zionist."

"You must understand," Eichmann said, "it wasn't the same then as it is now. I was a soldier. Like you. I had orders to follow." "Aren't you a soldier?" Eichmann asked. "Don't you follow orders? Who told you to come here and get me? What's the difference?"

During his trial, Eichmann revealed the same mode of thought. Eichmann said he was certain he was not what he called an *innerer Schweine-*

*hund*, a dirty bastard in the depths of his heart; and as for his conscience, he remembered very well that he would have had a bad conscience only if he had disobeyed orders (Arendt, 1964, p. 25). Eichmann maintained that it had been his duty to obey and that he had committed acts "for which you are decorated if you win and go to the gallows if you lose" (Arendt, 1964, p. 22). He claimed his obedience was a virtue that was abused by the Nazi leaders and that he was a victim of the ruling leaders. "I am not the monster I am made out to be," Eichmann said. "I am the victim of a fallacy" (Arendt, 1964, p. 248).

Eichmann told the court he was obeying orders and also obeying the law. Under the then existing Nazi legal system, Eichmann declared, he had not done anything wrong; what he was accused of were not crimes but "acts of state," over which no other state had jurisdiction. Robert Servatius, Eichmann's lawyer, went a step further. He declared that the only legitimate criminal problem of the Eichmann trial lay in pronouncing judgment against Eichmann's Israeli captors, which had not been done (Arendt, 1964, p. 22).

These statements show that Eichmann, like Milgram's subjects, sees himself as unaccountable for his actions. He explains his actions by attributing them to his obligations and conception of his duties as a soldier and not to any anti-Semitic or hostile tendencies. Eichmann does not deny the facts (collecting and transporting the Jews to the gas chambers), but he divests himself of responsibility by attributing all initiative to his superiors. From the moment he was charged with carrying out the Final Solution, Eichmann claimed, "I was no longer master of my own deeds" (Arendt, 1964, p. 136).

Although Eichmann is aware of the wrongness of his actions, he entrusts the broader task of assessing morality to the authority he is serving. He assumes the ruling leaders had good, idealistically based reasons for ordering a Jew-free Reich, so he complies. Consequently, Eichmann's moral sense of what is wrong and right gets a different perspective. Instead of focusing on his unjust actions, it now shifts to how well he carried out orders for the noble cause of the "National Socialist German Workers' Party." So Eichmann sees his murderous actions in a different context.

The meaning of his actions is now linked to the noble ideals and larger purposes of the party, which were defined as empowering the working class, liberating humankind from the rule of subhumans, and restoring the Reich to its former greatness. The most popular party slogan was "the battle of destiny for the German people" (*der Schicksalskampf des deutschen Volkes*). The slogan suggested that the National Socialist cause was started by destiny and was a matter of life and death for the Germans, who must destroy their enemies or be destroyed (Arendt, 1964 p. 52). Thus, the action of transporting men, women, and children to gas chambers, which in isolation appears cruel and inhuman, gets a different meaning when placed in the larger context of the Reich's noble, historic, and unique cause. Before he was hanged, Eichmann rejected an appeal by a minister that he repent. He spoke his last words in German. "I had to obey the rules of war and my flag. I am ready" (Malkin, 1990).

An act viewed in one perspective may seem cruel; the same action viewed in another perspective seems justifiable. That is why ideology, an attempt to define the context, is always a key feature of wars, revolutions, and other situations in which individuals are asked to do unjust actions. Allowing an act to be defined by its context is what makes cruel and inhuman action seem valid (Milgram, 1974). As Milgram says, new realities take over. In wartime, a soldier does not ask whether it is right to destroy a village or city; he does not experience shame or guilt in the destruction of a population; and he does not view that population as victims of his brutal actions. He does not view the victims as innocent people deserving his compassion but as impersonal objects.

The realities of victims and of those who, however remotely, might be victimizers tend to be different. Neither the facts nor their meaning will be experienced in the same way by the afflicted as by those who might have prevented or allayed the suffering. These people are too far apart to view things in the same way (Shklar, 1990). That's why the victims (and the public at large) did not believe Eichmann. They could not admit that a "normal" person, neither sadistic nor deviant, could be incapable of telling right from wrong. They assumed that Eichmann's reality and their reality were the same. Therefore they concluded that Eichmann was a liar and his statements just excuses devised for the court.

But it would be incorrect to think of Eichmann's statements (and Milgram's subjects' statements) as excuses devised for the occasion. Rather, they reflect a central mode of thinking for many people once they are in a context in which they surrender their autonomy for an ideology. People acting for a "noble cause" truly think their unjust behavior is "right" because it serves a higher purpose. And this fact is what makes injustice a complex matter.

Because no matter how "unjust" one might think some behavior is, it virtually always involves conflicting considerations. In most ethnic conflicts in Israel/Palestine, Cyprus, Bosnia, Northern Ireland—the list goes on—the conflict is routinely described in terms of injustices on both sides. In a more commonplace context, most marital and relational conflicts center on injustices allegedly perpetrated by each side. Even in extreme instances like Eichmann's case and Milgram's experiment, justice is two-sided: each side has a different perception of the meaning of unjust behavior. Each side thinks their perception is the right one.

## Summing Up

As a psychology professor, I use Milgram's experiment and Eichmann's case to introduce the complexity of justice. Inevitably, students denounce the actions of Milgram's subjects and Eichmann's actions and measure them against the standard of their own context. However, this is hardly an objective standard. Milgram's subjects and Eichmann felt strongly about the moral need to refrain from action against a helpless victim. They too, in abstract terms, knew what ought to be done. But this had little, if anything, to do with their actual behavior in a specific, ideological context. More than two thousand years ago Aristotle noted, "A man may commit an unjust or bad action without having become bad" (Aristotle, 1955, p. 155).

Thus, if our aim is to understand unjust behavior rather than judge it from a moral standpoint, we are required to consider different contexts and therefore consider different viewpoints. I don't say this lightly, because there is the fear that if we understand an unjust event objectively, then we overlook or forgive it. However, "hearing the other side," "seeing another view," only means that we think in an open manner, in contrast to a closed, dogmatic manner. The difficulty in seeing the other side—or going this more balanced way—is not just a problem for those who face injustice directly but, as we will see in the next chapter, for their children as well. As we explore justice further in the next chapter, we will examine how memories about past injustices are transmitted from generation to generation.

# 3

# JUSTICE AS INTERGENERATIONAL

Nazis' children and survivors' children are embraced in a symbiotic relationship, in part defining themselves in terms of the other—as opposites of the other. Imbued in their respective ethnic identities are stored injustices of the past, handed down from their parents and grandparents and based on their elders' experiences. Some Nazis' children rankle at the effects of the Treaty of Versailles and the plundering by Allied troops, while some survivors' children carry with them their ancestors' suffering in concentration camps.

A half century after World War II, a chasm of shame and vengeance still divides children from both groups. A similar generational animus is found the world over, from Northern Ireland to tribal Africa. Its roots are ancient, stretching back to Old Testament prognostications decreeing that the sins of parents will be visited on the sons and daughters.

In the contemporary world, however, Nazis' children and survivors' children appear to seek more than just vindication for their parents' or the righting of historical wrongs. Rather, having internalized the parables of their parents, each group of children also is seeking their own vindication, their own justice, and in some cases, their own expiation.

Eichmann thought that the courts lacked the "objectivity" needed for hearing his point of view. In the notes he made in preparation for an interview, he wrote a warning to "future historians to be objective enough not to stray from the path of this truth recorded here" (Arendt, 1964, p. 54). Still, Eichmann cooperated with the court authorities and confessed to incriminating details of which there could be no proof but for his confession. Specifically, he acknowledged his visits to the concentration camps, where he saw the atrocities with his own eyes. Even the judges who asserted that Eichmann was a liar had to admit they were puzzled by his confession: "Why did Eichmann confess?" (Arendt, 1964).

Eichmann's explanation, given in Israel, was striking:

> About a year and a half ago [in the spring of 1959], I heard from an acquaintance who had just returned from a trip to Germany that a certain feeling of guilt had seized some sections of German youth . . . and the fact of this guilt complex was for me . . . a landmark. . . . It became an essential point of my inner life, around which many thoughts crystallized. This was why I did not escape . . . when I knew the search commando was closing in on me. . . . After these conversations about the guilt feeling among young people in Germany, which made such a deep impression on me, I felt I no longer had the right to disappear. This is also why I offered, in a written statement, at the beginning of this examination . . . to hang myself in public. I wanted to do my part in lifting the burden of guilt from German youth, for these young people are, after all, innocent of the events, and of the acts of their fathers, during the last war. . . . (Arendt, 1964, p. 242)

The notion that descendants will be burdened by the evil acts of the fathers is as old as the Greek classics and the Bible. According to Plato, the evil acts of a wrongdoer impact the community and the next generation. Plato tells us that the temple robber and murderer are in danger of polluting those near them and of bringing divine wrath upon all. Not only one's community but also one's descendants are endangered, for unexpiated guilt will be inherited by them (Plato, 1980). Similarly according to the Bible, evil acts of a wrongdoer impact the next generation. In the Ten Commandments God threatens to punish "the iniquity of fathers on children, to the third and fourth generation." And throughout the Bible there are many moralistic stories of descendants who receive payback for the evil acts of their ancestors. For instance, God commands the destruction of Amalek throughout the generations for the crimes of one generation. The flood, the destruction of Sodom and Gomorrah, and the slaughter of the entire clan of Shechem are other examples of collective or familial punishment. "Sometimes the collective punishment is vertical (down through the generations), other times it is horizontal (within one generation, but extending to the entire family, clan, or city)" (Dershowitz, 2000, p. 233).

The Bible also states that it is wrong to punish anyone for the sins of another; punishment, if it is to be just, must be individualized. The movement from collective responsibility—of the family, the tribe, the nation, the race, the religion, and so on—toward individualized responsibility is shown in the early books of the Bible. However, it has not been a linear movement in history, because the emotional pull of collective accountability and of revenge remains powerful (Dershowitz, 2000, p. 234).

A concrete illustration may be helpful. Tom Segev (2000), an Israeli journalist, reports that after the war in Europe a well-known Holocaust survivor arrived in Palestine with a plan for revenge. (Rich Cohen describes the survivor and his plan for vengeance in a book titled *The Avenger: A Jewish War Story*). Abba Kovner, twenty-seven years old, had been a ghetto defender whom many considered as a symbol of Jewish resistance to the Nazis. When he arrived in Palestine, he enlisted a group of other young Holocaust survivors to poison the drinking water of several major West German cities; they hoped to murder six million Germans. The idea originated among Jews serving in the ranks of the Ukrainian partisans. "There were many debates," Yitzhak Avidov, then called Pasha Reichman, would later remember. The question was: What would happen "the day after?" One evening Reichman's people met Kovner, and the conversation turned to revenge. "It came of itself," Avidov said in a deposition he recorded for the Hebrew University's Institute for Oral Documentation. "We sat with our glasses and the idea flew out of us and suddenly it was no longer in the air but on the table. . . . Everyone wanted revenge." Then someone said it: mass murder of the Germans, by the millions. This person knew of a plant that grew in India from which poison could be produced. "We were very excited," Avidov related. Thus, the *Nakam* (Revenge) organization was born, with a command echelon of five members. Each enlisted additional members. "There was no doubt that we were taking action that God himself, were there a God, would have taken," Avidov related (Segev, 2000, pp. 141–142).

Segev reports that Kovner would later recount that the idea obsessed the group. Kovner said they saw themselves as messengers of fate. Kovner described their mental state in those days: "The destruction was not around us. It was within us. . . . We did not imagine that we could return to life, or that we had the right to do so, . . . to establish families, to get up in the morning and work as if accounts with the Germans had been settled." This was, in essence, an accounting between two nations. To be true revenge it had to precisely equal the dimensions of the crime. Kovner therefore set six million German citizens as his goal He thought in apocalyptic terms; revenge was a holy obligation that would redeem and purify the Jewish people (Segev, 2000, p. 142).

In his recorded testimony, Kovner said he met with Chaim Weitzman, leader of the Zionist Organization, who would become the first president of Israel. Professor Weizmann was a chemist by profession. According to Kovner, Weizmann sent him to a scientist whom he asked to make the poison. Kovner identified the scientist as Ernst David Bergman, later a leader of Israel's nuclear project. Bergman gave Kovner the poison substance. Kovner took the poison and sailed for Europe to carry out the vengeful mission, but was arrested on board and then jailed in a military prison in Cairo (Segev, 2000, pp. 143–144).

"The force that motivates them is the desire for revenge," reported a Jewish Agency leader returning from a mission among Holocaust survivors. "Extensive testimony confirms this. Years later, eight out of ten young survivors recalled that at war's end they longed for vengeance: no other emotion was so widespread among them—not agony nor anxiety, happiness nor hope" (cited in Segev, 2000, p. 140).

The spontaneous reaction to injustice of most victims of genocide and other human horrors is not just a call for fair punishment, but for revenge. Injustice not only makes victims angry, it moves them to get even. According to Aristotle, "It is just the feeling that, as one does, so one will be done by. . . . For men regard it as their right to return evil for evil—and, if they cannot, feel they have lost their liberty . . ." (Aristotle, 1955, p. 151).

To seek revenge for a serious wrong lies at the base of our sense of justice. If there is a chance to get back at the wrongdoer, their kin, or their descendants, the temptation for the sense of justice to express itself in revenge is powerful. As Solomon (1990) says, the desire for revenge is not just aggression but also a deep psychological sense of getting even, putting the world back in balance, supplying the retribution that will put things right and pay back the wrongdoer. "Whoever has done me harm must suffer harm; whoever has put out my eye must lose an eye; and whoever has killed must die. . . ." says Albert Camus in *Reflections on the Guillotine*.

In the eighteenth century, philosophers like Rousseau emphasized that simply to be aware of injustice proved that one was a moral being. He argued that a sense of justice was the one universal mark of our humanity and the natural core of our morality. Without the power to be offended or outraged and to revenge oneself there would be no sense at all of justice, dignity, or morality. He believed that this feeling of justice was with us from the moment of our birth. As a child Rousseau was treated so brutally that he left his home in Geneva to seek a life elsewhere (Grimsely, 1967). Personal experience had taught Rousseau that the unjustly treated child might never say or do anything at all in response, but such a child does not lose his moral awareness that an injustice occurred.

It is thus not surprising, given Rousseau's influence, that since the eighteenth century the sense of justice has been of concern to social scientists. Due to their findings, we know that primates respond to perceived injustices also. Retaliation in response to an injustice exists among primates. Revenge is a very old motivation that underlies many primates' responses to transgressions that they have received. Data on chimpanzees show that they keep negative acts in mind, repaying offenders with other negative acts—sometimes even after considerable time has passed (De Waal, 1996).

For instance, the primatologist Franz De Waal (1989) reports that among Arnhem chimpanzees, individuals may go as far as to feign a friendly mood to reach exactly the opposite goal: revenge. De Waal describes an adult female who was unsuccessful at catching her enemy during a previous aggressive incident. The female would approach her escaped enemy with an invitational gesture, such as an outstretched open hand, and keep her friendly stance until the other, who was attracted by it, had come within arm's reach. Then the female would suddenly grab and attack her naive enemy. De Waal says his impression was that the attacks were much too abrupt and vicious to have resulted from hesitation and conflicting emotions. "I believe, in short, that these were premeditated moves to square an account" (De Waal, 1989, p. 240).

Planned revenge or retaliatory reciprocity—an eye for an eye, a tooth for a tooth—is as common in human culture as in animal behavior. Planned revenge implies that there is a strategy involved in response to an injustice. The Kiwai-Papuans, for instance, place a bundle of small tally sticks on the village path to show how many enemy lives they intend to take in retaliation for a previous offense. In New Guinea every death was ascribed to some enemy from another family, who was then accused of witchcraft (now outlawed) and peremptorily clubbed to death (Solomon, 1990).

Planned revenge can also be a culturally imposed duty. For instance, in Sardinia according to the ancient code of vengeance (the vendetta), an individual has a culturally imposed duty to avenge one's kin for a previously offensive action. "An action is offensive when the event from which depends the existence of such offense is foreseen in order to damage dignity and honor" (cited in Solomon, 1990, p. 41). And in Albania revenge is a culturally sacred duty too. The *canon* compiled by Leke Dukagjini, a fifteenth-century Albanian nobleman, lists every variety of offensive action that calls for revenge (cited in Blumenfeld, 2002a, p. 76). They are organized under headings:

CXXVI:      Blood Is Paid for with Blood
CXXVII:     A Crime May Not Be Recompensed with Blood
CXXVIII:    Blood Is Not Paid for with a Fine
CXXIX:      Blood for Evil Acts

Whether vengeful acts are spontaneous reactions, planned strategies, or culturally imposed duties, they stem from a sense of justice and the need to get even, to counteract in some way an interpersonal offense. The need for revenge arises from the emotion of indignation, which is defined as "anger provoked by what is perceived as unfair treatment" (*The New Oxford American Dictionary*, 2001). When an offended person feels indignation, the need to seek revenge is increased. As the late psychiatrist and Auschwitz survivor Viktor Frankl put it, ". . . there are moments when indignation can rouse even a seemingly hardened prisoner—indignation not about cruelty or pain, but about the insult connected with it" (Frankl, 1963, p. 39).

An insult, and presumably any disrespectful act, evokes our sense of injustice because it creates a social imbalance. In Miller's words, "insults and injuries are understood as gifts, of negative moral value to be sure, but as gifts nonetheless and, as such, demand repayment" (Miller, 1993, p. 16). As mentioned above, one possible intent underlying revenge is the desire to "balance the scales," "get even," "get blood for blood" or "an eye for an eye." The expressions used for revenge show the perceived use of revenge for restoring a sense of justice and moral balance. Thus, revenge might be understood, at least from the vengeful person's viewpoint, as truly just.

Revenge also involves the desire to teach the wrongdoer a lesson (De Waal, 1996; Heider, 1958; Murphy & Hampton, 1988). Revenge, in this sense, is symbolic behavior designed to show the wrongdoer that the insult will not be tolerated or go unpunished. Victims typically attribute to their wrongdoers a belief that the victim was not worthy of better treatment (Heider, 1958). For instance, Frankl recounts the demeaning treatment he received from a guard. The guard threw a stone at him and did not think it worth his while to even say anything. Frankl describes the demeaning treatment like this:

> Strangely enough, a blow which does not even find its mark can, under certain circumstances, hurt more than one that finds its mark. Once I was standing on a railway track in a snowstorm. In spite of the weather our party had to keep on working. I worked quite hard at mending the track with gravel, since that was the only way to keep warm. For only one moment I paused to get my breath and to lean on my shovel. Unfortunately the guard turned around just then and thought I was loafing. The pain he caused me was not from insults or blows. That guard did not think it worth his while to say anything, not even a swear word, to the ragged, emaciated figure standing before him, which probably reminded him vaguely of human form. Instead, he playfully picked up a stone and threw it at me. That, to me, seemed the way to attract the attention of a beast. . . . (Frankl, 1963, pp. 36–37)

Using the psychologist Fritz Heider's language, revenge is a means for changing the belief-attitude of the wrongdoer that gave rise to the unjust act in the first place. Heider says the feeling of resentment is a wish to produce a change in the underlying belief-attitude of the wrongdoer, and revenge is the means of realizing this wish (Heider, 1958, p. 267). By reacting to the first unjust act with even more aggression, the victim tries to communicate an even stronger message to the wrongdoer about his or her self-worth. "In naive psychology this purpose is often recognized by such expression as: I will teach him; he has to learn that he can't do that; who

does he think he is; I can't take this lying down—my honor is at stake, etc."
(Heider, 1958. p. 267).

The concept of revenge, although not a traditional focus of psychology, is growing. In recent years a variety of researchers have been investigating the relationship between the nature of the revenge system, forgiveness, and aggressive acts. They have found that measures of attitudes regarding revenge are positively correlated with standard measures of ruminative thinking about the offense. It appears that ruminative tendencies and feelings of resentment interfere with people's abilities to forgive an interpersonal transgression. That is to say, "vengeful people ruminate on the injustices and harm they have suffered to keep themselves focused on the goals of balancing the scales, teaching the offender a lesson . . ." (McCullough et al., 2001, pp. 602–603).

In addition, researchers have found that vengeful people are high in negative affectivity and neuroticism and are low in agreeableness. Agreeableness reflects a prosocial orientation toward others that includes such qualities as altruism, kindness, and trust. People low in agreeableness have greater amounts of relational conflict and difficulties in relational closeness and commitment. They also have empathy deficits (Ashton, Paunonen, Helmes & Jackson, 1998).

Also, researchers have found that the desire for revenge is frequently cited as a motive for many destructive interpersonal behaviors, including homicide, rape, arson, and adultery (McCullough, 2001). And finally, researchers have found that the desire for revenge is frequently cited as a motive in ethnopolitical conflicts (Waldman, 2001). Put simply, a considerable amount of human misery can be attributed to people's difficulties in modulating their revenge motivations (McCullough, 2001, pp. 107–108).

At a societal level, there is the danger, of course, that one act of revenge can result in another insult to be righted. And when the revengeful act is perpetrated not against the same person who did the offense but another who is a descendant—part of the same tribe, nation, or family—the possibilities for escalation are endless. And in retrospect it is often hard to figure out which action represents the original injustice inflicted to a group and which the act of revenge. The extreme, as mentioned above, is the vendetta, a pattern of killing in revenge for some previous insult or injury that can go on for generations. "The Gilyak aborigines of Russia believed that the soul of a murdered man came back as a bird, pecking at his relatives to take revenge for up to three generations" (Blumenfeld, 2002a, p. 81).

Accordingly, we can readily understand the need to limit or eliminate the escalation of revenge through a legal system designed to keep revenge under control. Speaking very generally, legal justice exists to control all forms of revenge in the interest of social peace and fairness. The legal system (among other things it does) tries to dilute feelings of indignation and even hatred that victims typically direct toward wrongdoers. Legal punishment is a civilized and efficient way in which such emotions may be directed toward their proper objects, allowing victims to get legitimate revenge with the control of public order. In the present age, some of us are uncomfortable talking about the legal system in such terms. We prefer to think that civilized people are not given to indignation so intense that it generates the desire for revenge.

If effective, the legal system may preempt, neutralize, and dilute indignation. However, it cannot abolish it, either as an emotion or as a motivation to seek revenge. The desire for revenge is not easily eliminated by any legal system. The law is impersonal, detached, and rule bound, but the desire for revenge is personal, intense, and unruly (Jacoby, 1983). The law itself cannot eliminate the desire for revenge. And then there are crimes of such magnitude and scale that agencies of law seem inadequate to address the wrongdoing. In cases of genocide and other human horrors legal punishment may remain a frustrating substitute for revenge, neither eliminating nor satisfying its urging.

One can readily appreciate the need to limit acts of revenge through a legal system, and yet history shows us that, if it ignores the emotional and psychological needs of individuals, it may not serve its purpose. Justice is a matter of personal concern, not just of anonymous legal institutions, systems, and governments. If there is an opportunity to get back at the wrongdoer, the temptation for the sense of injustice to express itself in personal revenge is strong. Unlike legal punishment, revenge meets the specific case directly, indifferent to every other concern except the need to react to an unjust act or perceived wrong.

One need go no further than ethnic conflicts to see revenge at work.

Ethnic conflicts illustrate the translation of intensely felt personal injustice into political violence. Examples can be found in Northern Ireland, Bosnia, and the Middle East. In these ethnic conflicts one sees a collapsed sense of time, where ancient grievance is current grievance. The Irish Catholics and Protestants continue in a spiral of revenge that goes back more than 300 years. The Bosnian Serbs can recall all the injustices that Muslims perpetrated during their 500 years of rule. And Palestinians can remember all the wrongs that Israelis have committed since the establishment of Israel. Each has its list of grievances and atrocities.

Muslims have massacred Serbs; Protestants have massacred Catholics; and Israelis have massacred Palestinians. But each side has its "chosen trauma," which captures an injustice to the exclusion of any wrongs committed by themselves. The best description for that is what I call the bind of the "double victim," in which each thinks of itself as the legitimate victim. Examples of the double victim pattern abound.

Take the case of Palestinians and Israelis. Palestinians and Israelis both insist "we" are the indigenous people here, "they" are the invaders. "We" are the victims, "they" are the aggressors. Each group brings to the conflict a deep sense of persecution not recognized by the other side, which is preoccupied with its own unjust experiences (Heradstveit, 1979; Rouhana & Bar-Tal, 1998). Or take the case of Irish Catholics and Protestants. At the University of Ulster in Northern Ireland, social psychologist Hunter and his colleagues (1991) showed Catholic and Protestant students videos of a Protestant attack at a Catholic funeral and a Catholic attack at a Protestant funeral. Most students attributed the other side's attack to aggressive, bloodthirsty motives but its own side's attack to virtuous self-defense.

In ethnic conflict, each side thinks of itself as the legitimate victim. Each describes the other in similar terms of wickedness and evil, with their own list of historical injustices. Like the narcissism or self-centeredness of individuals who see themselves as having been so hurt in the past that they can tend only to their own needs, each side feels no compassion for the hurt they perpetrate upon others. Each side feels they have some kind of justification for what they do to the point of feeling righteous. Each has an almost mystical sense of their own victimhood.

One can see this sense of victimhood in *Mein Kampf*, in which Adolf Hitler asserts that Germans are being victimized by "world-conquering Judaism." According to Hitler's reasoning, Judaism attempted to extricate the feeling of pride from the soul of the Aryan race, robbing Aryans of their leadership. Therefore, to give back to this noble race their former sense of superiority, the Germans are justified in destroying the Jews. Hitler also claimed that Versailles was unjustified because it was a sign of the visible subjugation of Germany and was intended to destroy Germany. Hitler considered the unification of Austria, the Saarland, the Sudentenland, and Danzig into the Third Reich to be German domestic matters because they had been unjustly taken away in 1919. Thus, Hitler was convinced that Germany must be restored to its rightful position.

The feeling of victimization, which is stimulated and amplified by the memories and feelings of historical injustice, often ends in the desire to seek revenge. And the quest for revenge, as mentioned before, often ends in aggressive behavior (McCullough, 2001, pp. 107–108). Along with the egoism of victimization comes a tunnel vision that prevents individuals involved in the ethnic conflict from "seeing another view" or "hearing the other side." They see events through a single narrow viewpoint that blocks out context and perspective. As Mohandas Gandhi put it, "An eye for an eye makes the whole world blind." Victims avenge victims through repeated cycles that are transmitted from one generation to the other, backed by stories of atrocities and unjust acts committed by the other side and by the honorable acts carried out in revenge, in defense of one's own group and its transcendent values.

We can begin to see why claims for justice are rarely simply a matter of right or wrong but primarily a matter of ethnic identification with one's own group, whether it is on a family, religious, or national level. (As an aside, we are dealing here with claims for justice in ethnic conflicts, not in cases of criminal acts like murder, rape, and so forth.) The psychological functions served by ethnic identification are common to all human beings. Identification with one's group defines one's sense of integrity. The philosopher Hampshire (2000) puts it like this: When "Remember 1689" is chalked on a wall in Belfast by a Roman Catholic calling to mind William III's Protestant Settlements, it would most certainly be useless to respond: "Be fair and reasonable; forget the injustices of the past, as you see them, because the past cannot now be repaired; it is more fair and reasonable to start from now and to try to build a peaceful society for the future." The response comes back: "You are asking us to forget who we are. Like every-one else, we define ourselves by what we reject. We should cease to exist as a community if we thought only of the future and of what you call rea-sonableness. That would be disintegration, the loss of integrity, both as in-dividuals and as a community." Self-definition by opposition is the moral equivalent of the old logical principle *Omnis determinatio est negatio* ["I am what you are not. I am not what you are."] (Hampshire, 2000, pp. 25–26).

Looking at human evolution, identification with one's group is neces-sary for survival. Groups can share food, provide mates, and help care for offspring (Ainsworth, 1989; Barash, 1977; Buss, 1991). Our ancestral history prepares us to live in groups. Not surprisingly, we also define ourselves by our groups, write Australian social psychologists Hogg and Williams (2000) and John Turner (1981, 1987, 1999) and his colleagues. Our sense of who we are contains not just a personal identity but an ethnic identity also.

Turner and the late British social psychologist Henri Tajfel proposed social identity theory. They noted that we categorize people into groups, we identify ourselves with certain groups, and then we compare our groups with other groups, with a favorable bent toward our own group. We evaluate ourselves partly by our group memberships. Having a sense of "we-ness" strengthens our self-concept. It makes us feel good. More-over, taking pride in our groups and seeing our groups as superior helps us feel even better (Smith & Tyler, 1997).

The notion that we have a need to belong to a group is not new, of course. The psychologist Erikson (1968) writes that human beings as a species have survived by being divided into what he has called *pseudo-species*. First each horde or tribe, class, and nation, but then also every re-ligious association becomes *the* human species, considering all the others an odd invention of some irrelevant god. To reinforce the illusion of being chosen, every tribe recognizes a creation of its own, a mythology, and later a legacy: thus was loyalty to a particular tribe, nation, family, or religion secured (Erikson, 1968).

Like Erikson, Freud declares that ethnic identification encourages in-dividuals to believe that their tribe, race, or religion is "naturally" superior to others. Individuals become indoctrinated with the conviction that their "group" alone was planned by an all-wise deity, created in a special cosmic event, and appointed by history to guard the only genuine version of humanity under the leadership of divine leaders. To illustrate this point Freud writes, "We may start with one character trait of the Jews which governs their relationship to other people. There is no doubt that they have a very good opinion of themselves, think themselves nobler, on a higher level, superior to the others. . . . They [the Jews] really believe themselves to be God's chosen people. . . . When one is the declared favorite of the dreaded father one need not be surprised that the other brothers and sisters are jealous" (Freud, 1939, 134–135). And in an address to the Society of B'nai B'rith in Vienna in 1926 Freud said: ". . . I have always been an unbeliever and was brought up without any religion though not without a respect for what are called the 'ethical' standards of human civilization. Whenever I felt an inclination to national enthusiasm I strove to suppress it as being harmful and wrong, alarmed by the warning examples of the peoples among whom we Jews live. But plenty of other things remained over to make the attraction of Jewry and Jews irresistible—many obscure emotional forces, which were the more powerful, . . . as well as a clear consciousness of inner identity, the safe privacy of a common mental construction . . ." (cited in Erikson, 1968, pp. 20–21).

According to Freud, ethnic identification can cause prejudice and conformity, and it can restrict the intellect. Freud notes that an individual's acceptance of an ethnic identity is inseparable from authority acceptance. An individual's personal quest for distinguishing good from evil, just from unjust, is cut short because ethnic teachings are assertions about facts and conditions of reality which tell one something one has not discovered for oneself and which lay claim to one's belief rather than one's intellect. The beliefs are handed down from generation to generation, and the individual is forbidden to raise questions about their authentication. The individual becomes indoctrinated with the conviction that he ought to believe because his ancestors believed (Freud, 1961).

To ensure the acceptance of the beliefs, a system of rewards and punishments is used. Excommunication, whether employed by a church, a tribe, a religious group, or a family, is a powerful punishment for bringing about individual conformity and ethnic identification. According to Freud, countless individuals have been impaired by the compromises they are forced to make because of the pressure imposed on them to accept the legacy of their ancestors. Freud says many individuals, including the ancestors who bequeathed their legacies, probably had doubts about their ethnic beliefs, but the pressure was too strong to have dared to utter them. They had to suppress their doubts, writes Freud, and thereby their intellect, because they thought it was their duty to believe; "many brilliant intellects have broken down over this conflict, and many characters have been impaired by the compromises with which they have tried to find a way out of it" (Freud, 1961, pp. 25–27). This process is in itself a remarkable psychological problem, concludes Freud.

Social identity theory and these statements by Freud and Erikson serve to show a few dimensions of identity formation and explain why ethnic identification is so all-pervasive in justice matters—for the process of identity formation is located in the core of the individual and yet also in the core of his or her ethnic group. In psychological terms, it employs a twofold process. The psychological development of individuals (their personalities and view of themselves) goes hand in hand with the relations they establish to an ethnic group. The values and beliefs underlying the ethnic group become incorporated in one's self-identity and also place one in an ethnic group. We all carry with us tendencies that anchor our identities in some ethnic group. This process is for the most part automatic, transmitted from one generation to another by the ancient heritage of storytelling. Like material assets, legacies are handed down from generation to generation through stories about the past. Legacies transmit beliefs and feelings, conserve memory, and preserve the past.

Thus, as mentioned before, in ethnic conflicts one sees a collapsed sense of time where past injustice is current injustice. And whether in ethnic conflicts or in personal matters, an individual's sense of justice is never simply a matter of rationality. It is first a matter of feelings in defense of one's self, one's group, and inherent in this is the unwillingness of both sides to face the others' passions and viewpoints (Solomon, 1990). From one generation to the other, each side is told stories of unjust acts perpetrated by others, and of the loyal acts carried out in defense of one's own ethnic group and its honorable values. In view of all this, we can see that the experience of an injustice leaves a powerful imprint upon both sides that continues to be transmitted through the generations.

There are many psychological studies on the intergenerational effects of the Holocaust. Most studies on the intergenerational effects of the

Holocaust rely on a pathology model. Since most of these studies assume pathology is transmitted from parent to offspring, first I will review the psychological studies that focus on the effects of the Holocaust on the survivors and Nazi perpetrators. Then I will discuss the effects of the Holocaust on survivors' offspring and the perpetrators' offspring.

There are almost 2,500 studies in Krell and Sherman's (1997) bibliography that deal with the effects of the Holocaust on concentration camp survivors. Most of the studies have focused on the presence or absence of pathological effects of the Holocaust on survivors. Initial reports describe a high incidence of survivor guilt, chronic diffuse anger, sleep disturbances, anhedonia, flashbacks, hypervigilance, depression, psychosomatic and sexual dysfunctions, flashbacks and intrusive thoughts, inability to establish close emotional ties with others—in short, all the symptoms now subsumed under the diagnostic criteria for Posttraumatic Stress Disorder (PTSD) established in the *Diagnostic and Statistical Manual of Mental Disorders* (DSM-IV-TR). The DSM-IV-TR of the American Psychiatric Association is the professional guidebook for diagnosing psychopathology and specifying its prevalence in general and clinical populations.

Eventually, studies on the pathological effects of the Holocaust on survivors expanded to include the survivors' offspring. Terms such as vicarious and secondary traumatization, and direct and indirect have been used to describe intergenerational trauma transmission (Baranowsky, Young, Johnson-Douglas, Keeler & McCarrey, 1998; Weiss & Weiss, 2000). Most of the studies have focused on whether secondary PTSD syndrome, reflected in the current PTSD symptomology, is being transmitted from one generation to the next. Initial reports describe a high incidence of depression, anxiety, conduct disorder, personality problems, inadequate maturity, excessive dependence, and poor coping in survivors' offspring (Fryberg, 1980; Nadler et al., 1985; Podietz et al., 1984; Rakoff, 1966; Rakoff, Sigal, & Epstein, 1976; Rosenman, 1984; Sigal et al., 1973; Sigal & Weinfeld, 1985; Trossman, 1968). Other reports describe survivors' offspring as having a general fragility and vulnerability to stress and having high levels of fear and mistrust (Barocas & Barcocas, 1983; Danieli, 1985; Dashberg, 1987; Rowland-Klein & Dunlop, 1998; Yehuda, Bierer, Schmeidler, Aferiat, Breslau, & Dolan, 2000).

There are studies on the effects of the Holocaust on the perpetrators too, including some SS personnel and Nazi doctors. The studies have focused on the presence or absence of pathological personality traits. Researchers used psychometric instruments or content analyses to examine the perpetrators' personalities and family backgrounds (Dicks, 1972; Lifton, 1986). Initial reports describe the workings of several defense mechanisms. For instance, compartmentalization, which is the ability to raise cognitive and emotional barriers that wall off one domain of thought and activity from another, was thought to underlie the perpetrators' personality disorders. Dicks (1972) interviewed former members of the SS concentration camp personnel and Gestapo units and at the end of his study uses the term "splitting off" to explain how the perpetrators, whose day-long job was mass murder, could go home after work was done and enjoy a civilized family evening. Lifton (1986) interviewed physicians who had been significantly involved at high levels with Nazi medicine and at the end of his study uses the term "doubling" to explain the perpetrators' pathological behaviors. According to Lifton (1986), terms such as "splitting" or "dissociation" or "psychic numbing" denote something about Nazi doctors' suppression of feeling or psychic numbing in relation to their participation in murder, but to chart their involvement in a continuous routine of killing, another psychological term was needed, as it is in any "sustained psychiatric disturbance" (Lifton, 1986, pp. 419–420). So Lifton uses the term "doubling" to describe the sustained pathological behavior of Nazi doctors. "The key to understanding how Nazi doctors came to do the work of Auschwitz is the psychological principle I call 'doubling': the division of the self into functioning wholes, so that a part-self acts as an entire self. An Auschwitz doctor could, through doubling, not only kill and contribute to killing but organize silently, on behalf of that evil project, an entire self-structure (or self-process) encompassing virtually all aspects of his behavior" (Lifton, 1986, p. 418). According to Lifton, doubling included elements considered characteristic of sociopathic character impairment: these include a disorder of feeling (swings between numbing and rage), a pathological avoidance of a sense of guilt, and masked depression related to repressed guilt and numbing (Lifton, 1986).

Eventually, studies on the pathological effects of the Holocaust on the perpetrators expanded to include the perpetrators' offspring. Terms such as "born guilty" and "the inability to mourn" have been used to describe intergenerational pathology transmission (Mitscherlich & Mitsherlich, 1975; Schirovsky, 1988; Stierlin, 1981). Initial reports describe a high incidence of emotional turbulence, psychic damage, and lack of inner peace. Other reports describe perpetrators' offspring as having ambivalence about the past and an inability to work through the distortions of their parents (Bar-On, 1989; Lebert & Lebert, 2001).

Some therapists (Bar-On, 1989; Danieli, 1985; Fogelman, 1984; Kaslow 1997; and Stierlin, personal communication, 1993) came to see the descendants of survivors and perpetrators as in dire need of help. To this end, they have organized dialogue groups, sessions, and seminars, and encounter workshops, self-help groups, and therapy groups to help the descendants achieve solace and healing. Some apparently have remained in contact over the years, each continuing his or her own quest, trying to achieve healing and change. And some have gone on to form other groups committed to healing and working through the impact of the Holocaust.

The numerous reports and studies on survivors, perpetrators, and their children have been central to our awareness of the pathological effects of the Holocaust and the transmission of these effects on their offspring. However, there has been no systematic research that compares the effects of the Holocaust on these two groups of descendants. Previous studies have focused on the pathological effects on each group separately. Moreover, psychological studies have traditionally overlooked how stories about past injustices are transmitted from parent to child, how the offspring of both sides make sense of the stories, the way it influences their identities, and the way in which they rebalance an injustice in their lives. In short, there is practically no research relating to the actual experiences of offspring whose parents inflicted injustice or of those whose parents suffered injustice. There is little research on the quality of emotions or cognitive processes that follow perception of a past injustice. The research remains predominantly individuocentric, psychoanalytic, and pathological in focus, unconcerned with how historic injustices thread together the two sets of offspring as they adapt to an unjust historic event.

## A Study of Injustice in the Lives of Survivors' and Nazis' Offspring

To advance the research in this area, during the fall of 1991, with my husband Daniel Giacomo, then a Harvard psychiatrist, and a team of students at Harvard, we undertook a study to compare the generational legacy of the Holocaust for the descendants both of Nazis and of concentration camp survivors (Weissmark, Giacomo & Kuphal, 1993). We also undertook, as a later aim, to organize the first meeting between children of Nazis and children of concentration camp survivors to examine how injustice effects interpersonal behavior. We are confronted with a paradoxical analogy between the children of victims and the perpetrators; both share a common bond. They have had to cope with the same heritage.

How had these children of victims and of perpetrators dealt with their heritage, with the past injustices and their parents' involvement in those injustices? How had they found out about the past injustices? How had they made sense of the stories transmitted to them by their parents? What impact did it have on their identities? What coping responses did they use to deal with the past injustices? How had they tried to rebalance the past injustices in their present lives? Did the children of concentration camp survivors want to avenge the injustices their parents suffered? Did the children of Nazis feel their parents' roles in those injustices were justified? And how did they view the descendants of the other side?

We set out to ask children of Nazis and children of concentration camp survivors identical questions and then compare their responses. Our first task was locating the children. Luckily, we discovered Ilona Kuphal, a German businesswoman living in Cambridge and the daughter of a Waffen SS Nazi officer. After interviewing Ilona, I asked whether she would agree to travel to Germany to help us recruit other descendants of Nazis. She readily agreed. Also, Gerald Posner had just published a fascinating book on the sons and daughters of leaders of Nazis (Posner, 1991). Gerald spent much time locating German children of prominent Nazi parents. He generously shared his list of contacts.

The first person on the list we called was Klaus Saur. Klaus was the son of Karl Saur, a committed Nazi and the chief of the technical department in the armaments ministry. He was a trusted friend to Hitler and one of the few men named in Hitler's will. We called Klaus, described our research project, and asked if he would like to attend a meeting of descendants of Nazis and concentration camp survivors. Although Klaus declined to attend (his brother, however, Karl Saur, Jr. did attend), he unexpectedly sent us a check—a research grant to support the project. With the names from Posner and the grant from Saur, we began our study in earnest.

A form letter, a one-page description of the study, and biographical information about the researchers were sent to thirty-one people. Each was told that an interview study of children of concentration camp survivors and children of Nazis was being conducted and that a meeting with the children would be held later. We eventually chose to interview ten children of Nazis and ten children of concentration camp survivors.

Three criteria were used for choosing children of survivors: having at least one parent who was a survivor of either a Nazi concentration camp or slave labor camp, not having a parent who was a member of an organization that actively fought against the Nazis, and agreeing to participate in a meeting with children from the "other side" that would be televised on network television. Three criteria were used for choosing children of Nazis: having at least one parent who was an active member of the Nazi party during the Third Reich, not having a parent who was a member of an organization that actively fought against the Nazis, and agreeing to participate in the videotaped meeting.

Of the twenty interviewed, the average age was forty-three, ranging from thirty to forty-eight. Fourteen were female and six were male. Ten were born in Germany, one in Israel, and the remaining nine in the United States. Their parents' background varied. For survivors' children, some came from families where both parents were survivors of death camps and a large part of the family was killed. Others came from families where only one parent was a survivor of a labor camp and a limited part of the family was killed. Still others came from families that spent some time hiding in the forest before being transported to concentration camps. Similarly, Nazis' children came from varied backgrounds. Some were the children of high-ranking Nazis like the Gestapo chief, the deputy armaments minister, and lieutenants in the Third Reich's Waffen-SS. Others were the children of lowly Wehrmacht soldiers who served on the eastern front. Obviously, this is not a random group, but those who decided to speak on the record and agree to attend a televised meeting at Harvard.

The interviews were conducted in English and German, tape-recorded, and transcribed. They usually lasted about two hours and took place primarily in the Boston, New York, Hamburg, and Berlin areas. The ten children of Nazis were interviewed by Ilona Kuphal, and the ten children of survivors were interviewed by the author.

A semistructured interview was designed as the chief instrument of the study. The interview was designed to generate data by focusing on broad areas. We hypothesized that these areas would yield useful data for comparing (the similarities and differences) between the two groups of descendants. The areas also determined the sequence of inquiry followed during the interviews. The areas were: (1) subjects' developmental histories with special attention to the evolution of finding out about the war, the Holocaust, and their parents' involvement, (2) subjects' reports of their responses to information about the war and the Holocaust and of its influence on them, (3) subjects' perspectives on justice, and (4) subjects' views on descendants of the other side.

Subjects were told that the interview was designed to help provide an understanding of the lives of people whose parents were survivors of concentration camps or whose parents were Nazis. They were told that the schedule of questions the interviewer kept was aimed at helping this goal. The potential risks and benefits of being interviewed and attending a joint meeting were explained to the subjects. The subjects were told that there were no serious risks involved except for the issue of confidentiality. The subjects were also given information about the interviewers' backgrounds. They were told that Kupahl's father was an officer of the Waffen SS, and they were told that my mother was a survivor of Auschwitz and my father a survivor of Dachau. All subjects were cooperative and friendly toward the interviewers. The atmosphere during the interviews, however, varied. Although the interviewers had a general concern that they were intruding into a very private and difficult area of the subjects' lives, this was especially acute with particular subjects. At times, a few subjects would cry and say they never discussed these matters.

After getting verbatim transcripts, the major task of the study was to organize the mass of data into the areas the interview was designed to investigate. In the process, themes within each area were identified. Here, I compare the responses that emerged from the recollections of the sons and daughters of Nazis and of concentration camp survivors and their significance for understanding justice as intergenerational. In the next chapter, I will discuss the meeting with the sons and daughters of Nazis and of concentration camp survivors and its significance for understanding how injustice affects interpersonal behavior.

## Voices from the Interviews

The results showed that the responses of children and Nazis revealed similar threads of feelings and associations to the past that run through their lives. These include several themes that I mentioned earlier in this chapter: ethnic identification, double victimhood, feelings of indignation, and a personal sense of justice. Each is discussed in turn.

### *Ethnic Idenitification*

Although these second generation children were uninvolved in the events of their parents, the past injustices still affected them in profound ways. The offspring of both Nazis and of concentration camps survivors said they felt they inherited a dark legacy submerged into their identities, which consumed large parts of their lives.

Typical answers to the question "How did the information about the Holocaust and the war influence you?" showed that their parents' experiences influenced their identification with their ethnic group.

For example, a daughter of an Auschwitz survivor, who was six years old when her mother first told her stories about the camps, said,

■ My whole Jewish identity revolves around my parents' having been concentration camp survivors. I always felt, since I was a child, that I had to know more, so I could really understand why this happened to the Jews. Later it made me proud to be a Jew because we survived that, but also very hateful of Germans and mistrustful of all non-Jews. When I got older I became a Zionist because I felt Jews could only be safe if they had their own country. I remember in high school I use to have this pin that said 'Never Again.' It's hard really to describe the influence it had on me. But I guess I'd have to say my whole life has been determined by the fact that my parents were survivors. It is something that is deep in me, and I want my children to know what their grandparents went through.

A son of a Nazi, who was nine years old when his mother told him his father was a high-ranking Nazi, said,

■ The simple fact is that even those who were born after the War have grown up in a situation in which that happened. All Germans have this historical legacy. None of us can escape it because our identity as individuals and as Germans is woven into it. Since I found about my father's role in the National Socialist German Workers' Party, I was curious to know more. In school we got very little of it, so I had to search out the information myself. It consumed a large part of my life. I think any young German person growing up in Germany after World War II felt their identity was linked to that period. There were many untrue things said of what we Germans have been told about our history. The party was trying to save Germany's rightful position, to build a unified Germany, and to stop the Western Powers from destroying Germany. My father, like millions of Germans, thought they were doing their best for Germany. This historical legacy is still with us.

*Double Victim*

One difference that emerged from the recollections is that most children of Nazis reported their parents told them stories about the *war*, whereas children of survivors reported their parents told them stories about the *Holocaust*.

The daughter of a survivor put it like this:

■ I didn't even know there was a war until I was a teenager. I didn't even know fifty million people were killed during the war. I thought just six million Jews were killed. The stories I heard were always about taking the Jews to concentration camps. For my whole childhood I think I thought it was only the Jews who were killed. That it was just Nazis killing Jews. It wasn't until some history class that I realized this was a major war. But you know, still I think the Jews had it the worse, they suffered the most because every Jew was a victim like someone said.

The daughter of a Nazi officer put it like this:

■ I didn't know about the concentration camps until I was in my teens. First I heard about the party. Then I heard stories about the war, about bombs falling or about not having food. I would hear that my father was an officer in the army, and I remember seeing pictures of him in uniform. And I remember his black shiny boots. And I saw a picture of him on a horse. At first I remember feeling proud to find out my father was an officer in the army.

Because children of Nazis first heard their parents talk about the war, they believed their parents were victims too. In fact, many children of Nazis recalled their parents telling them stories about how they suffered during the war.

This is described by the son of a high-ranking Nazi: "At the end of the war, my family was forced to move from their large house to a small, cold apartment, and food was difficult to find. All our property was taken, and my mother literally had to go beg for food to feed the family. She really suffered to do this." Another son of a Nazi described it like this: "I remember my mother crying because of the bad situation they had. There were several years after the war when they did not have anywhere to live. They went from apartment to apartment. The British expropriated my father's business. I think that was unjust and wrong."

As expected, all of the children of survivors recalled their parents telling them stories about how they suffered in the concentration camps. One son of a survivor described the details of that suffering like this:

■ I remember my father would tell me stories about the camps, about how he was brutally beaten and starved. He told me if you were called a *Muselmänner* (one of the walking dead) that meant you wouldn't survive much longer. In my mind I could see the grotesqueness of the scenes, the image of my father neither dead nor alive. For me the picture of him and the other Jews being victimized by brutal Nazis was very strong.

Another son of a survivor, whose father was a Jewish "kapo," a concentration camp inmate to whom the Nazis had assigned supervisory positions, recalled his father telling him how he suffered too. The kapos had authority to impose punishment and many were famous for their cruelty.

As a result, the Ministry of Justice in Israel introduced an Act against Jewish War Criminals in August 1949, but the ministry preferred to avoid such controversial, sensitive matters, and by the mid-1950s, only a few Jews suspected of collaborating with the Nazis were under investigation for "crimes against humanity," and very few of these investigations led to indictments. "The kapo trials were a filthy and embarrassing story, and the courts and press in Israel did not want to get caught up in it," reports Segev (Segev, 2000, p. 261). No one knows how many kapos escaped justice after the war. Although survivors and Nazis have been the subject of many psychological studies, as far as I know, there have been few psychological studies on the kapos.

The son I interviewed admitted his father was a kapo, but he clearly defined himself as the son of a survivor (not the son of a war criminal or a Nazi collaborator), and he described his father's suffering like this: "My father said many good Jews then did all kinds of jobs because they had no choice. That it's not so horrible. That they suffered to do it and that to survive you couldn't refuse to accept the job of a kapo."

### Feelings of Indignation

Many children of survivors recalled their emotional reactions to the stories about the past injustices, which included feelings of indignation, which in turn incited the desire to seek revenge. The son of a survivor said,

■ When my mother talked to me about the camps and the torture and showed me pictures of dead relatives, she didn't have to say she's angry. You felt it. I think I have a much more powerful sense of anger and hate and wanting to get vengeance than most people do. There were times when I said I would just love to shoot a Nazi. I'm not stopped from doing an act of violence toward a war criminal on ethical grounds. I'm stopped by a practical issue. I don't want to go shoot some Nazi living in Argentina and then spend the rest of my life in jail. I know if I was going to die soon, I would love to have the option to do that.

Another child of a survivor described it like this:

■ I felt a deep sorrow and loss. They took everything from my family—they killed my family, they took all the properties, and money everything. My parents came here with nothing. And what did the Germans get for their crimes? I wish there was more I could do. But at least I'm involved in Jewish activities, and I do lot of lecturing, writing about the Holocaust so people can't forget. And to this day I will not visit Germany or buy any German products. I don't think the Germans have paid for what they did to us. Look at how well they live now.

Many children of Nazis recalled their emotional reactions to the stories about the past injustices, which also included feelings of indignation. The son of a Nazi said,

■ I was angry when I heard what the Allies did to my family. My father said the former Allies were wrong, and I think they were. I think the former Allies were wrong. They split Germany up like in Versailles and wanted history to say that every German was a Nazi and all Nazis were evil so that all of Germans would feel guilty. But that is not the truth. And I will do my part to see the Allies are repaid for the wrong they did and that things are discussed in the proper perspective.

Another child of a Nazi described it like this:

■ I think the Americans and the Allies went too far. I think the bombing of German cities like Dresden was unfair. And I don't think it was right that the Allies tried the Nazis. It should have been done by German courts. And the other thing is, not all Germans were Nazis. The first people killed in Dachau were German people, not Jewish people. I think the Jews want to make it seem like they were the only victims but they were not. The German people suffered too, and people need to know it, but Germans are afraid to talk about it.

*A Sense of Justice*

For both the children of Nazis and survivors, the stories of the Holocaust and the war provide visions of a perceived injustice and visions for understanding moral responsibility. In turn, those visions provide a framework for acting in the world. All the children reported that they felt their parents did not sufficiently engage in retributive actions—that is, actions aimed at restoring justice. Thus, both the children of Nazis and of survivors reported they felt the need to rebalance the past injustices in their lives.

For instance, the son of a Nazi said: "I feel I have a special obligation to let people know how unfairly Germany was treated. I think the real facts should come out."

The daughter of a survivor said: "It is important to me that my children know about the horrors of the Holocaust about how unfair and cruel Jews were treated. And I feel I have a duty to let others know too."

## Summing Up

It seems as if Adolf Eichmann's prediction that the second generation of Germans would be burdened by the deeds of their Nazi parents has come true. The recollections of Nazis' and survivors' children show this intergenerational process of ethnic identification at work. Summarizing the significance of the children's recollections, I would stress the indelible imprint of the parents' stories on the children's ethnic identities, on their loyalties to their parents, and on their need to rebalance the past injustices. Also the children's reports reveal the double victim phenomena described earlier. Both Nazi parents and survivor parents (and even a kapo parent) told their children stories about the injustices they suffered. These stories conveyed a sense of victimhood. Nazi parents told their children stories about how they suffered during the war, about the injustices perpetrated by the Allies, and about the injustices of the Versailles treaty. Survivor parents told their children stories about the injustices perpetrated by the Nazis in concentration camps and in the ghettos, and about anti-Semitic incidents before the War.

Although Nazi and survivor parents' descriptions and details of their experiences varied in detail and vividness, all the children reported the stories had an intense emotional impact on them. They felt a need to construct meaning out of the stories, which they thought would help to better understand themselves. Survivors' children expressed the need to redress the past injustices by educating others about the Holocaust and by seeking revenge. Also survivors' children expressed a deep loyalty to their

Jewish identities and a distrust of gentiles. Nazis' children expressed loyalty to their German identities and a desire to inform others that "not all Germans are Nazis." Also some children of Nazis expressed the need to redress the past injustices by educating others about how the German people suffered during the war and about the injustices perpetrated by the Allies.

Nazis' children and survivors' children have been locked into a special relationship. Both of their identities have been shaped by World War II and the Holocaust. What the Germans call *Vergangenheitsbewältigung*, mastering the past, coming to terms with their parents' experiences, is a painful and difficult legacy for both groups. The next chapter will look at the way this shared legacy links the two groups and reveals the interpersonal aspects of justice.

# 4

# JUSTICE AS INTERPERSONAL

People who feel they have been treated unjustly—and who still resent the perpetrators—choose one of two coping strategies, recent research suggests (Miller, 2001). They chose either to withdraw or to even the score. And victims of severe trauma, whose psyches have been marked with anguish of the event, seek to avoid any thoughts, feelings, or reminders that could make them relive that painful experience, research also shows.

Yet, redressing such injustices often requires both parties' willingness to suspend resentment and meet and talk.

Therein lies the paradox for survivors' children and Nazis' children. They seek to avoid the very thing that might ultimately resolve—or at least salve—their pain: a face-to-face encounter with each other. For to do so would give their past, as embodied in the memories of their parents' suffering, a new reality.

Indeed, even when some children of the Holocaust and Nazis' children agreed to make a historic meeting at Harvard Medical Education Center in 1992, their sense of a shared experience only took them so far. Although many participants from the two groups were able to relinquish some resentment and bond with the children of their parents' enemy, they could not shake their stake to the moral high ground. Survivors' children were the most intractable, feeling that there was no Nazi point of view that could justify, much less rectify, the suffering and death of their relatives in concentration camps.

The burden of confronting past injustices was transmitted to another generation. Coming to terms with their parents' dark past shaped the identities of both Nazis' children and survivors' children. The Holocaust and WWII legacy had a dominant influence on the children's lives and obligations.

For children of survivors, the legacy emphasized the exclusivity of the Holocaust. For children of Nazis, the legacy emphasized the general conditions of the war. The children of survivors' descriptions of how their parents suffered during the Holocaust are matched by the children of Nazis' descriptions of how their parents suffered during the war. This fact brings us to a problematic legacy of the Holocaust. Both survivors' and Nazis' accounts claim the status of victimhood. We are faced with symmetrical stories of victimhood, with the double victim phenomena.

One survivor parent told his child, "I want you to remember every Jew was a victim. Germany was a nation of murderers. They didn't have any pity for women or for children. What happened to the Jews was the greatest crime in history." A former Nazi's child recalls her father telling her, "I want you to remember. We were fighting a war. The Jews weren't the only ones who suffered. I was in prison too. We lost the war, so the Allies wanted people to believe all Germans were guilty, but the Germans were the first to be taken to the camps."

Nazis' children and survivors' children are challenged to confront a difficult past recalled with deep-seated emotions. The deep emotions are presented not only in the survivors' stories but in the former Nazis' stories too. These stories, passed down from the generation that experienced them to the generation that now remembers, compel the children to face the uncomfortable presence of earlier unresolved roles and injustices. In each case, the demand arises to understand the injustices wrought over a generation ago, which were not settled by the previous generation.

The experience of injustice involves more than an emotional reaction to physical or economic suffering. Appealing to our everyday experience confirms that. When we are treated unfairly by others (or those close to us are treated unfairly), it affects us in profound ways. We are likely to suffer not only from the physical harm done to us, but also from the psychological injury of having been treated unfairly. The reason most people are affected by injustices done to them is not simply that they hurt in some tangible way; it is because such injuries are also messages—interpersonal communications. They are ways a wrongdoer has of saying to us, "I am superior to you" or "I have the right to decide who should and who should not inhabit the world" or "I count and you do not" (Murphy & Hampton, 1988). When people are intentionally denied the respect to which they believe they are entitled, people feel as unjustly treated as when they are denied the material assets to which they believe they are entitled (Miller, 2001).

An intentional injustice is insulting and degrading, and thus involves an injury that is interpersonal. As Aristotle asserted, ". . . a man can give something away if he likes, but he cannot suffer injustice if he likes—there must be somebody else to do him the injustice" (Aristotle, 1955, p. 163). Research from studies of the layperson's understanding of everyday injustices supports the notion that the experience of everyday injustice involves some form of disrespectful interpersonal treatment. For instance, when people are asked to describe unjust experiences they have experienced in daily life, the most frequently mentioned are violations of interpersonal codes of conduct like giving orders in an inappropriate tone, unjustified accusation and blaming, or ruthless use of one's status and power (Lupfer, Weeks, Doan & Houston, 2000; Mikula, 1986; Mikula, Schere & Athenstaedt, 1998).

Princeton University psychologist Dale Miller says that people care whether their treatment is just or unjust because it suggests something critically important to them—their self-worth. The right to be treated in a way that fosters positive self-worth plays an important role in an individual's experience of injustice. According to Harvard University philosopher John Rawls (1971), one of the entitlements individuals are due by virtue of their humanity is the right to be treated in a way that fosters positive self-worth. Recent research on what has been called "interactional justice" (Bies & Moag, 1986; Cropanzo & Greenberg, 1997; Skarlicki & Folger, 1997) confirms that people believe they are entitled to respectful treatment from others. "Concern for justice and respect for personhood are powerfully and inseparably linked" (Miller, 2001, p. 17).

When we (or those we love) are treated unjustly by others, it hurts us in profound ways. Our sense of dignity and self-worth is offended. So we are likely to react by feeling angry, resentful, or bitter toward those who have hurt us. These feelings function in defense of our self-esteem, of our perception of our own worth, and of what we are owed. It is a response that is chiefly concerned with our (the victim's) relationship to the wrongdoer.

The psychologist Bernard Weiner (1993) adopts the metaphor that victims are godlike, and life is a courtroom where interpersonal dramas are played out. Like God, victims regard themselves as having the right to judge others as innocent or guilty, as good or bad. These inferences then cause affective reactions that are also ascribed to God, including anger, resentment, and compassion. Weiner gives the example of a spouse failing to appear at a designated time to go to a movie. The waiting wife believes that the errant husband went somewhere else instead. The wife is angry and, upon seeing the partner, refuses to speak to him. The husband then confesses his "sin" and asks forgiveness. The wife is merciful and withdraws her sentence.

The wife's forgiveness can be an act of goodwill, but it can also be an act of arrogance (Murphy & Hampton, 1988, p. 31). Because negative emotions like anger and resentment create unequal moral relations among persons, the wife may feel her husband owes her an apology. Seeing it this way, the husband might resent the forgiveness. "Who do you think you are to forgive me?" "I don't owe you anything," the husband might respond to his well-meaning wife.

Besides creating unequal moral relations, negative emotions can stand as a fatal obstacle to the restoration of a relationship. We can see this clearly in close relationships such as marriage and friendship. Because of the nature of attachment, interpersonal injuries here are not just ordinary injustices but also betrayals (Murphy & Hampton, 1988). Because, when we relate to people toward whom we feel deeply attached, our feelings are highly susceptible to emotional extremes. When such a person does something that is contrary to our expectations it has a greater potential to hurt us. So resentment here can be deep and nearly intractable. In the example above, the wife might have been unmoved by the pleas of her husband. She might have refused to forgive him because in her mind her husband was now untrustworthy.

In ethnic relationships too, anger and resentment can stand as an unyielding response—as revealed in this statement by a daughter of survivors: "I don't feel a need to give up my grudge. My blood is not ready to cool. The Germans cannot be redeemed. They must pay for what they did to us. And we must impress hatred of the Germans upon our children and their descendants." And we can hear the voice of resentment in this statement by a son of a former Nazi: "Every major nation has had its own Hitler period with its own atrocities. What is the Allied bombings of Hiroshima and Nagasaki? I think this talk of collective guilt has gone on for too long. I am tired of the Jewish people trying to make us Germans feel guilty. The Nazi regime forced the German people to be Nazis. If they hadn't obeyed, the Gestapo would torture them."

The law tries to redress injustices by institutionalizing and reducing feelings of anger and resentment. James Stephen, the famous Victorian judge and theorist of law, claimed that the law gives "distinct shape to the feeling of anger" and provides a "distinct satisfaction to the desire of vengeance." He wrote: "The . . . law gives definite expression and solemn ratification and justification to the hatred which is excited by the commission of the offence . . ." (cited in Murphy & Hampton, 1988, p. 3).

Concerning the Holocaust, the Western Allies and the Federal Republic of Germany tried to institutionalize feelings of resentment by setting up a system of reparations to redress the past injustices. They established legal sanctions and a financial reparation program. The money from Germany was to be compensation for the property stolen by the Nazis and for the physical and economic damage suffered by the Holocaust survivors. The program was identified as *Wiedergutmachung*, which literally translated means "to make good again."

However, it was widely recognized that these measures had the opposite effect and were equally resented by survivors and Germans alike. The program failed to remedy feelings of hatred and resentment; in fact, it perpetuated such feelings. *Herut*, an Israeli newspaper, printed a quotation from the section of Maimonides's legal code devoted to murderers: "And one should take care not to take ransom from a murderer even if he gives all the money in the world. . . ." To the left was a picture said to be taken at the death camp; it showed two words in Yiddish, purportedly written in blood: *Yidn nekome*—Jews, revenge (cited in Segev, 2000, p. 214).

Many survivors supported the news release. They resented the monetary amends of West Germany, calling them "blood money." They declared that such amends could not avenge for the suffering they endured or make up for the degradation. And some West Germans have expressed their resentment because Germany is still stigmatized although "Nazi criminals were hunted down and put on trial. Guilt was accepted, and billions were paid in restitution to survivors and heirs" (Joffe, 1998, pp. 222–223). Thus, the *Wiedergutmachung* program was unsuccessful at redressing past injustices or reducing feelings of resentment.

One can readily appreciate the desire to redress past injustices through institutionalized programs like the *Wiedergutmachung* program. But redressing an injustice sometimes demands more than establishing legal sanctions or financial reparations. An injustice is committed when rules of conduct are willfully broken. This violation, as mentioned before, results in some form of harm that violates interpersonal codes of conduct. So, whether in policy or in close relationships, redressing an injustice is more than simply a matter of jurisprudence or economics but, first, a matter of personal concern. It is decidedly intimate, whether involving individuals, a whole family, or a whole nation of people. Redressing an injustice, therefore, requires personal involvement. It requires both parties' willingness to meet and redress the injustice (Weissmark, Giacomo & Kuphal, 1993).

Most of us would dismiss this thought. Our response is to shun those who have wronged us or to strike back. Recent research of people's responses to being treated unfairly confirms that the most common responses to injustice fall into two broad categories: withdrawal responses or attack responses. For example, giving one's partner the "silent treatment" is a common withdrawal response; whereas "evening the score," as mentioned before, is a common attack response (Miller, 2001).

When we are treated unjustly by others, it affects us in profound and deeply threatening ways. There is an emotional response. We are affected not only by what happens to us, but also by what happens within ourselves. Since we are all, to some extent, sensitive to how others treat us, it is natural to respond by hating and resenting those who treat us unjustly and to "want to separate ourselves from them—to harm them in turn or at least banish them from the realm of those whose well-being should be our concern" (Murphy & Hampton, 1988, p. 25). Our sense of self-worth is social in at least this sense, and it is part of human nature that we respond in these ways.

Surprisingly, during his trial, Eichmann expressed the sentiment that he would like to meet with the victims to redress the past injustices. He said he "would like to find peace with [his] former enemies"—a sentiment he shared with Himmler, who had expressed it during the last year of the war, and with the Labor Front leader Robert Ley, who, before he committed suicide in Nuremberg, had proposed the establishment of a "conciliation committee" consisting of the Nazis responsible for the massacres and the Jewish survivors (cited in Arendt, 1964, p. 53).

Arendt described Eichmann's sentiment as an "outrageous cliché," "a self-fabricated stock phrase," "devoid of reality." She thought it unbelievable that many ordinary Germans reacted in the same terms at the end of the war. And she concluded that the desire to meet with the victims was merely self-serving. Arendt wrote: ". . . you could almost see what an 'extraordinary sense of elation' it gave to the speaker the moment it popped out of his mouth" (Arendt, 1964, p. 53).

It is impossible to know what was in Eichmann's mind or other former Nazis' minds when they uttered this sentiment. But we can, I think, understand Arendt's response. Hannah Arendt was a German Jew. She was born in 1906 in Hanover, Germany. She studied philosophy with Martin Heidegger at the University of Heidelberg, where she earned her doctorate. Her own experience with anti-Semitism forced her to leave Germany. Her former teacher and lover Martin Heidegger had joined the Nazi party. It is reasonable to assume, therefore, that Hannah Arendt herself felt betrayed and was deeply affected by the experience of injustice.

"What was decisive," Arendt recalls in 1965, "was the day we learned about Auschwitz. That was the real shock. . . . It was really as if an abyss had opened. Because we had the idea that amends could somehow be made for everything else, as amends can be made for just about everything at some point in politics. But not for this. This ought not to have happened" (cited in Kohn, 1994, pp. 13–14).

As mentioned in Chapter 1, Hannah Arendt was widely attacked in the Jewish press and by Jewish organizations for her controversial interpretation of the Eichmann trial and for her description of the Jewish leadership's cooperation with the Nazis. But the Jewish press and Jewish organizations praised Arendt's response to the Holocaust—the idea that amends with the Germans could never be made. The Israeli newspaper *Herut* published a declaration saying that any hands raised in favor of negotiations with Germany would be "treasonous hands" (cited in Segev, 2000, p. 213). Menachem Begin, a member of the Knesset and a staunch opponent of reparations, said at an Israeli Knesset session, "There are things in life that are worse than death itself. And this is one of those things. . . . We will leave our families, bid our children farewell, and there will be no negotiations with Germany. . . . We are prepared to do anything, anything to prevent this disgrace to Israel . . ." (cited in Segev, 2000, pp. 219–220). "Twelve million Germans served in the Nazi army. There is not one German who has not murdered our fathers. Every German is a Nazi. Every German is a murderer" (cited in Segev 2000, p. 216).

This understandable response to resent those who have treated us unjustly explains the reluctance to meet or to talk with those who have treated us unjustly. Furthermore, clinical evidence shows that our reluctance to meet with those who have wronged us stems from the traumatic psychological effects of the injustice itself.

Clinical data show that victims of injustice experience intense psychological distress at exposure to external cues that symbolize or resemble an aspect of the unjust event (Figley, 1985). Exposure to reminders of the unjust event may trigger images, flashbacks, or a sense of reliving the painful experience. Most victims, therefore, avoid thoughts, feelings, or conversations associated with the unjust event. And most victims avoid activities, places, or people that arouse recollections of the unjust event. The reluctance to meet with the wrongdoer stems from the victims' needs to protect their mental well-being. These findings may help to explain why most survivors avoided meeting or having discussions with former Nazis.

But if we accept the notion put forth here—that injustice is an interpersonal injury, that resentment can lead to bad consequences, and that resentment is a fatal obstacle to redressing an injustice—then it follows that avoidance or attack cannot always be the final response we take to those who have wronged us (Murphy & Hampton, 1988, p. 17). Redressing an injustice, sometimes, requires both parties' willingness to meet and discuss the injustice.

But getting both parties to discuss the injustice is first a matter of getting them to reason or be reasonable. And this involves "getting them to acknowledge or at least face the others' passions and points of view" (Solomon, 1990, p. 47). As Solomon says, this is why the most tragic ethnic conflicts, such as those in Northern Ireland, Bosnia, Cyprus, and the

Middle East, perpetuate themselves with a refusal to acknowledge the others' points of view.

Reason has the key function of promoting mutual awareness. Whether in policy matters or in personal relationships, reason in justice involves more than proving the validity of one's point of view; instead it involves curbing one's emotions. This, in turn, can help one understand others' circumstances. Given the controversial and possibly misinterpreted implications of this idea, let me make clear that I am not suggesting one overlook or forgive an injustice. As I mentioned in the first chapter, if our aim is to understand unjust behavior and the reactions and legacies resulting from this behavior rather than judge it from a moral standpoint, then we are required to consider different contexts and viewpoints. "Hearing the other side," "seeing another view," means we use thinking in a unbiased, open manner, in contrast to a biased, closed manner. It does not mean we forgive a person's unjust actions or seek to redress the injustice at all costs.

A story may make this clearer. Recently, the journalist Laura Blumenfeld (2002) chronicled her journey to meet with the Palestinian terrorist who shot her father. The attack had taken place in Jerusalem in 1986. For twelve years, Blumenfeld says she was haunted by the idea of somehow avenging the crime. "It was like a fracture that never healed," she says (Schindehette & Seaman, 2002, p. 129).

Though the bullet only grazed her father's scalp, Blumenfeld was deeply shaken. "It was my first brush with evil," she says. "It made me angry . . ." (Schindehette & Seaman, 2002, p. 129). The idea of confronting the terrorist who shot her father never left her. "I had two impulses," she says. "One was to physically shake him and scream, 'Do you know what it is that you did?' The other was to reach inside him and shake up his soul" (Schindehette & Seaman, 2002, p. 130).

Blumenfeld learned that the man who shot her father was in a pro-Syria breakaway faction of the Palestine Liberation Organization. Several Palestinians had been tried and convicted in an Israeli court in 1986 for the shooting of foreigners. The man who had shot her father was named Omar Khatib and was now serving twenty-five years in an Israeli prison.

Identifying herself simply as an American journalist interested in "hearing his story," Blumenfeld went to the West Bank to meet Khatib's family. She asked the gunman's father, "Why did he do it?" The father's response was brief. "He did his duty," he said. "Every Palestinian must do it. Then there will be justice" (Blumenfeld, 2002b, p. 38). Khatib's parents showed Blumenfeld their son's report cards and high-school certificate of graduation that read, "The school administration certifies that Omar Kamel Said Al Khatib was a student . . . His conduct was very good" (Blumenfeld, 2002b, p. 38).

Only immediate relatives were allowed contact with prisoners, so Khatib's brother offered to take letters from Blumenfeld to his brother in prison. In her letters to Khatib, Blumenfeld explained that she was an American journalist and was interested about his life in an Israeli prison, about his family's history, about the events that led to his arrest, and what, in particular, had inflamed his feelings against Israel. Khatib wrote her back several times. In one letter he wrote:

> This city [Jerusalem] has shaped my identity; she planted in my mind un-forgettable memories. I witnessed the Israeli aggression of the Six Day War. I was four years old then, but enough aware to understand what was going on. I remember when my mother used to hide us. . . . We were so frightened by the darkness and the sound of the guns. . . . At the end of the '60s my brother was arrested and sent to prison. . . . I saw the painful time that my family went through, searching to know the fate of my brother. I remem-ber visiting him with my mother once or twice, but after that he was ex-pelled to Jordan. . . . There he was sent to prison for no reason but under the pretext of crossing the borders illegally. We were such a poor family at that time, we didn't have enough money to eat. . . . I will never forget the ex-haustion and pain of the journey when I accompanied my mother to visit my brother. . . . Do you know when I saw [my brother] next? It was 25 years later. This time I was the prisoner, and he was the visitor. (Blumenfeld, 2002b, p. 39)

In her reply to Khatib, Blumenfeld asked him why he shot the Ameri-can tourist. Khatib wrote back: "With regard to David Blumenfeld—I hope he can understand the reasons behind my act. If I were him I would. I have thought a lot about meeting him one day" (Blumenfeld, 2002b, p. 40). To give Khatib a better sense of David Blumenfeld, Laura Blumenfeld replied that she had contacted David, and discovered that his grandpar-ents had been killed in the Holocaust, and that he had come to Israel to gather material for building a Holocaust museum in New York. Blumenfeld told him that David was not hostile to the Palestinian cause, but that he was concerned about whether Khatib would ever again resort to violence against anyone, innocent or not (Blumenfeld, 2002b, p. 40). When Khatib learned that David felt sympathy for the Palestinians, he wrote that he had hoped they could one day be friends.

In his next letter, Katib wrote: "Back to David, I do admire his talking to you and I appreciate his understanding, his support for my people. If these feelings are really from the depth of his heart, his may contribute a lot to our friendship. Of course my answer to his question [about committing an act of violence again] is NO" (Blumenfeld, 2002b, p. 40).

In July 1999 Khatib was scheduled for a hearing on a possible medical parole. Blumenfeld returned to Israel, stood in the courtroom, and proclaimed that she was the daughter of David Blumenfeld, the man Khatib shot at. Blumenfeld says she tried to explain why she had concealed her identity for so long: "I did it for one reason. This conflict is between human beings, and not between disembodied Arabs and Jews. And we're people. Not military targets. We're people with families" (Blumenfeld, 2002b, p. 40). Blumenfeld says, "I wanted them to know me as an individual, and for me to know them. I didn't want them to think of me as a Jew, or as a victim. Just Laura. And I wanted to understand who they were, without them feeling defensive or accused. I wanted to see what we had in common" (Blumenfeld, 2002a, p. 362).

Blumenfeld argued for the prisoner's release. Khatib and his family stared in shock. His family wept and embraced her. The meeting, says Blumenfeld, "felt like the defining moment of my life" (Schindehette & Seaman, 2002, p. 131). Blumenfeld's story shows that her meeting with the Palestinian terrorist and his family was a transforming experience.

Similar stories of transformation have been reported in journalistic accounts of families of murder victims who have had face-to-face meetings with a wrongdoer. For example, correspondent Joseph Kahn describes a mother's face-to-face meeting with her son's killer (*Boston Globe*, January 20, 1994). Sue Molhan met Alfred Lemerich, her son's killer, in 1992. "It felt good," she says. "It felt right. . . . Now I know that for me there is life after murder. . . Alfred understands the pain he caused me now and what he took away from me" (*Boston Globe*, January 20, 1994, pp. 45, 50).

Still, it is true that some emotional wounds are too deep to ever really be transformed. The survivors of the death camps endured a traumatic experience of systematic injustice and cruelty. The look in my mother's eyes, when she told me stories about Auschwitz, has never left me. Her parents are buried at Auschwitz, her little brother, and a part of my mother was buried there, too. She was a 15-year-old girl when she was taken to the camps. Imagine now that young woman who lost everyone she loved, and at the same time everything she possessed. Her head was shaved. She was clothed in a striped uniform with a Star of David sewn on the jacket. And she learned one thing quickly: to say "Jawohl" (Yessir), and never to ask questions. She learned the only values that counted were finding food, staying warm, and getting shoes that fit. She became a hollow person, reduced to suffering and needs. It is in this way that one can understand, as Primo Levi (1961) says, the double sense of the term "extermination camp."

My mother's number was 47021. I can't recall if it was tattooed on her left arm or her right. But I know she carried that tattoo on her arm until she died, just a few years ago. And I know the look in her eyes, as they stared into mine, was tormented. Her pain was permanent, branded in blue numbers on her forearm. The experience of someone who lived for years merely as a thing in the feelings of others is unlikely to emerge willing to hear others' passions and points of views. But if survivors' wounds can never heal, the question remains: must they be passed on to the children of the wounded and to their children?

And what about the children of Nazis, must they inherit their parents' memories too?

■ "My father was a 17-year-old boy when they took him into the Waffen SS," says the son of a former Nazi. "I say took because I'll never forget when my father told me the story. Like most Germans growing up after the war, I thought my father volunteered for the Waffen SS. But he told me an SS officer came by and introduced himself and asked if anyone wanted to volunteer. No one came forward. So the SS officer said, 'If you want to be German soldiers you'd better know, then: either you volunteer for the Waffen SS right now, or else you'll wind up in the *Strafb Atallion*' [Delinquent Battalion]. My father said there was a procedure. He had to undress naked, and he had to see the SS doctor, and it was always under these kinds of floodlights, and, uh, there were all these SS officers and other officers and senior headquarters staff and commissioned officers, and then my father came to the final part, he had to sign that he volunteered for the Waffen SS. My father said, it was a way of being forced. He didn't want to sign it, but he was afraid. When he came home and told his mother she said to him, 'You should never have done that.'"

He went on to explain: "My father's brother refused to sign it, and they sent him to the delinquent camp. He was tortured there. One thing led to another and he killed himself, or so it was reported. When my grandmother died, just before she died, my father asked her about what happened to his brother. She told him, she visited him in the delinquent camp. And he told her 'I learned one thing, and this is it say jawohl, jawohl, jawohl' [yessir, yessir, yessir]. That's how badly they had tortured him. Then my grandmother said to her son, 'Isn't' that awful?' And her son said—and this my father got out of his mother's diary—'Yes, it sure is. But what are you going to do about it? In our country, in Germany, you are simply not allowed to tell the truth.' Only by looking in my father's eyes could you see what my father had to endure. It was a mental torment for him to be forced to join the Waffen SS. It was cruel and unjust. I know he regretted this decision. I know it as only a son can know such things. But the German people were being terrorized. No one wants to hear this but it's time for the world to know. My father was there and he experienced the terror."

After the war, most former Nazis and survivors wanted to get on with rebuilding their lives. To some extent, both distanced themselves from what had happened. By distancing themselves from that dark period in their lives they could remove it from their everyday consciousness so that it did not intrude on their thinking or interfere with rebuilding their lives. Within a few years, former Nazis and survivors reconstructed themselves and their lives and became useful and productive members of a society. To do so necessitated significant changes on their part, both in terms of behavior and in their outlook.

Survivors who had been so debilitated, both physically and psychologically, could recover and immigrate to new countries, adapt to the new conditions, and raise a family and function on a day-to-day level (Helmreich, 1992). Also, most former Nazis, upon returning to their homes could cast off their Nazi self and view themselves as essentially ordinary citizens (Lifton, 1986; Ryan, 1984). Both survivors and former Nazis could shed their former selves, reconstruct their lives, and form new identities. There was no reason, therefore, to contemplate meeting the other side.

Indeed, the very notion of meeting the other side is an idea many survivors and former Nazis feel should not even be mentioned, an impossibility that should never be proposed. But what about the children? Do survivors' children and former Nazis' children want to meet the 'other side'? How would children of survivors react to hearing children of Nazis tell stories about how their parents suffered during the war? How would children of Nazis react to hearing children of survivors tell stories about how their parents suffered during the Holocaust? Could they face the others' passions and points of view? Could children of survivors and Nazis talk to each other about World War II and the Holocaust and understand the anxieties of each about the other as a gateway to reestablishing a relationship? Could children of Nazis understand and acknowledge the roots of children of survivors' pain that goes back to the Holocaust? On the other hand, could children of survivors understand and acknowledge the roots of children of Nazis' fear that goes back to World War II? Or would resentment and anger stand as a fatal obstacle to restoring equal moral relations between Nazis' children and survivors' children?

## A Study of Interpersonal Justice: Descendants of Survivors, Nazis Meet

I knew the answers could only be found by bringing the groups together and observing them interact. So as mentioned in the last chapter, with my husband, the daughter of an SS officer, and a team of students, we organized the first meeting between children of Nazis and children of survivors. Our aim was to study their interpersonal behavior. There was no published work in this area, so a study of children of survivors and Nazis coming to terms with the past and each other would benefit our understanding of the interpersonal aspects of injustice.

The idea to bring together children of survivors and Nazis was a simple, intuitive idea. But it was also seen as shattering a taboo, almost as a revolutionary event. Although research aims to understand events, not change or influence them, many people feared that our research study would be interpreted as a justification of Nazism or as a challenge to the Holocaust's status as the symbol of absolute evil. This fear may have inhibited other researchers and may explain why books like Hannah Arendt's and Raul Hilberg's works on the Holocaust remain untranslated in Hebrew. Like Arendt, Hilberg examined the role of Jewish leadership in helping the extermination program. The roles of the Jewish leadership and of the kapos are still the most sensitive issues of the Holocaust (Segev, 2000).

Segev reports that in July 1981 the Israeli Knesset passed a law that essentially made the Holocaust a doctrine of truth—no longer a subject for the historians or for the researchers. According to Israeli law, "The publication, in writing or orally, of work that . . . downplays their [Nazism or Nazi crimes] dimensions with the intention of defending those who committed these crimes or of expressing support for or identification with them is liable to five years' imprisonment" (cited in Segev, 2000, pp. 464–465). Thus, according to Segev, the Holocaust had become a national doctrine of truth, protected by law, similar in legal status to religious faith. "Indeed, in one way the Holocaust has even a higher status than religion: The maximum punishment for 'crass injury' to religious sensibilities or tradition—including, any denial of God's existence—is one year in prison" (Segev, 2000, pp. 464–465). Likewise, Finkelstein, the author of *The Holocaust Industry* (2000), argues that ". . . the Holocaust has proven to be an indispensable ideological weapon" (Finkelstein, p. 3). According to Finkelstein, the Holocaust has become an ideology and like most ideologies is immune to criticism.

Although our research study had no intention of defending those who committed Nazi crimes or of expressing support for or identification with them, our plan was to allow the children of Nazis to express their point of view too. Since our aim was to study injustice rather than judge it from a moral point of view, we planned to allow spontaneous expressions of thoughts and feelings of any kind. We intended, in other words, to allow stories on both sides to be told, and to observe how individuals reacted to hearing the others' point of view.

We expected there might be conflicting claims advanced by individuals, including downplaying Nazism, equating Nazis' actions with the Allies' actions, comparing recruitment into the SS with being taken into concentration camp, and relating how German people suffered during the war with how Jews suffered in the concentration camps. Still whatever the subject matter, whatever the response, this "hearing the other side" was precisely the point of our research. Prescribing a doctrine of truth would have foiled the purpose of our study.

As mentioned in the last chapter, in organizing the research study, we wrote to potential subjects inviting them to participate in a joint meeting. We explained that we were conducting a research study of the influence of the Holocaust and World War II in the lives of descendants of Nazis and survivors. We explained that the meeting was not a therapy group or an encounter group. There was no goal other than to observe their interpersonal behavior. Some individuals wrote back saying they were not interested in meeting the "other" descendants.

"I really cannot fathom why people would choose to meet with the descendants of their families' murderers," said the daughter of a survivor. "The only thing they could do for me is to bring back my grandparents, my aunts, uncles, and cousins who were all murdered. Other than that, I have no interest in helping them to work through their guilt."

"I don't feel guilty for what my father did," said the son of a high-ranking Nazi. "The title 'war criminal' for my father means nothing. In some years history will take a different perspective. It will be seen that the former Allies are anything but moral and just. As for meeting with children of KZs [shorthand for *Konzentrationslager*, concentration camp], I don't think they are ready to hear a factual examination of the truth."

Most individuals, however, wrote back saying they were interested in attending the meeting. For one son of survivors, the opportunity to interact with former Nazis' children provided him with a chance to get answers.

"The meeting will be a way for me to fill in the blacked out part of my father's life," he said. "I want to see the second generation—my contemporaries—where they were at. Did they deny the Holocaust ever happened?"

Another child of a survivor said, "I think the word I'm looking for is remorse, or something that's going to make me feel better, but I also recognize that I can't make children of Nazis feeling something just because I want them to feel it, or say something because I want them to say it."

For the daughter of a former Nazi, the opportunity to interact with survivors' children provided her with a choice: "I feel I can either choose to live with this legacy of shame or I can choose to do something useful with it," she said. "I feel a responsibility to do something with this legacy that might be helpful, to let people know not all Germans are Nazis."

Another child of a former Nazi said, "I am comfortable with my past. I want to go to the meeting because I want to recognize my heritage and to teach people that not everyone feels hatred mistrust and fear. I want to reveal the truth about what our parents had to go through too."

We interviewed each applicant, choosing individuals from different economic, social, professional, and religious backgrounds. We chose to include a daughter of a survivor whose mother, a Polish Catholic, spent the war in a Nazi labor camp; her uncle died at Buchenwald. (Interestingly, this applicant reported that she had tried to find a group of survivors' children to whom she might express her feelings. Composed of just Jews, they were unwilling to admit her because individuals of Polish background were perceived to be traditionally anti-Semitic.) Locating, interviewing, and choosing participants took seventeen months. Finally, in September 1992 and 1993, twenty-two individuals met. For four days, the group met in discussion sessions, facilitated by my husband, a psychiatrist from Harvard Medical School who is neither German nor Jewish. Each discussion session was videotaped and later transcribed. One discussion session was televised on the CBS program *Sunday Morning News with Charles Kuralt* and on NBC.

## Voices From the Meeting

### Betraying Their Legacies

For many of the survivors' children, the initial foray into the conference room felt like a shameful act. There was the concern that if they got close to the Germans they would be betraying their legacy. On the first day a child of a survivor asked, "I've been thinking about how this is going to impact my family. Am I betraying my parents by being here? Am I minimizing their trauma? Am I forgiving? It's certainly not in my power to forgive. And no—and it is too presumptuous even a thought about—about forgiveness."

For many of the former Nazis' children, the initial foray into the conference room felt like a disloyal act. On the first day a child of a Nazi asked, "My *Mutter*—that's the way we call her, my mother—she never wanted us to talk about it. And I haven't even said much. It was just that my father was—an officer in the Waffen SS. But there was suddenly this feeling for me—oh my God, you know, how is my family going to react. You know, am I betraying my family. You know, what am I doing. And how are the other Germans going to react?"

### Nazi Death-Camp Stories

As participants gathered in a circle, stories poured forth from all of them (except the son of the kapo, who did not talk about his father's camp experiences during the conference). The survivors' children related Nazi death-camp stories. They talked about how their parents were transported to the camps, about the brutal conditions in the camps, about liberation from the camps, and then resettlement in the United States. They talked about how their parents' death-camp experiences affected their lives. They described the anger, fear, rage, and resentment they felt when hearing about the camps.

### Wartime Stories

The former Nazis' children outlined the flip side of the Nazi regime. They talked about how their parents were forced to join the Nazi party, about the brutal tactics of the Gestapo, and about a disrupted post-World War II Germany. And, they talked about how their parents' wartime experiences affected their lives. They described the fear, anger, and resentment they felt when hearing about the war.

### Resentment and Rage

As participants gathered in a circle many survivors' children spoke about their resentment and rage. "Deep down inside, I can feel all my rage," the daughter of a survivor said. "My whole life I've had the image of bad Germans. And when I look across the room now and I see all your

German faces, the blond hair and the blue eyes, I can feel my resentment bubble up. I feel the six million dead people between us. And part of me wishes to see you all suffer for what was done."

## Fear of Retaliation

Many former Nazis' children spoke about their fear. At one point the daughter of a Nazi began to cry. "I was afraid that I would be subject to understandable accusations, anger, and rage," the daughter of a Nazi officer said. "I thought you children of the victims would want to kill me. But I chose to participate at any cost. The fear did not stop me. Because I am not guilty. Yes, my father's generation was. But I want to make this very clear. I've carried my father's burden. I don't want it anymore."

## Looking for Retribution

The child of a survivor replied, "I understand you did not do it. Your parents, the perpetrators are responsible, they're guilty, they should be dealt with. But the problem is my bitterness. I don't feel enough, they [the Nazis] are not enough caught, enough tried, enough convicted, and enough who paid any price. I'm looking for some kind of retribution that I don't, and I don't know what the amount is, and I don't know how much is enough because it'll never be enough, and no one can make up for my lost family, and nobody can make up for my lost childhood."

As the meeting progressed, stories poured forth from the participants about how their parents' lives had affected them.

## Distrust

Weeping, a daughter of survivor said: "I've lived with their experience. It did happen. They have numbers on their arms to prove it. It happened once. What I have to speak about here is how imprisoned I am because of it. And how imprisoned I've been all my life. How afraid I am of the—of the world, the universe. I grew up terrified. Everything frightens me, the door has to be locked, I look behind me, I'm not safe anywhere. I have a lot of claustrophobia in elevators in closed places. Any room like that reminds me of the gas chamber. I can't sit in a room without windows. I need windows and air. I grew up distrusting everyone and with a lot of rage and no place to vent it. And I need you to explain to me why it will never happen again, when I have such distrust. That I can look into the face of—of a child of German Nazis and I don't see that look anymore. I've come here to see that. I want to look into your face and believe you, that you don't hate me. And that you're not going to kill me."

### "Never Said Anything Bad About Jews"

A daughter of a Nazi offered comforting words: "It would be a positive experience for me to make you feel safe. And it's almost like you have a memory stored in your head that's not yours." Then she explained, "When my parents told me stories about their youth, they never said anything bad about Jews, and you didn't know to what degree they were involved. I also carry the—you know, the experience of my—my grandmother and, you know, a lot of other relatives who lost their home in Russia. And my father definitely transmitted that to me too, you know. The world my parents talked about, sometimes, with nostalgic feelings, it had absolutely nothing to do with those times. A lot of those things have to do with German culture. And a lot of those things are good. A lot of those things have to do with what is my heritage. It is a sense of identity that I wasn't allowed to have. More than half a century has passed since the war, and some Germans are tired of seeing their history reduced to the 12 years of the Nazi regime."

### Disbelief

Unconvinced, the daughter of a survivor asked: "So you want me to believe that your parents never said anything bad about the Jews. They just joined the Nazi party, supported the killing of Jews, and then never mentioned a thing about it to their children?"

The daughter of a Nazi officer replied: "That's right, everybody would always say, 'We didn't know anything about the concentration camps,'" adding that her history books in school only covered up to the nineteenth-century Prussian chancellor Bismarck. "When I was smaller, I would hear, 'Oh, this store belonged to a Jew,' and I didn't even know what a Jew was. The minute we tried to talk to our parents, they felt attacked and accused. . . . They would say things like you are green behind the ears, you wouldn't understand those times. When I needed to speak to someone, I felt isolated and alone. I had a friend who said, 'You Germans started the war, you lost it, I really don't give a damn what Germans are feeling right now.' I felt like I was not allowed to have any feelings about this."

Irate, a daughter of survivors replied: "You're saying that the children of Nazis endured silence, and then they endured having the identity of being a person of a culture that made others move away from them and not see them as people. You know, I look at you and the other descendants of the Nazis here, and I'm thinking now you know what it's like to be a Jew at that time, when people moved away and didn't want to associate."

### "Not Just the Germans"

The most provocative hours came on the third day. A daughter of a Nazi officer said: "I don't think that just Germans lost their innocence; I think all humanity lost its innocence. Now we know that this is possible. I don't want to judge my father. He was only 17 years old. He disappeared after World War II. I don't know what he knew. I don't know what he did. And I honestly cannot say that if I lived in those times, that I would have been a decent person. I don't know that. I hope I would have been. But you know, it's something that I can never resolve."

### "Don't Listen"

A daughter of a survivor replied: "You know I'm in a bind when I hear you talk. I can't ignore my feelings, which is to not deal with my anger, not to deal with my rage, because they were inappropriate in my own home because they could be destructive to my father, the victim. So I'm in a bind. I want to be true to my feelings. On the other hand, I believe there does need to be a space for something like this, for you to be heard. And when you said your father was 17 years old. I immediately said, 'He was a kid, of course.' And then I said, 'You're betraying, don't listen to her, because you're betraying your parents.' I mean at 17, I did some things I probably wouldn't do now. So I—I understand. But then I hear my mother crying, 'Don't understand.'"

Another child of a survivor said: "From the stories I've heard from my mother and her friends, that by the time these Jews were 17 years old, these people were no longer children. So I don't think age is the issue here. Your father had a choice. My mother told me some of the greatest *Antisemiten* [anti-Semites] were kids who were in the Hitler youth and they were just 14 years old. What you're asking me to believe is that because your father was 17 he wasn't guilty."

A daughter of a Nazi replied: "None of us can understand it. I came to show some compassion for a tragedy I don't think any of us will ever understand. I wasn't there. I didn't do it, but that's not the issue. I can't judge my father whether he was 17 or not. Would I have acted differently? Could I have acted differently during those times? That's not the issue. Someone has to say they're sorry. I want to help close that wound—to get a little bit of balm, not vinegar, on these wounds."

### "No Restitution"

For the children of concentration camp survivors, the impassioned apologies could do little to ease the pain many still feel over the death of their relatives. One daughter of a survivor explained: "There is no restitution for the loss of our families. We carry the pain of it and the rage of it. We cannot change what happened in the past, but I don't think I can forgive it."

### "We're All Victims Here"

The daughter of a Nazi replied: "But, in a way, we're all victims here. We share a legacy of pain. The German people suffered too. They were forced into the army and to join the Nazi party. Not all of them wanted this. I always saw my parents as the real victims of World War II—until I learned of the Holocaust during a history course."

*"We Are Different"*

The son of a kapo declared that his history and inheritance were unlike those of a Nazi child's. He said he was at the meeting so he could learn more about how his history differed from the children of Nazis. He also declared that the tendency to compare the histories was a way to obscure and diminish the memory of one's parents.

(As mentioned before, a kapo was a concentration camp inmate who collaborated with the Nazis. The kapos had authority to impose punishment, and many were notorious for their cruelty. After the war, the kapos mixed with the survivors, trying to hide their pasts. Many, however, were identified while in the DP camps, and then lynched by other Jews. Interestingly enough, the son of the kapo wanted to be identified as a child of a survivor, not as a child of a collaborator. Also, he wanted to emphasize the differences between himself and the descendants of Nazis. And finally, he was the only participant who refused to share stories about his father's concentration camp role and experiences.)

A son of a Nazi replied: "We have no choice about our inheritance. None of us. Both sides, everybody in the room. We did not ask to be born to a Jew or a Nazi. It happened to us and we have to deal with this. The question is why didn't anyone resist?"

The son of a survivor added: "I think it's important that we make a distinction, in my mind, to make the distinction between the child of the survivor and the child of Nazi. I can't in my mind forgive and forget about the perpetrators. And I can't do it, and I haven't reached that level or whatever that is, and I don't know if you call it bigotry or hatred or whatever the hell it is, but I still got it, and I can't forgive."

Another child of survivor added: "I find this conversation offensive. It is dangerous to talk about resistance in general because what that does is shift the blame onto the Jews. And it changes the whole way you look at it and is very convenient shorthand language for moving everything to the Jews did it themselves. And that is always convenient in a room where there are a group of Germans as well. And my reaction is, it is dangerous."

The son of a Nazi asked: "Aren't we just all asking, the Germans and Jews, why didn't our parents resist? How can we understand those times?"

Despite these provocative exchanges the anguish of those Germans who were themselves children (or not even born) at the time of the Holocaust helped cement the two groups together in an emotional bond as strong as the legacy they both share.

The daughter of a survivor said: "I think we were able to grieve together because we all have a lot to grieve over, and to do that together is very powerful."

The daughter of a Nazi said: "In a way, we're all children of trauma here. Attending the conference has made a major difference in my life. I feel like a lot of the shame has been lifted, and because of that it's much easier for me to believe in my own sincerity."

### What Was Gained

After four days of telling each other their personal and family histories and revealing their deepest emotions, the participants began to sense that they had accomplished something beneficial. Both the children of Nazis and survivors who chose to take part in the meeting felt they gained from it.

The daughter of a Nazi explained: "I feel an incredible sense of relief and of a new beginning. I really feel I've arrived somewhere. I've—what I've been looking for and I have a lot of hope. And I know that is—you know, cynicism will come back and fear will come back and despair will come back, but the process has started."

The daughter of a survivor explained: "There is a tremendous feeling of relief. There is a sense that I am leaving behind—metaphorically speaking—a lot of anger, a lot of resentment, a lot of fears—the burden of having carried this legacy."

The son of a Nazi said: "When we speak together about the repercussions of hatred and what it's done in our lives . . . I could not have done that a year ago because I could not have believed that I could be believable to children of survivors. It's a very strange process."

The son of a survivor explained: "While I was at the meeting and talking to the people, the connection and the ability to transform some of the pain and the rage that I think I carried over from my mother turned into acceptance and a desire to act from a state of tolerance and love."

For another daughter of a survivor, the fear of being "disloyal to my family who perished" was replaced by an experience she called "an exploration of my humaneness." Her experience was echoed by the daughter of a Nazi Waffen SS officer, "What better way to remember the victims than through working on something new—on people seeing each other as human beings? If we remained enemies, then we would continue Hitler's work."

## Summing Up

Summarizing the significance of the conference, I would stress the children's cathartic experiences. At the end of the conference, all the participants reported feeling relieved. The participants said the conference experience brought about a satisfying release from tension. They described the experience as uplifting. Telling the "other participants" stories about their personal and family history had the effect of bringing terrible memories to consciousness, affording them expression, and then inducing relief.

A daughter of survivors said, "I felt I gained something by [their] laying eyes on us and by [our] laying eyes on them. I could not believe that there were Germans with such backgrounds who were interested in meeting us and hearing our stories."

The daughter of a Nazi said of the conference: "It was a powerful experience."

The daughter of a survivor said: "The main surprise was that we liked each other. At the end of the four days we were one happy family. I made friends."

The daughter of a Nazi officer said: "It did not take long for us to become [so] involved in each other's stories that the differences and fears faded away."

A daughter of a survivor said: "One of the participant's fathers committed suicide after the war. We were riveted by her story."

### *What Was Not Gained*

Despite these impressive statements testifying to the participants' cathartic and bonding experiences, the participants' experiences during the conference failed to modify their understanding or acknowledgment of the others' passions and points of view. This was especially true of the survivors' children. Survivors' children resisted thinking from the standpoint of Nazis' children. Instead, they insisted on proving the validity of their viewpoints. Their reluctance to acknowledge the former Nazis' children's viewpoints stemmed from their overwhelming feelings of resentment and anger. These negative emotions, in turn, had the effect of creating unequal moral relations between former Nazis' children and survivors' children.

We can see this effect occurring during the most provocative hours, which came on the third day of the conference when a daughter of a Nazi officer declared, "I can't judge my father. He was so young then. He had to join the German army. They were fighting a war." Later that day another child of a Nazi said, "The German people suffered too. Many of them did not agree with the policies, but they had not choice." And still later that day the son of a Nazi declared, "We did not ask to be born to a Jew or a Nazi. It happened to us and we have to deal with this. The question is why didn't anyone resist?"

In each instance, the responses of the children of survivors were unyielding. "Your father's age is no excuse for what was done to the Jewish people," replied the child of a survivor. "There is no restitution for the loss of our families," explained another daughter of survivors. "We come from different pasts. And to try and blur that to me minimizes the memory of our parents," declared the son of a kapo. "I find this conversation offensive. It is dangerous to talk about resistance in general . . . " said the daughter of a survivor. "My blood is not ready to cool. Nothing can make up for the fact that I had to grow up without grandparents, aunts, uncles. I can't forgive the Germans. And my children will learn that too," declared the child of a survivor.

The unyielding responses of the children of survivors suggest that the desire to restore justice is a double-edged sword. At one level, survivors' children exert tremendous effort to right a previous wrong. At another level, however, their desire to right a previous wrong leads not to justice but to inequity and exclusion. Of all the statements spoken by survivors' children 66% were statements that emphasized the exclusivity of their parents' suffering and victimhood. On the other hand, of all statements spoken by Nazis' children 70% were statements that stressed their parents' wartime suffering.

The significance of these conference findings is that it documents the way in which the responses of the children of Nazis and the responses of children of survivors, wittingly or not, invalidate the others' points of view. Their parents' views and feelings were passed down to them, and stand as obstacles to establishing equal moral relations. (By contrast, when discussing their *own* hurts and sufferings, which will be spelled out in more detail in chapter 6, the participants did acknowledge the others' view and establish an equal moral relationship.) The depths of the offspring's emotions, especially survivors' children's emotions, in discussions about their parents' hurts and sufferings, overrule their mental abilities to see justice as two-sided, to keep an open mind.

The next chapter will look at the way our existing views affect the way we see and interpret information. Once we adopt a view, we become more closed to information that challenges our views, research suggests. A major effect of this constraint is that people tend to become entrenched in their own one-sided views on history and justice, which makes it more difficult to acknowledge and access the view of the other.

# 5

## JUSTICE HAS TWO SIDES

Hearing the other side requires more than anecdotal exchanges between children of Holocaust survivors and children of Nazis; it calls for a willingness—and an ability—to suspend—and perhaps even discard—ideas that have shaped their respective worldviews for a lifetime.

The demand is daunting for anyone because it militates against the human tendency to cling to one's inbred belief system, a phenomenon known as belief perseverance. In other words, new facts can be "heard" and merely interpreted in ways that reinforce an individual's original mindset.

In clinging to the known there is comfort and perhaps even pride, while altering a fundamental view could require admitting that past beliefs were mistaken.

For the intractable, psychologists suggest "hypothetical reasoning" could be a useful tool. For example, survivors' children could be asked to "make-believe" that Nazis weren't all evil and spin out the possibilities that might stem from that leap. That is, they could be asked to use the new premise to develop "the other side of the story."

This predilection to a one-sided view also infiltrated scholarship, with the taboo of exploring both sides finally broken in the 1980s, in a very unexpected way. The catalyst was then-President Ronald Reagan's proposed visit to the German military cemetery at Bitburg to lay a wreath in celebration of the 40th anniversary celebration of V-E Day. The revelation that 49 Waffen SS troops also lay buried in the cemetery incited calls from Jewish leaders imploring Reagan to cancel the trip. But Reagan seemed to concur that the Nazi soldiers were victims along with those attacked by the Nazi state, and the public airing of that notion freed scholars to debate the possibility of more than one truth.

Still, for survivors' children and Nazis' children the shackles of past thinking seem not to be so easily lifted. Not only is their worldview at stake, but also their very group identity, an identity forged through visceral stories handed down directly from parents, brothers and sisters, aunts and uncles.

Thus, for many, truly hearing the other side means to deny more than closely held ideas and passionately told tales; it means to deny their ancestors, their history, and themselves.

## The Power of Existing Views

The depths of the descendants' feelings of family loyalty compelled them to keep their existing view. "There is the fear that if Jews get close to Germans," said the daughter of a survivor, "we will be forgetting the past." "And there is the fear that if we get close to the Jews," said the daughter of a Nazi, "we are incriminating and blaming our parents." When discussing their parents' feelings and points of view, the participants at the conference were unlikely to revise their existing views even when new information dictated such a change.

Social psychologists have conducted striking experiments that reveal the extent to which existing views can bias the way we see and interpret information. Given the same information, opposing groups of people each assimilate it to their existing views and find their views strengthened.

For example, an experiment by the psychologists Robert Vallone, Lee Ross, and Mark Lepper (1985) showed how powerful existing views can be. They showed pro-Arab and pro-Israeli students identical news segments describing the 1982 massacre of civilians in refugee camps in Lebanon. Participants from the two opposing groups interpreted the media's sample of facts and arguments differently: in light of their own existing views. Each group perceived the network news as hostile to its side and believed the news coverage was against their point of view.

Another experiment by Lord, Ross, and Lepper (1979) asked students to evaluate the results of two supposedly new research studies. Half the students believed that capital punishment was good and half opposed it. One new research study confirmed and the other disconfirmed the students' views about the deterrent effect of the death penalty. The results showed that both proponents and opponents of capital punishment readily accepted information that confirmed their view but were critical of disconfirming information. Showing the two sides mixed information had, therefore, not changed their views or lessened their disagreement but, rather, preserved their views and increased polarization through the mechanism of biased assimilation: that is, each group quickly assimilated or accepted at face value the evidence that seemed to support its view but subjected to critical scrutiny the evidence that threatened or undermined its view. And in follow-up studies, people exposed to mixed information have been discomfited by the challenging evidence and incited to refute the contrary information. Each side ends up perceiving the information as supporting its existing view and believes even more strongly (Edwards & Smith, 1996; Kuhn & Lao 1996; Munro & Ditto, 1997).

Other experiments have revealed that it is difficult to change an existing view, once the person invokes an explanation for it. For instance, psychologists Anderson, Lepper, and Ross (1980) asked people to decide whether people who take risks are better firefighters than those who do not take risks. One group of subjects was given concrete cases to review showing that a risk-prone person was a successful firefighter and a cautious person was an unsuccessful firefighter. The other group of subjects reviewed cases considering the opposite conclusion.

After forming their view that risk-prone people make better or worse firefighters, the subjects wrote explanations for their views—for example, that risk-prone people are brave or that cautious people are careful. When information was presented that discredited their explanations, the people still held their views and therefore continued to believe that risk-prone people really do make better or worse fire fighters. The experiment showed that the more people examined their explanations and how they might be true, the more closed they became to information that challenged their views.

Thus, taken together, these studies suggest that our existing views affect how we see and interpret information. The studies suggest that our existing views, or what some social psychologists call *prejudgments*, endure despite challenging evidence to the contrary (Davies, 1997). The studies reveal that it is surprisingly difficult to revise an existing view, once a person conjures up a rationale for it. This phenomenon, named *belief persever-*

*ance*, shows that existing views can take on lives of their own and outlast the discrediting of the information that produced them (Myers, 2002).

*Assimilation and Accommodation*

The notion that existing views can bias the way we see and interpret information is not new, of course. The Swiss psychologist Jean Piaget spent a half-century studying the relationship between how people interpret new information and mental development. Piaget's observations have greatly influenced psychology's current position on how we think, reason, and use our intelligence to cope with new information. Piaget discovered that our mental growth—which he defined as an increased ability to adapt to new information—takes place because of two key processes that he calls *assimilation* and *accommodation*.

Assimilation is the process of incorporating new information into one's existing view of the world. Accommodation is the process of changing one's view of the world when new information dictates such a change. To develop a view of the world that is realistic we must occasionally revise our worldview and extend our understanding to include new information. The process of accommodation, that is to say, revising our worldview is essential for mental growth (Piaget, 1952, 1971).

Sometimes, however, our emotional reactions block our mental growth. In such instances, we avoid accommodating altogether. Instead of changing our worldview when new information dictates such a change, we cling to our existing view through the process of assimilation. When we cling to our existing view, usually unknowingly, we ignore, deny, or downplay new information and disregard inconsistencies or dismiss them as oddities.

Some examples may make this clearer. First, we'll consider the young daughter of a survivor. Then, we'll consider the prosecution team at the Eichmann trial. And, finally, we'll consider a young daughter of a former Nazi.

Imagine a young daughter of a concentration camp survivor whose mother survived Auschwitz. Her mother told her stories about the ghetto and the camps. She told her how the police entered the ghetto and were shouting in the street: "All Jews outside! Hurry!" One by one the houses emptied, and the Jews were taken to the station where cattle wagons were waiting. There the police beat them, without reason, indiscriminately, old men and women, children, and invalids alike. If people tried to escape, the police shot them. Here her mother, who was 15 years old, received the first severe blows.

Then she was loaded on the train, the doors closed. It was one of those notorious transport trains that never returned. Hundreds of men, women, and children pressed together. There was no water or food. The train traveled slowly to Auschwitz. Suddenly the doors opened with a crash. Some strange-looking prisoners dressed in striped shirts lunged into the wagon. They held clubs and flashlights. They began to strike out to the right and left, shouting: "Everybody get out! Quickly! Quickly! Leave you luggage on the train!" They behaved like simple police officers doing their normal everyday job. Here her mother received the second severe blows.

Suppose that the meaning of this story goes deep, that the daughter thinks of her mother and the other Jews as helpless victims and Nazis as evil persecutors. She interprets her mother's stories. She acts in relation to this interpretation. She identifies with her mother and the Jews and therefore acts out the part of being unconditionally loyal to her family and heritage. This quality of loyalty she feels to her family and Jewish heritage is claimed with pride and gives her security. She sees herself as loyal, protective, responsible, and responsive to the legacy of her mother's sufferings.

Later, the daughter hears a new, shocking fact: without the cooperation of the victims, without Jewish help in police work and administrative work by the members of the Jewish Councils (the *Judenrat*) and the Jewish leaders, it would have been impossible to round up the Jews and send them to concentration camps. Yes, this fact was mentioned in her mother's story. Yes, it was a Jewish police guard and a Jewish prisoner dressed in a striped shirt who beat her mother, but the daughter ignored those disturbing facts in her interpretation of the story. The daughter remembers only that her mother suffered unjustly.

Then the daughter hears more new facts. The Jewish councils, she hears, compiled the lists of persons and heir property, secured money from the deportees, kept track of vacated apartments, and supplied the police forces to help capture Jews and get them on the trains. Jewish officials distributed the yellow Star of David badges and armbands, sometimes turning this distribution into a business: for sale were ordinary armbands and fancy, washable armbands. In the manifestos issued by the Jewish Councils, the Jewish leadership unabashedly announced their new power—"The Central Jewish Council has been granted the right of absolute disposal over all Jewish spiritual and material wealth and over all Jewish manpower," as one manifesto phrased it (cited in Arendt, 1964, p. 118).

The daughter hears that over the whole way to the concentration camps the Jews got to see rarely more than a handful of Germans. And in Auschwitz the SS men were few, and were seen infrequently (Levi, 1959, p. 28). She hears that in the concentration camps the SS could not have functioned without the cooperation of the victims. "That the SS state could not have functioned without the cooperation of the victims, I can testify to from my own camp experience. The SS would have been unable to run the concentration camps without the cooperation of many of the prisoners—usually willing, in some cases reluctant, but all too often eager cooperation" (Bettelheim, 1980, p. 269). "The Jews who worked for the Germans, and almost every Jew with even the ribbon of a deputy kapo on his arm, murdered—all but an exceptional few" (cited in Segev, 2000, p. 259).

In brief, the survivors' daughter hears that "wherever Jews lived, there were recognized Jewish leaders, and this leadership, almost without exception cooperated in one way or another, for one reason or another, with the Nazis" (Arendt, 1964, p. 125). About half of the Jews could have saved themselves if they had not followed the instructions of the Jewish Councils (Arendt, 1964, p. 125).

When confronted with these shocking facts, the survivors' daughter's first impulse is to assimilate the new information into her existing (one-sided) view that Jewish survivors were guiltless victims. So her first impulse is to ignore, to deny, to question the accuracy of the facts, to justify them, or to conclude that the victims' cooperation with the Nazis was uncommon. To a survivor's daughter—indeed, to most Jews—the cooperation of the Jewish Councils and Jewish leaders in the destruction of their own people is the most disturbing information in the whole disturbing story. The information threatens the one-sided view of a clear-cut division between Nazis and survivors, and therefore, it threatens the survivors' legacy of exclusive suffering.

The role of the Jewish Councils and leadership was mentioned twice during the Eichmann trial. One survivor-witness testified that the ghetto police and the *Judenrat* were essential in helping the Nazis; and the Judge found out from Eichmann in cross-examination that the Nazis had considered this cooperation as the foundation of their Jewish policy (Arendt, 1964). Eichmann asserted that without the Jewish leadership's cooperation the extermination would have run into serious difficulties. He said, "The formation of the Jewish council and the distribution of business was left to the discretion of the Council. . . . The functionaries with whom we were in constant contact—well, they had to be treated with kid gloves. They were not ordered around, for the simple reason that if the chief officials had been told what to do . . . that would not have helped matters any. If the person in question does not like what he is doing, the whole works will suffer . . ." (cited Arendt, 1964, pp. 123–124).

The prosecution team, however, avoided bringing this side of the story into the open. They deliberately refrained from asking witnesses questions about the cooperation of the Jewish leadership. Supreme Court Justice Gabriel Bach, who had been a member of the prosecution team at the Eichmann trial, told the journalist Segev (2000) that there was a danger of the whole trial becoming the trial of the Jewish councils instead of Eichmann and the Nazis. Bach told Segev that "One day Eichamnn's German defense counsel, Robert Servatius, came and showed me [Bach] fifteen letters he had received from Israeli citizens, all of whom offered to appear as defense witnesses for Eichmann. They were not interested in defending Eichmann; instead, they hoped that while testifying they would have the chance to close old accounts with members of their local Judenrats. These people were boiling cauldrons waiting to explode. . . . Imagine what would have happened if all those witnesses, Jews from Israel, had appeared in court and told Judenrat stories," Bach said. "No one would have remembered Adolf Eichmann" (cited in Segev, 2000, p. 465).

Indeed, the prosecution's case would have been weakened if it had acknowledged the whole truth that the rounding up and transportation of Jews who were sent to their deaths had been, with few exceptions, the job of the Jewish administration (Arendt, 1964). Moreover, the prosecution's one-sided picture of a "clear-cut division between persecutors and victims would have suffered greatly" (Arendt, 1964, p. 120). The prosecution feared, perhaps, that acknowledgment of the whole truth would be interpreted as a challenge to the abstract, almost mystical legacy of Nazis as the symbol of absolute evil. And it would challenge the survivors' legacy as the symbol of exclusive suffering.

Thus, both the young survivors' daughter and the prosecution team deliberately refrained from questioning facts inconsistent with the survivors' legacy of exclusive suffering. Instead, through the mental process of assimilation they incorporated the new information into their existing view of the world. When people assimilate new information into their existing views, they must ignore new facts, deny them, or dismiss them as oddities. In the instances above, the technique used was to avoid bringing another side of the story into the open. When people avoid changing their views and behavior when new information dictates such a change, their mental abilities weaken. They cling to old categories and act from a single perspective. In my previous book, *Doing Psychotherapy Effectively*, and in various articles I describe how people often get stuck in rigid, fixed, one-sided views and act in passive-observant ways (Giacomo & Weissmark, 1986, 1987, 1992a, 1992b; Weissmark & Giacomo, 1994, 1995, 1998).

We saw this happen at the conference too. Children of survivors disregarded the uncomfortable fact that a participant's father was a kapo in a concentration camp. The participants avoided discussing the subject. They were only too glad not to elaborate on this side of the story, and they shifted the discussion to anti-Semitism. Similarly, when a daughter of a survivor mentioned that her mother threw knives at her and physically abused her, the other participants ignored the statements. And when some children of Nazis talked about how loving their fathers were, the other participants disregarded the reports. The kapo, the abusive survivor parent, and the loving Nazi parent are inconsistent with a clear-cut, one-sided view.

As noted earlier, former Nazis' children grew up hearing a viewpoint different from what survivors' children heard. Former Nazi parents stressed historic wrongs going back to the Treaty of Versailles, the conditions of World War II, and the injustices perpetrated by the Allies in postwar Germany. So, when children of Nazis heard information about the Holocaust, it was inconsistent with their existing view of reality. It caused tension between assimilation (using their old view to fit the new information) and accommodation (changing their old view to fit the new information).

As an example, imagine a young daughter of a Waffen SS officer. Her father told her stories about the army and the war. He told her how a Waffen SS officer came by and introduced himself, and "he talked about peace, about a final victory, and about our beloved Führer." He asked who wanted to volunteer. Here her father, who was 18 years old, volunteered for the Waffen SS. Her father returned home to tell his widowed mother that he joined the Waffen SS. "We are Christians. You should never have enlisted even though they would imprison you," said his mother.

"To go to the Waffen SS or not to go the SS? I don't know," the father said to his young daughter. "Things were just different then. I was scared. I didn't want to go to the labor camps for prisoners. The Nazis used those labor camps to terrorize us. Any German person who tried to oppose would be sent to the camp. The Nazis spread terror of punishment for opposition among the German population. The Nazis wanted to force all of us Germans to turn ourselves into willing and obedient subjects of the Nazi Reich. So I was afraid. I wish I could say I would have the courage to be different, even today, but I don't know."

The father told his daughter that the Waffen SS had served primarily as a military elite, shock-troop division used to stiffen the collapsing fronts as the Allied forces advanced. He told her stories of how he managed to get out of the Waffen SS. He arranged to go to the war front instead. He was a radio operator in a tank. He told his daughter about the night he arrived close to Leningrad, the night of retreat, in the middle of winter, 25 degrees below zero. "I was locked in because of the cold, and saw villages burning on fire and bombarded by the tanks and grenades. All of us thought we would die that night," he told his daughter.

When the war was over, he returned home to Germany. He found that his mother was put into an American detention camp, and his sister was living with a relative. Later, his family was forcibly moved from their home to a small, cold-water flat, and food was hard to find. Their personal property was seized and looted by some Jewish displaced persons. His younger sister had to go out and beg for food. "Once an American GI was drunk and he lined me and my little sister up against a wall and waved his rifle, threatening to shoot us."

The meaning of this story is one formed by stories that the daughter has heard. It is the only one the daughter knows: her father was being forced to join the Waffen SS, and her grandmother, uncle, and aunt are helpless victims. She interprets and assimilates her father's stories. And she identifies with her father and the Germans, and she therefore acts out the part of being unconditionally loyal to her family and heritage. This quality of loyalty she feels to her family and her Christian German heritage is claimed with pride and gives her security. She sees herself as loyal, protective, responsible, and responsive to the legacy of her father's hardships.

Later, the daughter sees a new shocking and inconsistent fact: a newspaper picture of a death camp. At first, she didn't believe it. She heard it was just Russian propaganda. But she asked her father, "Did you have anything to do with this?" And he quickly replied, "No, I promise you I had nothing to do with it." Decent Germans like her father, she concludes, were shocked by it. They did not like this type of destruction.

But then the daughter discovers even more new facts. She was about ten years old and the Eichmann trial was taking place. Suddenly during the Eichmann trial there were things in the paper and on television. She saw pictures of young Jewish children going to the concentration camps. She saw piles of their dead bodies (Weissmark, Giacomo & Kuphal, 1993). She couldn't believe that anybody could kill innocent children. She discovers that there were about 20 concentration camps and about 165 slave labor camps. Nobody knew exactly how many had died in the camps. But the estimates varied from 11 million to well over 18 million. She read that between 5.5 and 6 million of these were innocent Jews.

The daughter hears that the death camps were staffed by the most trusted and fanatic followers of Hitler, the SS troops. About 40,000 SS were assigned to rule the various camps. Later when the SS expanded, elite formations were created whose officers administered and ruled the death camps while the soldiers served as guards. In brief, the former Nazi's daughter hears that German soldiers served as guards in the death camps and that Nazi SS troops cooperated in overseeing the destruction of millions of innocent Jewish people. They played a great and disastrous role in the systematic herding of these millions of innocent people— men, women, and children—into the gas chambers. These innocent people were murdered in consequence of the Nazis' belief about what was required to protect the purity of their race and the living space they believed they needed.

When confronted with these shocking facts, the Nazi's daughter's first impulse is to assimilate the new information into her existing (one-sided) view. So she insists that the German people were themselves victims, forced to join the Nazi party. Her first tendency is to ignore, to deny, to question the accuracy of the facts, or to justify them. She concludes that the Germans' cooperation with the extermination policy in the death camps was uncommon ("excesses of the East"). To a former Nazi's daughter, indeed to many Germans, the cooperation of the German people in the destruction of innocent human beings is the most disturbing information in the whole disturbing story. The information threatens the Nazis' legacy of a justified war.

This example shows that the tension between assimilation and accommodation for Nazis' children comes from having to accommodate to information about the death camps and the role of the Germans in the destruction of innocent people. On the other hand, as illustrated above, the tension between assimilation and accommodation for survivors' children comes from having to accommodate to information about the war and about the role of the Jews in the destruction of their own people.

For both Nazis' children and survivors' children, however, the tension between assimilation and accommodation stems from the same demand: to change their clear-cut views and to acknowledge another viewpoint. This creates tension, because there is the fear that in acknowledging another viewpoint, their own view becomes discredited. It is precisely when they are most likely to ignore, to deny, or to downplay new information to maintain their existing worldview. There is the threat that what they have deeply believed over many years might be invalidated.

The tendency, therefore, is for Nazis' children and survivors' children to defend the beliefs of their group with all their might. Otherwise, if their own view becomes discredited—and indeed, the threat to it is great enough—then their identity collapses. So it is often a matter of trying to maintain their secure one-sided view of reality against the uncertain possibilities of revising their worldview. We might call this way of being "seeking-self protection" or "acting in defense of self" or "preserving one's identity."

*One-Dimensional Views and the Need to Belong*

The need to belong impels Nazis' children and survivors' children to defend their group's worldview. Recent research shows that the need to belong to a group is a powerful, fundamental, and extremely pervasive need. According to Baumesiter and Leary (1995), much of what human beings do is done in the service of belongingness. "Even though many psychological theorists have noted human affiliative tendencies in one form or another, the field as a whole has neglected the broad applicability of this need to a wide range of behaviors" (Baumesiter & Leary, 1995, pp. 497–498). To the psychologists Roy Baumesiter and Mark Leary (1995), a large body of empirical findings conclusively show that people have the need to belong and therefore resist the dissolution of existing bonds.

As noted earlier, the device of excommunication, whether used by a religious group, an ethnic group, or a family, is a powerful device for maintaining loyalty to a worldview. Baumeister and Leary note that "[a] general pattern may well be that cultures use social inclusion to reward, and exclusion to punish, their members as a way of enforcing their values" (Baumeister & Leary, 1995, p. 521). This was apparent in the conference. The participants raised questions about how their groups would judge them. Many Nazis' children were concerned about "betraying their families," and many survivors' children were concerned about "diminishing the pain of their parents' suffering." These concerns, in turn, may have limited their abilities to revise their worldview. Abundant research "attests that the need to belong shapes emotion and cognition" (Baumeister & Leary, 1995, p. 520).

In defending a worldview, the usual cases are individuals who, from the beginning of their lives, find themselves loyal to a group, whether it is an ethnic group, a religious group, or a family. Loyalty and the need to belong to a group, as mentioned earlier, are part of our social and biological evolution. By telling stories, we pass the legacy from one generation to the next and secure each individual's loyalty. Individuals are expected to accept uncritically all the teachings and assertions that the legacy put before them and even to overlook inconsistencies.

They become indoctrinated with the conviction that they ought to believe the teachings and assertions because their ancestors believed. Their personal quests for distinguishing good from evil, for allowing different points of view to be heard, are cut short because the legacies are teachings and assertions about facts of reality that tell individuals something they have not discovered for themselves that lay claim to their beliefs and feelings rather than their intellects. As Freud puts it, "Their truth must be felt inwardly, and need not be comprehended" (Freud, 1961, p. 28).

When individuals accept uncritically the teachings that the legacy puts before them and overlook the inconsistencies between them, we need not be surprised, then, at the weakness of their intellect and ability to accommodate to new information. Feelings of loyalty make no demands on individuals' intellectual capacities. Instead, loyalty demands the process of incorporating new information into one's existing view of the world. Thus, loyalty to a legacy blocks the full mental development of individuals because feelings of loyalty are outside the control of critical reasoning.

But although this is one aspect, there is another one too. Acceptance of a legacy spares individuals the task of challenging the validity of cherished views. Also, loyalty to a group legacy gives individuals a feeling of security and of owning a valued tradition. They feel they belong to, they are rooted in, a structuralized heritage in which they have an unquestionable place. "It seems that nothing is more difficult for the average person to bear than the feeling of not being identified with a family or group" (Fromm, 1941, p. 234). They may suffer from hunger or suppression, but they do not suffer from the worst of all pains—aloneness, doubt, and anxiety (Fromm, 1941).

Thus, it is reasonable to conclude that children of Nazis and of survivors, like most people, have a deep need to feel connected to their family and group. The need to belong is so compelling because it is biological. It begins in our childhood, somewhere between mother and infant. Human babies are born with a tendency to become attached to the adults who take care of them. It is a deeply emotional process anchored in the very core of an infant's being.

During the first two years of life, attachment takes the form of a strong tendency to approach particular people, to be receptive to care and comfort from them, and to be secure and unafraid in their presence. Young children show a strong preference for their mothers—especially when they are afraid or distressed by the unfamiliar or unexpected. Studies have shown that young children, separated from their mothers, became more agitated, depressed, and withdrawn; they also cried more and experienced increased heart rate and awakenings from sleep. However, when their mothers returned the symptoms decreased (Kagan & Segal, 1968, p. 516). More recent research confirms the physiological effects of attachment. According to Panskepp, Siviy, and Normansell (1985), both the tendency to form attachments and the loss of attachments (e.g., sadness and fear) are mediated by opioids. In their view, the tendency to seek attachment ties is based on psychophysiological mechanisms (cited in Baumesiter & Leary, 1995, p. 518).

The inborn tendency to attachment is a valuable asset in survival. It helps infants find affectionate nurturance and protection from pain and dangers, real or imagined. Because the child is unable to take care of itself, relating and forming an attachment with others is a matter of life and death for the child. "The possibility of being left alone is the most serious threat to the child's whole existence" (Fromm, 1941, p. 36).

Attachment to a caregiver gives the child security. Attachment ties are natural in the sense that they are part of a normal human development. They are the ties that connect the child with its family, and then later in human development, the individual with his or her ethnic group, or the individual member with their religious group. And then later in development, they give a sense of belonging to, being rooted in, a structuralized group heritage.

But if the tendency to remain closely attached to a parent persisted, children would never outgrow their dependence on their caretakers. Slowly the child comes to regard these ties as limiting. As the child grows older, he or she is confronted with the task of becoming autonomous. Psychologists have noted that adolescence is a time of separating from parents and defining one's personal, independent self (Myers, 2002). But the process of separating and becoming independent is a gradual one.

The more the child grows, the more it develops a quest for freedom and independence. To become self-sufficient, the child must explore the environment, encounter new experiences and information, and learn how to cope with them. The fate of this quest depends on the child's ability to resolve the tension between assimilation (which, in essence, represents the use of old views to meet new situations or information) and accommodation (which, in essence, is a change of old views to meet new situations or information). The resolution of this tension results in intellectual and developmental growth (Piaget, 1971).

As a simple example of how this tension can be resolved (taken from Kagan and Segal, 1968), consider a young boy who has many toys. To these familiar toys we add a new one—a magnet. The boy's first impulse will be to assimilate the new toy into his view of other toys: he may try to bang it like a hammer, or throw it like a ball, or blow it like a horn.

But if the boy realizes that the magnet has a new quality—the power to attract iron—he accommodates his view of "toys" to include this previously unfamiliar fact. He now plays with the magnet according to his changed view that some toys are not designed to bang, throw, or make noise, but to attract metal. The boy actively changes his original view to fit the new information. Thus, this example shows we can develop our mental skills only by revising our old views. We need an environment that exposes us to new information and thus challenges us to exercise and increase our mental skills.

However, if the environment discourages us from exploring new information, then our mental growth and quest for self-sufficiency will be hampered. For instance, imagine the boy's mother notices him banging the magnet. She gets angry at his behavior, takes the magnet away, and then says in a stern voice, "Don't ever bang new toys on the table." The boy cries and stretches his arms out to seek his mother's comfort. Mother withdraws and says, "You are a bad boy." Now the boy's attempt to accommodate his view of toys is inhibited by fear, doubt, and anxiety. Maintaining the relationship overwhelms the context. Instead of feeling challenged to explore new information, the boy feels threatened. He is anxious about the punishment and withdrawal of his mother's love. As long as this goes on, he is likely to be immobilized. His inborn need for attachment and security will overrule his quest for autonomy.

This example shows that mental growth and independence is influenced by parental, or more broadly speaking, social pressures. Social pressures do not end in childhood. As Freud points out, countless adults have been impaired by the compromises they are forced to make because of the pressures imposed on them to accept the legacy of their ancestors. They have had to suppress their doubts, writes Freud, and by that, their intellect and abilities to accommodate their worldview, because they thought it was their duty to believe; "many brilliant intellects have broken down over this conflict . . ." (Freud, 1961, pp. 25–27).

A particularly telling example of the conflict between changing versus maintaining one's worldview is offered in the biblical story of woman's exile from paradise. The story identifies the beginning of human history with a daring act of accommodation (changing one's old view), but it puts all emphasis on the sinfulness of this first act and the suffering resulting from it. The story from Genesis is titled "The First Sin and its Punishment."

Man and woman live in the Garden of Eden. They live in complete harmony with each other and with nature. There is peace and no need to work; there is no choice, no freedom, no thinking either, no knowing good and evil. Man and woman are allowed to eat of the fruit of the trees of the garden except one tree, which is in the midst of the garden. God tells them, "Ye shall not eat of it, neither shall ye touch it, lest ye die."

Man and woman's first impulse is to assimilate this information into their existing view of the garden. But then the woman is confronted with an inconsistent fact. She notices the fruit of the tree in the midst of the garden looks just like the fruit of the other trees. She "saw that the tree [in the midst of the garden] was good for food, and that it was pleasant to the eyes, and a tree to be desired to make one wise." So the woman accommodates her view of "garden" to include this previously overlooked fact. And she actively changes her behavior to fit the new facts. She decides to take the fruit of the tree in the midst of the garden, to eat it, and share it with her husband.

In so doing, the woman acts against God's command; she thinks for herself; she changes her old neatly divided clear-cut view of what is forbidden and what is not. For God, who represents authority and environmental pressure, this act is essentially sin. For the woman, however, this is the beginning of mental growth and reason. She changes her existing view of the world when new information dictates such a change: "It looks just like the other fruit, so why not eat it?"

The woman's decision to disobey God is not an act that comes easily. It is tinged with fear. The woman finds herself locked into a comfortable, close, harmonious relationship with God, man, and nature. Woman's relationship with God, man, and nature is predictable. To break out of the assigned relationship is to create a form of uncertainty and anomie. So for Eve there is fear about what will follow disobedience, tinged with the fantasy of God's retribution, that she will die for disobeying him. So the woman seeks encouragement and support from the serpent. The serpent reassures her that she will not die if she eats from the forbidden tree. And the serpent tells the woman, "Ye shall not surely die." The only reason God doesn't want you to eat from that tree, says the serpent, is because "then your eyes shall be opened, and ye shall be as gods, knowing good and evil."

This encouragement seems to work. With the serpent's help, the woman decides to act against the environmental pressures. Acting against God's orders means the woman frees herself from obedience, which in turn frees her from old views when new information dictates such a change. Acting against the environmental pressures, committing a sin, is in its positive human aspect the first act of accommodation, that is, the first human act of self-initiated change. The act of disobedience as an act of accommodation is the beginning of mental growth and reason. But the myth emphasizes the negative results of this act.

Man and woman are exiled from the garden. They are ashamed, afraid, and powerless. The original harmony between nature, man, and woman is broken. God proclaims that he will put enmity between man and woman and between nature and man. And God punishes woman. He says, "I will greatly multiply thy sorrow and thy conception; in sorrow thou shalt bring forth children. . . ." And God punishes man and the serpent too. Thus, the myth stresses the suffering and conflict that results from this first act of accommodation. Man and woman are free from the bondage of obedience, but they are not free from fear, anxiety, and loneliness. These negative emotions inhibit their abilities to develop their mental growth, to realize their individuality.

When a story or legacy has been told and retold through the centuries, as this one has, it is one that will go deep, which a person will be unable to forget. The biblical story shows that mental growth may require an act against the sweet ties to paradise. (This, of course, does not mean that sinful behavior is always equal to helpful growth.) When woman disobeys God's orders, she frees herself from coercion, and she emerges from a mindless existence to the level of a rational human being. But the point of the story, the part that goes deep, is that woman's newly won mental growth appears as a curse.

If every step in the direction of mental growth and independence were matched by social approval, then the process of accommodation would be harmonious. This does not occur, however, as the biblical story illustrates. There are social pressures imposed on us to accept assertions about conditions of reality that lay claim to our beliefs rather than our intellect. We are expected to conform to a one-sided view of reality. This, in turn, compels us to ignore new facts, to deny them, or to treat them as oddities. Otherwise, we may risk the threat of isolation, punishment, the loss of identity. The psychic cost of changing one's view of reality is considerable, as the story from Genesis makes clear.

The phenomenon of Eden is present today too. Regarding knowledge about the Holocaust, in 1979 the Israeli Ministry of Education Committee drafted a study program. The intention was to shape and preserve the legacy of the Holocaust. Like the forbidden tree of knowledge, information was prohibited. The program announced that Holocaust studies should be taught from only a single viewpoint, emphasizing the student's emotional involvement. "The Holocaust must first of all be felt," declared the committee chairman, and "it must be felt as a fact and of itself not as part of the larger historical context and not in the framework of scholarly inquiry" (cited in Segev, 1991, p. 482). The committee prohibited anyone from attempting to understand the Holocaust in a wider context.

Social prohibitions and pressures have deterred many individuals, Jewish and gentile, both writers and the public, from attempting to understand Nazism from different standpoints. Hannah Arendt once told Segev (cited in Segev, 1991, p. 465) of the pressures that prevented the Israeli publication of her controversial book on the Eichmann trial. In the United States Arendt became the object of scorn, even slander. The American Jewish Press claimed her views on the Eichmann trial were lies told out of "self-hatred." Since Arendt was a German Jew and her second husband Blücher was a gentile German, this made her especially vulnerable to such slander. I suspect if Arendt herself was a gentile, then she would have been even less fortunate and lived in fear of being accused of anti-Semitism.

Social pressures also have prevented Raul Hilberg's basic work on the Holocaust from being translated into Hebrew. Like Arendt, Hilberg presented the controversial view that the Jewish leadership cooperated with the Nazis. Similarly, when my colleagues and I embarked upon the controversial work of bringing together Nazis' children and survivors' children, the Jewish press and some organizations claimed the idea was a desecration of the Holocaust.

Gentile German writers like Martin Broszart and Hans Mommsen have presented the controversial view that "Nazism should not be treated as an extraordinary, exclusive, metahistorical event." And Ernst Nolte has presented the controversial view that "Auschwitz need preoccupy the Germans no more than Hiroshima or antebellum slavery, say, haunts Americans" (cited in Maier, 1988, p. 18). All of them have risked being labeled revisionists and anti-Semites. Any German who questions whether Nazism was unique in the annals of mass murder, compares Nazism to other fascist regimes, or argues that the Allies deliberately developed a course of conduct that led to war with Germany is subject to accusations of revisionism.

For instance, Wolf Hess, the only child of Rudolf Hess, the deputy führer of the Nazi party and one of Hitler's closest confidants, has argued that his father was a "man of peace." Hess asserts that his father was subjected to "improper and unfair justice of the victors" (Posner, 1991, p. 41) and argues that the Allies tried to distort history with postwar propaganda. "The Americans came here in World War I and Wilson didn't know what he was doing and they carved up Europe. Then after World War II, they still put their nose in everyone's business. . . . The victors split Germany, gave away German land. . . . It's the same as Versailles. . . . I always predicted reunification in my lifetime. . . . Even our lands the victors gave away after the war will come back . . ." (cited in Posner, 1991, pp. 67–68). Hess's views have been challenged as revisionist (Posner, 1991, p. 41).

Another telling example of the pressures imposed on individuals to follow a one-sided view of the Holocaust and World War II was evident during the Bitburg controversy in the late 1980s. At the German military cemetery at Bitburg, it will be recalled, President Ronald Reagan was scheduled to lay a wreath in celebration of the 40th anniversary of V-E Day. The visit was intended as a ritual of reconciliation, but it ended in controversy (Maier, 1988).

West Germans felt that the visit would be a show of reconciliation because it would be one that recognized that most West Germans had no individual role in perpetrating or supporting the Nazi deeds of the past. However, after the visit was scheduled, it was discovered that Bitburg turned out to be more than a military cemetery. It turned out to be the resting place as well for forty-nine Waffen SS troops, and from this point the controversy began.

The West Germans did not want the visit shifted to another cemetery. They insisted on the difference among segments of the SS and claimed that the Waffen SS had served primarily as a shock-troop division used to stop the collapsing fronts as the Allied forced advanced. "Should not the remnant of the Waffen SS forces lying at Bitburg be considered just as soldiers, entitled to share in the obsequies due the brave?" (Maier, 1988, pp. 10–11). The West Germans wrote American senators that a cancellation of the visit would be an affront and insisted that all fallen soldiers were entitled to equal honor (cited in Maier, 1988, p. 11). President Reagan seemed to agree with the "notion that the SS boys buried at Bitburg were equally victims with those attacked by the Nazi state" (Maier, 1988, p. 11).

However, many Jewish organizations, spokespeople for governments, and Jewish organizations were opposed to the visit. Elie Wiesel and other renowned "guardians of Holocaust memories pleaded with Reagan not to travel to Bitburg" (Maier, 1988, p. 10). Some declared that Reagan's effort at sympathy "unites oppressors and victims, Nazi perpetrators of violence with those who were struck down by it" (Maier, 1988, p. 14). It was pointed out that Waffen SS units had been assigned guard duty at concentration camps. They insisted that West Germany as a society must accept responsibility for the Nazi past.

The Bitburg controversy was important because, for the first time, it publicly unleashed the "undebatable." Before the Bitburg controversy social pressures placed questions and answers about Nazism off limits (Maier, 1988). But with President Reagan's recognition of another viewpoint, scholars began to openly debate the plurality of truths. Reagan's actions and the other participants at Bitburg helped dissolve the inhibitions of scholarly discourse, especially in Germany.

The Bitburg controversy unleashed a change in attitude. The time had come for considering two-sided views. For the first time, "Neither genuine questions nor good-faith answers should be placed off limits. If [scholarly] investigations undermine the founding 'myths' of one group or another, the scholar still believes that its members should revise their self-awareness and learn to live with complexity. . . . When some knowledge is put off limits and received traditions are shielded from objective reconsideration, we enter the realm of hallowing and sanctification—perhaps one necessary activity for communities, but not to be confused with [intellectual] activity" (Maier, 1988 p. 12).

Throughout this book, I have noted that the children of survivors and children of Nazis tend to view reality as one-sided. Similarly, in most ethnic conflicts and even in intimate conflicts, there comes a tunnel-vision that prevents individuals involved in the conflict from "seeing another view" or "hearing the other side." Individuals become indoctrinated with the belief that their side is "right." Attachment to a family loyalty, social obligations and pressures make it difficult for individuals to develop a broader vision. (On the positive side, however, there are many beneficial parts of belonging to a group like safety, comfort, order, and so forth. There are reasons we follow social norms, other than to exclude the other).

In growing up, most of us have learned to inhibit behaviors that go against social expectations. But the culture has failed in teaching us internal controls on destructive behaviors that have their origins in social obligations, group values, and familial legacies. Therefore, such actions can be far more dangerous to society (Milgram, 1974). Consider Riley, an Irish Protestant person living in Belfast who, in everyday life, is gentle and kind and a loving father, yet becomes a militant and feels justified in throwing bombs that target schoolchildren only because they are Catholic.

"I never was a militant, but see me now," says Riley. "I'm not only a militant, I'm a bigot." Then, according to *Chicago Tribune* correspondent Liz Sly, "Out poured a litany of grievances, great and small, old and new: the murders of his loved ones by Catholics who will never be punished," the stones thrown at his windows by Catholic youths living across the street, and perhaps above all, the steady encroachment of Catholic households into his shrinking Protestant enclave (*Chicago Tribune*, September 9, 2001). Riley sees the act of throwing bombs at Catholic schoolchildren as fulfilling a social duty to his Protestant enclave. Thus, he does not care that his actions caused others to suffer. He does not feel compassion for the other side's hurts.

Are there ways of teaching internal controls on destructive actions that have their origins in social obligations, group values, and familial legacies? In other words, is there a remedy for belief perseverance? Are there tools to make it easier to acknowledge and hear the view of the other?

Rationality is a tool for revising one's view, for thinking logically, for opening one's mind to possibilities contrary to what was regarded as obvious. The rational operation of the intellect encourages individuals to accommodate to new information. The use of the intellect and adherence to a legacy are very different.

The conference showed us that adherence to a legacy demands individuals to maintain a narrow frame of reference. (Obviously, this does not imply that the legacy of the Holocaust is just a myth or that survivors' children are irrational for having anger or saying that the Holocaust is wrong.) Unconditional adherence to a legacy encourages the mental process of assimilation—of ignoring or denying that which does not fit with a one-sided view of reality. The key words are "incapable of correction," "belief," "preserve," and "old." Individuals are discouraged from revising and extending their knowledge to include new information, to enlarge their frame of reference. In this sense adherence to a legacy or worldview compels individuals to be biased, close-minded, and dogmatic in their thinking.

By contrast, the rational operation of the intellect is an activity of skepticism. It encourages the mental process of accommodation and the expansion of knowledge. *Webster's Third New International Dictionary of the English Language Unabridged* (1981) tells us that intellectual activity consists of: "Studious inquiry; usually critical and exhaustive investigation . . . having for its aim the revision of accepted conclusions in the light of newly discovered facts." The key words are "examination," "knowledge," "distrust," "revise," and "new." In this sense, the rational operation of the intellect compels individuals to be unbiased, open-minded, and rational in their thinking. It encourages them to continually expand their realm of knowledge through the digestion and incorporation of new information. Kant's answer to what was the activity of the Enlightenment is still valid for intellectual activity: *sapere aude*, dare to know (cited in Maier, 1988, p. 12).

The drive that leads individuals to adopt an intellectual or rational attitude includes the notion that new things can be discovered and that greater depth of understanding is achievable. Intellectual activity, then, is a form of optimism about the human condition. It is an activity that assumes individuals can transcend their personal experiences into a more inclusive view of the human condition (Katsenelinboigen, 1984). Individuals must begin by distrusting what they already believe, by actively seeking the unfamiliar, by intentionally challenging the validity of what they have previously been taught and perhaps hold dear. The path to rational thinking lies through questioning old views and beliefs.

## Hypothetical Reasoning

At first, most individuals are uncomfortable questioning their old views— they prefer to stay where they are, to avoid revising their beliefs and to avoid the threat of uncertainty. But there are ways of helping individuals pass the crisis of threat. There are ways of helping them keep their minds open to possibilities contrary to what was regarded as obvious or true. The psychologist George Kelly (1969) calls it the way of "make-believe," "the invitational mood," or "hypothetical reasoning." Nothing has contributed so much to the adventuresome development of intellectual thinking as hypothetical reasoning (Kelly, 1969, p. 152).

Hypothetical reasoning invites us to make believe *as if* something is true. Instead of insisting that old truths are about to give way to new truths, we can say that we are shifting from one possibility to another. Suppose we assume we *cannot* place Nazis in a category labeled EVIL, but also, more importantly, one labeled NOT US. That is to say, suppose we assume most people will do what they are told to do. They will obey orders irrespective of the content of the order and without limitations of conscience, if they perceive that the command comes from a legitimate authority. We approach the truth, by forward steps, through the door of make-believe, writes Kelly (Kelly, 1969).

The point is that hypothetical reasoning serves to make an unrealistic possibility tenable for a sufficient time for the person to pursue its implication *as if* it were true (Kelly, 1969). The fact that it is regarded as a possibility, and as a possibility only, has a great psychological importance, for it enables us to break through the moment of threat. It is, after all, only make-believe, just a possible guess. Hypothetical reasoning invites us to get on with understanding the human condition. It bids us to test, to calculate new experiences and information, to profit from mistakes, rather than to be overwhelmed with guilt or fear for trying to accommodate to another viewpoint (Kelly, 1969).

There is something in stating a new outlook as a hypothetical possibility that leaves one free to explore new viewpoints. It implies we approach knowledge, whether it is a viewpoint about the external world, the Holocaust, World War II, or about ourselves, by successive approximations, each of which is subject to further examination. Truth, then, is regarded as something to be adventured and tested, not something revealed to us whole by God or passed down to us by a legacy (Kelly, 1969, p. 156).

Hypothetical reasoning assumes nothing is ever confirmed. The moment we find evidence to conclude, for instance, that many ordinary persons, just like us, will act like a Nazi if they perceive that the command comes from a legitimate authority, we don't conclude we proved the truth. Instead, we always post a little note on it that says "But maybe it's something else too"—or instead, "I'll be back later to test another possibility" (Kelly, 1969, p. 159).

Thus, hypothetical reasoning is a process of learning to live with doubt and uncertainty, with a plurality of truths, and with a willingness to revise some or add some. Hypothetical reasoning demands that we be open-minded and willing to construe knowledge and values from multiple perspectives. It compels that we are as conscious as we can be about the values that lead us to our perspectives. It asks that we be responsible for how and what we know.

According to the philosopher Stuart Hampshire, the study of how the human mind works shows that we all can think alternatively, come up with different perspectives, imagine possibilities. In his book *Justice Is Conflict*, Hampshire writes that the idea of individuals considering different perspectives has sense for us, because we know what it is for a legal procedure or public discussion to consider different perspectives. We imagine ourselves hearing two or more contrary cases presented and we listen to them, allowing the evidence on both sides to be heard; then, and only then, we are to reach a conclusion. This is the process of reflecting on different possibilities (Hampshire, 2000).

## "Hear the Other Side"

The weighing of evidence for and against an inner conflict; the weighing of evidence for and against a theory in a social science; the weighing of evidence in a historical or criminal investigation all demand this process of reflecting on different possibilities. This is a list of some activities that all involve the weighing and balancing of contrary possibilities bearing on a disputable issue (Hampshire, 2000). (I want to emphasize, however, that I am not implying that the facts of the Holocaust are disputable, but rather that the notion that all Germans are evil is disputable. And, that some facts are focused on more than others.) In all these activities the individual acquires the habit of balanced, two-sided thinking. Different skills are required in each of these activities, but they can be grouped together as hypothetical reasoning in conditions of uncertainty. They are all subject to the single prescription *auid alteram partem*—"hear the other side" (cited in Hampshire, 2000, p. 8). This "hearing the other side" is precisely what identifies thinking with the exercise of the intellect, in contrast to dogmatic, biased thinking. "Hearing" becomes a metaphor. Most of the verbs, writes Hampshire, that denote reasoned thinking are also pictured with these metaphors: seeing, weighing, reviewing evidence, judging, deliberating, adjudicating, examining, evaluating, and many more. They all denote a rational process of reflecting on two-sided views of reality, on hypothetical possibilities (Hampshire, 2000).

Experimental research attests that reflecting on hypothetical possibilities is an effective strategy for debiasing one-sided views of reality. Social psychologists have been interested in studying ways to inhibit an uncritical biased assimilation of new information to existing views and attitudes. So, Lord, Lepper, and Preston (1984) repeated the capital punishment study described earlier and added two variations. First, they asked some of their subjects when evaluating the evidence to be "as objective and unbiased as possible." This instruction had no impact on their views. Those who received this instruction made evaluations as biased as those who did not. Next, the researchers asked another group of subjects to consider opposite possibilities. Specifically, they described the process by which biased assimilation is thought to occur and reminded subjects "to consider the other side of the coin" (Lord, Lepper, & Preston, 1984, p. 1240). After imagining an opposite finding, these people were much less biased in their evaluation of the information for and against their views.

Likewise, psychologists Anderson (1982) and Anderson and Sechler (1986) found that explaining why an opposite view might be true—why a cautious rather than a risk-taking person might be a better firefighter—reduces or eliminates biased assimilation and one-sided thinking. And more recently, psychologists Hirt and Markman (1995) found that considering any plausible alternative outcome, not just the opposite, reduces biased thinking.

Thus, taken together the research suggests that hypothetical reasoning is an effective remedy for reducing or eliminating belief perseverance. Hypothetical reasoning drives people to ponder various possibilities. This, in turn, promotes acknowledging and accessing the views of others. Thus, it stimulates accommodating one's beliefs and views to include new information.

### Real-World Issues

However, the applicability of these results to real-world contexts is questionable. The applicability of these results to real-world contexts depends upon many factors and conditions. One issue, for instance, is whether hypothetical reasoning is effective when the views involved have a strong emotional component, such as beliefs concerning the injustices of the Holocaust. Such emotional commitment may prevent one from considering other views even when presented with another perspective. Simply requiring that one hear the other side does not guarantee that all points of view will be considered. The findings from the conference, as mentioned earlier, suggested that the participants' emotional commitment to their legacies may have prevented them from considering other views.

A second issue concerns the relational component. Hypothetical reasoning may be an effective remedy for belief perseverance in an individual. But it may not be a very powerful remedy between persons, and may fail as a remedy when there are strong passions on two sides of the victimizing barricade, so to speak. The findings from the conference, as mentioned earlier, suggest that the participants' view of the other as an "enemy" made it difficult for them to consider and access the view of the other.

A third issue concerns the situational demands. Certain situations are likely to elicit one-sided thinking. In group settings, there may be strong pressure on participants to think and act in the same way, preserving the group identity. The findings from the conference, as mentioned earlier, suggest that the participants were concerned about appearing loyal to their group.

And a final issue concerns the time frame in which the views are acquired. We might expect little influence of hypothetical reasoning on a view transmitted from generation to generation. If the view has been acquired years ago and has been assimilated with other knowledge structures and the identity of the individual, it is reasonable to assume that this may prevent one from considering other points of view. The findings from the conference, as mentioned earlier, suggest that the participants' views were deep-seated and rooted in their sense of justice.

So, the question remains: what sentiment can reinforce hearing the other side when there are strong passions and views on both sides? What could possibly override the pressures and loyalties to a legacy? The next chapter will look at what is involved in relinquishing some resentments.

## Summing Up

Because the National Socialist past imposed so many limits on postwar debate, compelled so much silence, the passage of time naturally evoked new questions and debate. The fading of silence and consensus may appear disturbing. There is the chance for confusion, but also the opportunity for accommodating our view to fit new information.

The rational operation of the intellect encourages us to revise our outdated views. Hypothetical reasoning is a helpful tool that was unavailable to our ancient ancestors. It was not until the past century or so that hypothetical reasoning became systematized. It can help us take the step forward to develop our intellect and expand our knowledge. Hypothetical reasoning causes a spirit of "make-believe." It causes a particular attitude toward knowledge and truth. It invites us to explore possibilities even when examining horrific events like the Holocaust and World War II. Hypothetical reasoning encourages us to be unbiased, open-minded, and rational in our thinking.

Hypothetical reasoning alone, however, is apt to fail when we have inherited a one-dimensional view. The next chapter will examine the way former survivors and former Nazis have remembered the past. It will look at how their one-dimensional views of the past affect the way their children remember the past today. Then, it will show that despite the tendencies toward one-sided thinking, when people experience a measure of compassion for another person's well-being a transformation occurs.

# 6

# JUSTICE AS COMPASSION

The survivors' children and the Nazis' children who met face-to-face at the Harvard conference confronted much more than each other, their parents' past, or even their own prejudice and fear.

They confronted their ability to understand another's suffering, even that of a perceived enemy, and found that they could offer not only clemency, but also compassion. They told their stories—their histories, and in releasing anger and sorrow over the past, they captured something that had long eluded them—compassion.

To be sure, the participants' transformation of thought took time, with their ideas evolving through discernible stages during the conference.

In stage one, the "generalizing" stage, survivors' children expressed the view that Nazis' children were merely part of a blanket group—"anti-Semitic Germans"—not individuals who might be good or kind or otherwise distinguishable from each other.

In stage two, the survivors' children began listening to the Nazis' children, realizing that the descendants of the Nazis were not the malefactors. What's more, many of the Nazis' children expressed regret, sorrow, and shame over their elders' misdeeds. Suddenly, the survivors' children found that it was not so easy to continue blaming the Nazis' children for the sins for their fathers.

By stage three, the survivors' children were bewildered, for if the Nazis' children were not to blame, if they could be distinguished from their parents, who then could be held accountable for the atrocities committed against the Jewish people? The survivors' children still felt justifiable anger, but now, with the Nazis' children exculpated, against whom could their rage be directed?

During the final three stages, both sides were able to overcome long-held negative impressions, with survivors' children, in particular, recognizing that the Nazis' children had been imprisoned by their own parents' past as much as survivors' children had been locked in their parents' past.

Finally, the two groups were able to build a new relationship based on compassion, bred of their common humanity.

The earlier confusion many survivors' children had felt about no longer having an outlet for revenge was replaced with quite different feelings: understanding and relief. Many survivors' children had concluded that their anger had been just another burden to carry—and one that, thankfully, the Nazis' children helped lift from their shoulders.

While I sat at the kitchen table, my mother stood beside the stove, cutting up potatoes and preparing dinner. "Mommy, how did you survive Auschwitz?" I asked when I was about thirteen.

"I was young and I wanted to live," said my mother matter-of-factly.

I persisted. "But what did you do to survive?"

"You know, I was lucky. I had a good job. I was in the Canada barracks."

The prisoners gave the concentration camp barracks nicknames. The buildings holding looted Jewish property were called the "Canada barracks" because Canada was considered the rich New World. When the transports arrived at Auschwitz, the prisoners on the trains were told to climb down with their luggage and deposit it alongside the train. If someone dared to ask for his or her luggage they were told "luggage afterwards" (Levi, 1961, p. 15). The luggage would then be brought by a transport detachment to Canada, where it would be sorted. The luggage of those who had been gassed was also brought to Canada.

My mother's job, I learned, was to sort the shoes.

"I was fortunate because it was indoor work and I could trade the shoes for food," said my mother. She looked at me in a way that encouraged me to say, "I understand."

She continued, "The transports of the Hungarian Jews were coming so fast and so many. The crematoria couldn't keep up with the gas chambers. The arrival of these Hungarian Jews with their luggage offered me many opportunities. If you had things to trade, you were better off. I could buy the best food."

"You mean, Mommy, you traded things that came from the suitcases of those Hungarian Jews that were sent to the gas chambers?" I knew that I was probably being too direct, but I was eager to get an answer.

My mother's response was puzzling. "I remember one day some new girl joined our work force. We were sorting through the shoes and suddenly this girl started crying out loudly. 'Look at the fires burning and the smoke. Fire, fire everywhere. It never stops burning.' We thought the new girl was crazy. She wouldn't stop crying out. You know we were doing this work for a long time. We didn't even notice the fire or smoke anymore. Maybe we were the crazy ones?"

Then my mother's voice changed. "Sometimes I feel ashamed of it, but that's how it was. I know the attitude wasn't right. But was it wrong? I was young and I wanted to live. You can't judge, Mona, you never know what you would do in those circumstances. Things were different in the camps."

My mother continued, "Upon arrival in the camp everything was taken from you. In an instant all our possessions were taken, our families disappeared. When we got off the train Mengele pointed his finger and said: 'You go over there. You go here.' He decided who would die and who would live. If you were young, pretty, and looked healthy maybe you would be selected to work. Everything happened fast, fast. They shaved your head. They tattooed numbers on your arm. Most of the people on my train were sent to be gassed. Of course when I first arrived at the camp I didn't know what happened to the other people. But in the evening I asked someone and I was told, 'Look at the chimney, they are there in the smoke.' I could not understand really what she was saying. The whole thing was unreal. But one thing was clear; the life I had been living was ended. I was not the same person in the camp that I was in real life. In the camp one didn't think. One was thinking of the next piece of bread, how to save it, where to put it so it isn't stolen from you. In the camp everything one did was acceptable as long as it contributed to helping you survive."

## Influence of Camp Conditions

Many accounts have been written about the horrific circumstances in the camps. I assume that the reader is familiar with these facts, but it should be reiterated that the prisoners were deliberately humiliated and tortured.

They were subjected to the most severe physical abuse. They suffered from extreme malnutrition and were inadequately clothed. They were forced to do hard labor for as long as eighteen hours a day, seven days a week. They were exposed to heat, snow, and freezing temperatures.

Every moment of the prisoners' lives was strictly regulated and controlled. Twice a day all the prisoners had to line up outside their barracks and stay there until everyone in their block was counted, which could involve counting as many as twenty or thirty thousand prisoners. Sometimes it took three hours each morning and three hours each evening to count all the prisoners. The roll calls began before dawn, adding sleep deprivation to the torture.

Besides the torturous physical conditions, camp conditions were designed to break up common bonds, an *esprit de corps*, existing in the members of a prisoner group. Conditions were designed to break the prisoners as individuals and change them into submissive masses from which no individual or group act of resistance could arise. Rudolf Hoess describes how this was done:

> In the concentration camps . . . enmities were keenly encouraged and kept going by the authorities, in order to hinder any strong combination of the part of all the prisoners. Not only the political differences, but also the antagonisms between various categories of prisoners, played a large part in this. However strong the camp authorities might be, it would not have been possible to control or direct these thousands of prisoners without making use of their mutual antagonisms. The greater the number of antagonisms, and the more ferocious the struggle for power, the easier it was to control the camp. *Divide et impera!* This maxim has the same importance, which must never be underestimated in the conduct of a concentration camp as in high politics. (Hoess, 1959, p. 121)

Thus, conditions in the camps were such, that to survive, prisoners had to constantly be active in their own behalf. "It is easy," Frankl reminds us, "for the outsider to get the wrong conception of camp life, a conception mingled with sentiment and pity. Little does he know of the hard fight for existence which raged among the prisoners. This was an unrelenting struggle for daily bread and for life itself. . . . The selection process was the signal for a free fight among all the prisoners, or of group against group.

All that mattered was that one's own name and that of one's friend were crossed off the lists of victims, though everyone knew that for each man saved another victim had to be found" (Frankl, 1963, p. 5).

Still, even under the extreme conditions of the camp there was considerable variation among prisoners in the way they adapted to the unrelenting struggle for life. The prisoners' actions and attitudes were guided, in part, by their values. Some prisoners, like my mother, underwent a process that caused a basic change in their emotional attitudes. My mother was unmoved while thousands of Hungarian Jewish corpses were burned before her eyes. The dying and the dead became routine sights to her and could not stir her any more. Pity, disgust, and horror were emotions that she did not feel. "I couldn't cry or feel; I tried to tell myself it wasn't happening," my mother said. Those changes protected my mother from recognizing the full extent of the harm being done to her and to others. Prisoners who worked in the extermination process removing the gold teeth, cutting the hair from women, lifting up the bodies and placing them in front of the ovens, and digging out and burning the corpses buried in the mass graves did the tasks with apathy. Some prisoners, including friends of my parents, who did less gruesome tasks like playing violin for the SS guards while they had orgies, did so with dulled indifference.

But some prisoners, like the new girl mentioned above, were either unable or unwilling to develop such attitudes and behaviors. The new girl, who my mother described, never reached that phase. She decided to "run into the wire," an expression used in concentration camp to describe one method of suicide—touching the electrically charged barbed wire fence. Bettelheim (1980) describes a prisoner who openly declared he was unwilling to survive by means of adapting himself to the life in camp. He was a prominent radical politician, a former leader of the Independent Socialist Party in the Reichstag. This prisoner asserted that he could not endure changing his attitudes so radically that he could no longer be considered the same person he used to be. He saw no point in continuing to live if he developed those attitudes and actions he saw developing in all old prisoners. Therefore, he decided to commit suicide (Bettelheim, 1980, p. 69.)

Other prisoners, my mother said, committed suicide by simply giving up the will to live and turned into walking corpses—the so-called "Muslims" (*Muselmänner*). Usually this happened quite suddenly. The prisoner would refuse to eat, to get dressed, to wash, or to report for roll call. Threats and blows had no effect. Nothing at all bothered the Muslims. Within a few days they died.

At the other extreme, some prisoners when in charge of others changed their attitudes so completely that they behaved like SS guards. My mother and other camp survivors like Bruno Bettelheim, Viktor Frankl, and Primo Levi have described how cruel some prisoners could be. My mother said the treatment they received from the guards, however cruel and brutal, never affected them psychologically to the same extent as did this attitude by their fellow prisoners. Some Kapo prisoners tormented their fellow-prisoners both mentally and physically and even beat them to death. Frankl writes:

> While these ordinary prisoners had little or nothing to eat, the Capos [sic] were never hungry; in fact many of the Capos fared better in the camp than they had in their entire lives. Often they were harder on the prisoners than were the guards, and beat them more cruelly than the SS men did. These Capos, of course, were chosen only from those prisoners whose character promised to make them suitable for such procedures, and if they did not comply with what was expected of them, they were immediately demoted. They soon became much like the SS men. . . . (Frankl, 1963, p. 4)

Bettelheim writes that some prisoners even took over the attitude of the SS toward the so-called "unfit" prisoners (Bettelheim, 1980, pp. 78–79). Unfit prisoners in the work gangs endangered the whole group. A prisoner who did not stand up well to the strain tended to become a detriment for the other prisoners. Unfit prisoners generally died in the first few weeks, so it seemed as well to get rid of them sooner. The prisoners were sometimes instrumental in getting rid of their "unfit" fellow-prisoners. "This was one of many situations in which some old prisoners would demonstrate toughness, having molded their treatment of these 'unfit' prisoners to the example set by the SS. Self-protection required elimination of the unfit prisoners, but the way in which they were sometimes tortured for days by the old prisoners and slowly killed was taken over from the gestapo" (Bettelheim, 1980, p. 79).

Prisoners who identified themselves with the SS did so not only in respect to aggressive behavior, but according to Bettleheim, they would try to acquire old pieces of SS uniforms too. Bettelheim and Hoess describe how some prisoners tried to sew and mend their uniforms so that they would resemble those of the guards. "The length to which prisoners would go in these efforts seemed unbelievable, particularly since the SS punished them for their efforts to copy SS uniforms. When asked why they did it, the old prisoners admitted that they loved to look like the guards" (Bettelheim, 1980, p. 79).

Some of us might condemn prisoners who worked in any capacity for the Nazis in the camps as "collaborators," by the harshest definition. But when my mother insisted that the circumstance in which she found herself was "different," she was asking me to dispel as misconception the idea that choice is merely an internal issue, immune to circumstance and chance. In the extreme conditions of the camps, some prisoners decided to abandon all values in their fight for existence; ". . . they were prepared to use every means, honest and otherwise, even brutal force, theft, and betrayal of friends, in order to save themselves" (Frankl, 1963, p. 7). Other prisoners did things they would not normally have done, but internally there were limitations derived from the values they held in freedom. Whether one abandoned all values or not, nonetheless to survive, prisoners had to block out the suffering of others. If a prisoner, like the girl that my mother mentioned, was unwilling or unable to watch the destruction of others, then survivorship was unlikely. Survivorship required prisoners to witness thousands of people perish in front of their eyes.

Elie Wiesel has said, "I am still here, because a friend, a comrade, an unknown died in my place" (cited in Bettelheim, 1980, p. 298). When his father lay dying in a camp bunk, Wiesel recalled, ". . . I thought in the most secret region of my heart, but I dared not admit it. It's too late to save your old father, I said to myself. You ought to be having two rations of bread, two rations of soup . . ." (Wiesel, 1969, p. 122). And when his father died, Elie Wiesel said, "I did not weep, and it pained me that I could not weep. But I had no more tears. And, in the depths of my being, in the recesses of my weakened conscience, could I have searched it, I might perhaps have found something like—free at last!" (Wiesel, 1969, p. 124).

Was Wiesel's or my mother's way of surviving wrong? When my mother insisted that the circumstances in which she found herself were different, she was asking me to abandon traditional evaluations about moral conduct and the usual distinctions between right and wrong that motivate such evaluations. It is clear from my mother's account that she distinguished between two worlds: the one of survival then; the other of moral evaluation now. Given the conditions, her apathetic reaction to the mass killings of the Hungarian Jews was permissible since it contributed to helping her survive.

The deadening effect of concentration camp life upon my mother's feelings was a kind of emotional death that marked the second phase of concentration camp life (Frankl, 1963). Locked into a concentration camp, she adapted to madness. She had that ability, which could be interpreted either as insanity or as an astonishing skill. She could stare evil in the face and remain detached.

Immediately after liberation from the camp, my mother described her experience of adapting to normal life like this:

■ We just walked out. But I was still looking at the world with concentration camp eyes. The only thing we thought about was food. Many girls got sick after liberation because they ate too much. It's wrong to think we were happy. There was so much sorrow and bitterness afterwards. I looked for my family, but no one was left. My former life was gone. After the camp, it took time to relearn how to feel pleased again, to love again. I had to relearn it step by step. When I met your father, and my girlfriends met their husbands, then I began to feel happy that I was alive. Your father was the kindest person. Not a mean bone in his body. When your father and I decided to have a baby and I got pregnant, I remember I cried. And a [survivor] friend said, 'Be happy, you're starting a new family.' But rebuilding my life was difficult. You never forget what was lost, what was taken from you. I was very bitter. It took me a long time to learn that the bitterness was only hurting me. Bitterness is like a cancer.

After liberation, survivors had to cope with survivorship. My mother called it "surviving the survival." Besides the original trauma of having been imprisoned in a concentration camp and subjected to terrorization and degradation, there was the problem of giving meaning to one's survivorship. Bettelheim (1980) writes that many survivors asked the question: "Why was I saved?" "What is the meaning of my suffering?" To many survivors, it seemed that a reasonable way to give meaning to their suffering was to reintegrate oneself essentially the same way one had been before imprisonment.

> As a matter of fact, to be able to return to life after liberation the same person one had been before was a wish fervently held by many survivors; to believe that it could happen made the utter degradation to which prisoners were subjected more bearable psychologically. The Nazis had destroyed the world the prisoner had been living in, had tried to destroy his very life. If so, the greatest defeat he could hand them was to demonstrate that they utterly failed in their design by taking up life after liberation as closely as possible to the way it had been before imprisonment. (Bettelheim, 1980, pp. 31–32)

According to sociology and Judaic studies professor William Helmreich, most survivors dealt with survivorship by working hard to rebuild their lives and reestablish families. About 80 percent of survivors married other survivors (Helmreich, 1992). For many the decision to have children was accompanied by the need to replace those who were murdered and by a belief that having children proved that Hitler's plans failed. This belief is expressed in Elie Wiesel's book *The Fifth Son*, where, in an imaginary dialogue with his son, the father says, "Your mother and I told ourselves that not to give life was to hand over yet another victory to the enemy. Why permit him to be the only one to multiply and bear fruit? Abel died a bachelor, Cain did not: it falls to us to correct this injustice" (cited in Helmreich, 1992, p. 127).

In order to return to "life as before," survivors who immigrated to the United States generally formed little enclaves, befriending one another and sending their children to the same schools. Most survivors spoke in Yiddish and clung to the old and the familiar, becoming only as American as seemed necessary (Helmreich, 1992). Most identified very strongly as Jews and maintained a distinct sense of group identity. They formed organizations like the *landsmanschaften*, the Bund, and the Jewish Labor Committee. These organizations served as a place for survivors to mingle and also as vehicles for perpetuating Jewish traditions, attitudes, and values. They held annual services commemorating the destruction of their communities.

Helmreich (1992) points out that many survivors identified themselves as religiously observant Orthodox Jews. While about 10 percent of American Jews in general claim affiliation with the Orthodox community, Helmreich's survey found that about 41 percent of the survivors identified with Orthodoxy, and most practiced, in varying degrees, the dietary laws and maintained the Sabbath observances. Helmreich explains that in practical terms, Orthodox Jews are limited in their social contact with the larger society because of religious restrictions. So, the high level of observances found among survivors also lessened the likelihood that they would assimilate quickly.

Preserving their Jewish values and identities, working hard to rebuild their lives, and reestablishing families helped survivors return to life as before. And it helped them to overcome the emotional apathy they experienced in the camps and to slowly become human beings again. As Frankl writes: ". . . being human is always directed, and pointed, to something or someone other than oneself: to a meaning to fulfill or another human being to encounter, a cause to serve or a person to love" (Frankl, 1978, p. 38). However, as Frankl explains, ". . . the meaning found in suffering belongs to a different dimension than the meaning found in work and love . . ." (Frankl, 1978, p. 45). Thus, many survivors felt their past suffering also bestowed on them a special obligation to bear witness—to tell the world of the horrors, so that it could be prevented from ever happening again.

But for many survivors, rebuilding their lives and reestablishing families required distancing themselves from the past horrors. Many survivors tried to ban the past horrors from their consciousness so that they did not interfere with rebuilding their lives. "What happened in the camps was so horrible, and one's behavior while there open to so many perturbing questions, that the desire to forget it all, as if it never happened, is most understandable" (Bettleheim, 1980, p. 31).

In order to return to "life as before" many survivors detached themselves from painfully upsetting thoughts, feelings, and memories. The experience of having been a concentration camp prisoner was such a painful and traumatic experience that, for many survivors, discussing and evaluating their own and other persons' behavior could hardly be touched upon in conversation. As mentioned earlier, the psychological reaction of many victims of extreme trauma is to avoid thoughts, feelings, and memories associated with the trauma. Memories of the past event may trigger images, flashbacks, or a sense of reliving the painful experience. Many survivors, therefore, were selective about the memories they discussed.

According to Helmreich (1992), one of the most difficult issues for the survivors was that of teaching their sons and daughters about the Holocaust. On one hand, many survivors felt the meaning of their lives was to bear witness and to tell their children about the past horrors, but on the other, survivors had the psychological need to avoid memories related to their camp experiences. Telling their children all the details about life inside the camps would have required discussing the disintegration of their personalities and the complexities of behavior patterns and values in the camps. Bettelheim writes: "[The] separation of behavior patterns and schemes of values inside and outside of the camp was so strong that it could hardly be touched in conversation; it was one of the many 'taboos' not to be discussed" (Bettelheim, 1980, p. 63). So, many survivors avoided discussing the variation of behavior patterns and values among the Jewish prisoners inside the camps.

Although the variation among the prisoners' values, attitudes, and behavior might have been mentioned, many children of survivors grew up, like I did, with the one-dimensional view that all Jewish people were victims of "the Germans." My parents used the term "the Germans" interchangeably with "the Nazis." My parents' stories bristled with the phrase. Sometimes, their stories seemed to use the term "the Germans" not so much as a term of description, as one of condemnation. The term implied that the German people as a whole were involved in murdering Jews. It implied that "they" (all the German people, not just a "nazified" sector) were anti-Semitic. My parents didn't have to tell me they were angry at the Germans. When they talked about the camps and the injustices they suffered and showed me pictures of their murdered relatives, I sensed it. My parents' anger was generalized. It was not personal; it was collective. They were indicting the entire German people, not just the German SS guards.

And what of the German SS guards? Did camp conditions influence the SS guards' actions and attitudes? Was there variation among the German SS guards' actions and attitudes as there was among the prisoners? Or were all of the German SS guards brutal, sadistic, anti-Semitic Nazis? Base and cruel by nature? Is it reasonable to believe that none of them was human enough to take pity on the prisoners?

## Influence of the Nazi Regime

The first concentration camps were established right after the Nazis came to power in 1933. These were not yet for the purpose of killing those whom the Nazis considered undesirables, but mainly to terrorize those Germans who might try to oppose the Nazis, and to spread terror of punishment for opposition among the rest of the German population. Lord Russell of Liverpool explains that Hitler introduced what was called *Schuthaft*, or protective custody, into the legal system. "Under it anyone who showed any signs of active opposition to the Nazi regime could be kept under restraint and supervision, and during the next six years thousands of Germans were thrown into concentration camps for what was euphemistically called 'treatment'. Many of them never regained their freedom. To the Gestapo was entrusted the task of 'eliminating all enemies of the Party and the National State', and it was the activities of that organization that supplied the concentration camps with their inmates, and the SS staffed them" (cited in the introduction to Hoess' memoirs, 1959, p. 15).

The SS, like the rest of the German population, could themselves be subject to punishment. According to Hoess, any SS guard who was caught having dealings with the prisoners, whether with criminal intent or from pity, would be regarded as an enemy of the State and could be sentenced to long terms of imprisonment or executed. Hoess gives an example of an SS officer who was executed because "Out of kindness the SS officer had let a man [a prisoner under his supervision] pay a last visit to his home, to change his clothes and say goodbye to his wife" (Hoess, 1959, p. 86). The prisoner escaped out of the back. The SS officer was arrested inside the Gestapo building while reporting the incident, and one hour later was sentenced to death (Hoess, 1959, p. 86).

Hoess provides another example of four SS men caught at Dachau being involved in ". . . an immense racket organized in the butcher's shop by the prisoners . . ." (Hoess, 1959, p. 67). The SS men were paraded in front of the entire guard unit, personally degraded by Theodor Eicke, the first inspector of concentration camps, and discharged from the SS ranks. According to Hoess, Eicke himself tore off their badges of rank and SS insignia, then handed the men over to prison authorities to serve their sentences. Afterwards Eicke delivered a long speech and told the entire SS guard unit that a similar fate would overtake anyone who helped prisoners (Hoess, 1959, p. 68).

"It was Eicke's intention that his SS-men, by means of continuous instruction and suitable orders concerning the dangerous criminality of the inmates, should be made basically ill-disposed towards the prisoners. They were to 'treat them rough' and to root out once and for all any sympathy they might feel for them. By such means, he succeeded in engendering in simple-natured men a hatred and antipathy for the prisoners which an outsider will find hard to imagine. This influence spread through all the concentration camps and affected all the SS-men and the SS leaders who served in them . . ." (Hoess, 1959, p. 79).

Still, even under the influence of these instructions there was considerable variation among the guards in the way they treated the prisoners. According to Frankl's account and many other survivors' accounts there were decent men among the guards. "It is apparent that the mere knowledge that a man was either a camp guard or a prisoner tells us almost nothing. Human kindness can be found in both groups, even those whom, as a whole, it would be easy to condemn. The boundaries between groups overlapped, and we must not try to simplify matters by saying that these men were angels and those were devils. Certainly, it was a considerable achievement for a guard or foreman to be kind to the prisoners in spite of all the camp's influences . . ." (Frankl, 1963, p. 136).

It is surprising and disturbing to see, as noted below, the extent to which Hoess' account corroborate Frankl's account of the variation among the guards' actions and attitudes. Frankl (1963) writes that the guards could be divided into three distinct categories. The first category, writes Frankl, were made up of guards who were "sadists in the purest clinical sense" (Frankl, 1963, p. 134). Frankl explains that among the guards there were some sadists that took pleasure in torturing the prisoners and watching them suffer. "When the SS took a dislike to a person, there was always some special man in their ranks known to have a passion for, and to be highly specialized in, sadistic torture, to whom the unfortunate prisoner was sent" (Frankl, 1963, pp. 134–135).

Hoess' account corroborates Frankl's account. In his memoirs, in a sober and relatively dispassionate account, Hoess writes that the first category of guards consisted of the "Malicious, evil-minded, basically bad, brutal, inferior, common creatures . . ." who regarded "the prisoner as an unresisting object on which they can exercise their unrestrained and often perverted desires and whims and so find relief for their inferiority complexes. They do not know the meaning of pity or of any kind of warm fellow-feeling. They seize every opportunity to terrorize the prisoners . . . , especially those against whom they have a personal grudge. . . . They spend their time thinking up new methods of physical and mental torture" (Hoess, 1959, pp. 71–72).

The second category, Frankl writes, was made up of guards who were basically indifferent. Frankl writes, ". . . the feelings of the majority of the guards had been dulled by the number of years in which, in ever-increasing doses, they had witnessed the brutal methods of the camp. These morally and mentally hardened men at least refused to take active part in sadistic measures. But they did not prevent others from carrying them out" (Frankl, 1963, p. 135).

Again Hoess' account corroborates Frankl's account. Hoess writes, ". . . the overwhelming majority of guards consists of those who were uninterested or indifferent. They carry out their tasks stolidly and discharge their duties, so far as they must, in competent or indolent fashion. . . . They have no deliberate wish to do the prisoners harm. But because of their indifference and narrow-mindedness and their desire for an easy life, they do cause a lot of harm and inflict much physical and mental anguish upon the prisoners quite unintentionally" (Hoess, 1959, p. 72).

The third category, Frankl reports, consisted of guards who were kindly by nature.

Frankl writes, ". . . it must be stated that even among the guards there were some who took pity on us. I shall only mention the commander of the camp from which I was liberated. It was found after liberation — only the camp doctor, a prisoner himself, had known of it previously — that this man had paid no small sum of money from his own pocket in order to purchase medicines for his prisoners from the nearest market town. But the senior camp warden, a prisoner himself, was harder than any of the SS guards. He beat the other prisoners at every slightest opportunity, while the camp commander, to my knowledge, never once lifted his hand against any of us" (Frankl, 1963, pp. 135–136). My parents' accounts confirm the existence of the variety of guards. When my father was imprisoned at Dachau, he recognized an SS guard there. The man was a former neighbor. He would secretly give my father pieces of bread, which meant he was endangering his own life. For the system of terror that prevailed within the camp, my father said, posed a risk for any individual, guard or prisoner, who dared to help the sufferer.

Again Hoess' account corroborates Frankl's account. Hoess writes, "The third category consists of men who are kindly by nature, good-hearted, compassionate and able to sympathize with a fellow-human's trouble. Within this category the individual guards vary considerably. First there are those who stick firmly and conscientiously to the regulations and will overlook no departure from them on the part of the prisoners, but who, out of kindness of heart and good nature, construe the regulation in favor of the prisoners and endeavor, so far as this possible, to alleviate their situation, or at any rate not to make it unnecessarily hard. There are others who are simply good-hearted, and whose naivety borders on the miraculous. They will try to gratify a prisoner's every wish, and out of sheer good nature and boundless sympathy will attempt to help him in every way. They are unable to believe that evil men exist among prisoners, too" (Hoess, 1959, p. 72).

Life outside the concentration camps, during the years of the Nazi dictatorship, was also marked by considerable variation in how people reacted to the conditions. For Americans and others, raised in democracy, it is hard to understand the conditions of the Nazi dictatorship. To comprehend the nature of a dictatorship it is worthwhile remembering that a dictatorship allows no opposition: those who opposed the Nazi regime were crushed. "So lethally dangerous was the Nazi regime to its opponents that, as with the cobra, hitting out at the tail was likely to result only in being destroyed by the head" (Kershaw, 2000, p. 212).

The Nazis tried to force all Germans to turn themselves into willing and obedient subjects of the Nazi government. Any German who dared to oppose the Nazi regime was fighting against a national government. Hannah Arendt's *Origins of Totalitarianism* describes the destroying inbuilt characteristics of Nazism that has been supported by later research (Kershaw, 2000). And Carl Friedrich's works, written from a standpoint of constitutional theory, describe the famous "six-point syndrome" highlighting what he saw as the central features of Nazism, which included "an official ideology, a single mass party, terroristic police control, monopoly control over the media, a monopoly of arms, and central control of the economy" (cited in Kershaw, 2000, p. 24).

From a psychological perspective, the Nazi dictatorship was a terrifying regime that knew no bounds in crushing its perceived enemies. Any German who lived under Nazi rule knew that resistance ran the risk of imprisonment or death or at the very least losing their jobs. Hundreds of thousands of ordinary citizens were persecuted for political "offenses" against the Nazi dictatorship (Kershaw, 2000, p. 214). According to Ian Kershaw, a Professor of History at the University of Sheffield, "'Keep quiet or you'll end up in Dacahu' was a common sentiment indicating an all-pervasive fear and caution sufficient to deter most people from challenging the regime in any way. Passivity and cooperation—however sullen and resentful—were the most human of responses in such a situation" (Kershaw, 2000, pp. 207–208). Was this way of responding to the Nazi regime wrong?

Yet, even under the terrifying conditions of the Nazi dictatorship there was considerable variation among ordinary Germans in the way they responded to the regime. Though most Germans were loyal to Hitler's regime, resistance was undertaken by some Germans (McDonough, 2001). This tells us that even under a repressive system like the Nazi regime, an individual's attitude and behavior were guided, in part, by his or her values. Within the category "German police," "German Nazi," and "German soldier" individuals assumed their roles in noticeably different ways. The personality traits of the Germans did not fall into a single mold. In each category there were Germans who eagerly did the destructive work, Germans who viewed themselves as powerless, as having to adapt to the circumstances, and Germans who actively resisted the regime (Hilberg, 1993). The three distinct ways of responding to the regime have been extensively documented in the literature.

For instance, Daniel Goldhagen provides evidence that some Germans eagerly did the destructive work. He presents a wealth of archival data, including testimony from German men working for the order police (*Ordnungspolizei*). The order police, according to Goldhagen, consisted of a total of 131,000 officers and men on the eve of the war to 310,000 men and officers by the beginning of 1943, of whom 132,000 were reservists (Gold-hagen, 1997, p. 182).

Drawing on the testimony of these German men who worked for a battalion of the order police, Goldhagen shows that some Germans (who "were not particularly Nazified in any significant sense") voluntarily killed Jews, tortured them wantonly, then posed cheerfully for pictures with their victims, and then spoke boastfully about their deeds (Goldhagen, 1997, p. 182). Goldhagen writes:

> Their [the German police] assiduousness in killing is not to be doubted. They applied themselves diligently to their task with telling effect. The gruesomeness of it revolted some, but not all, of them. One killer describes a vivid memory from that day: 'These Jews were brought into the woods on the instruction of [Sergeant] Steinmetz. We went with the Jews. After about 220 yards Steinmetz directed that the Jews had to lay themselves next to each other in a row on the ground. I would like to mention now that only women and children were there. They were largely women and children around twelve years old. . . . I had to shoot an old woman, who was over sixty years old. I can still remember, that the old woman said to me, will you make it short or about the same. . . . Next to me was the Policeman Koch. . . . He had to shoot a small boy of perhaps twelve years. We had been expressly told that we should hold the gun's barrel eight inches from the head. Koch had apparently not done this, because while leaving the execution site, the other comrades laughed at me, because pieces of the child's brains had spattered onto my sidearm and had stuck there. I first asked, why are you laughing, whereupon Koch pointing to the brains on my sidearm, said "That's from mine, he has stopped twitching." He said this in an obviously boastful tone. . . .' (cited in Goldagen, 1997, p. 219)

Similarly, early in 1995, The Hamburg Institute for Social Research launched a photographic exhibition referred to in the German media as the '*Wehrmacht* exhibition.' The exhibition explored the theme of *Wehrmacht* soldiers' involvement in acts of brutal, genocidal killings in Eastern Europe. The exhibition impressed on the viewer, in a similar way to Goldhagen's study, evidence that some German soldiers eagerly did the destructive work. Bill Niven, a Reader in German at the Nottingham Trent University, points out that as of 1942, German soldiers were forbidden to take photographs. That they still took them could be interpreted as the "expression of voyeuristic enjoyment, even pride. After all, such photographs were often sent home as trophies" (Niven, 2002, p. 154).

In hundreds of photographs, German soldiers were shown in various stages in the killing of Jews, communists, and others arrested as "partisans" or during grotesque reprisal actions. Victims were shown being shot or hanged.

> They were shown lying in mass-graves, or dangling from balconies, trees, telegraph poles and makeshift gallows. In other photographs, their bodies lay in haphazard piles, or strewn across the ground, cast away like spent matches. Soldiers could be seen arresting civilians, accompanying them to their execution, looking on as the victims dug their own graves, or standing by as preparations for killing got under way. Soldiers were seen cocking their rifles, shooting into crumpling bodies, and placing nooses around necks. Worst of all, there were photographs of soldiers gazing listlessly and indifferently at dead bodies, on occasion, they were smiling. Many photographs suggested that killing was mechanical; some suggested it was a source of satisfaction, even pleasure. (Niven, 2002, p. 152)

The exhibition triggered a strong response in many former *Wehrmacht* soldiers. Many wrote letters to the newspapers protesting the exhibition. "Mostly, . . . former soldiers were indignant at the exhibition" (Niven, 2002, p. 156). "Not that they denied there had been crimes. . . . Where *Wermacht* crimes were admitted, these were regarded as [deviations]" (Niven, 2002, p. 156). "Particular exception was taken by former front soldiers to the exhibition's title, which, they felt implied that the whole *Wehrmacht* was implicated in crimes. Would it not be better, they suggested, to rename it 'Crimes in the *Wehrmacht*', or 'Crimes of individual *Wermacht* units and soldiers'?" (Niven, 2002, p. 156).

According to Niven, most former *Wermacht* soldiers denied that they had been involved in, witnessed, or even heard of *Wermacht* crimes. Instead, many former soldiers viewed themselves as powerless citizens forced to adapt to the circumstances of war. About 18 million Germans had served in the *Wehrmacht*. Many of these Germans viewed themselves as honorable soldiers. They saw no choice but to serve their country.

For instance, Bartius Streithofen, who served in the Luftwaffe's Herman

Göring Division, writes: "Heroes and saints make up only a very small portion of humanity. Most people are opportunists who simply adapt themselves to circumstances. . . . There may be such a thing as 'collective adaptation.' That was certainly my experience during the war. Initially a bunch of my friends and I signed up for the Waffen-SS. I was only 17 and hadn't started to shave—political considerations weren't determining my choice. . . . A friend of my mother's pulled some strings, and I wound up in the Herman Göring Division as a radioman. . . . It was a hard war, and the Herman Göring Division was a tough outfit. . . . But we were soldiers, not butchers" (Steinhoff, Pechel & Showalter, 1994, pp. 279–280).

However, there are accounts of those in the *Wermacht* who witnessed crimes and responded by actively resisting the Nazi regime. In conditions of terroristic dictatorship, where individual opposition was doomed to failure, resistance against the Nazi regime was impressive. Kershaw points out that by 1939, around 150,000 German Communists and Social Democrats were put in concentration camps for resistance toward the Nazi regime. And "40,000 Germans had fled the country for political reason; 12,000 had been convicted of high treason; and a further 40,000 or so had been imprisoned for lesser political offences over the same period" (cited in Kershaw, 2000, p. 208).

As Kershaw explains, "During the war, when the number of offences punishable by death rose from 3 to 46, some 15,000 death sentences were handed out be German civilian courts. One jail alone, the Steinwache prison in Dortmund, has records of the imprisonment for political 'delicts' of 21,823 Germans during the Nazi dictatorship, . . . In the Rhine-Ruhr area, a total of 523 mass trials, involving 8,073 persons, resulted in 97 instances of the death penalty and the imposition of a total of 17,951 years of imprisonment on the convicted members of the worker resistance groups. It is reckoned that over 2,000 working-class members of illegal resistance organizations in this region lost their lives to Nazi terror. It amounts to a moving testimony to bravery, dignity, and suffering" (Kershaw, 2000, pp. 208–209).

(The extent of the literature on Nazism is so vast that even history experts have difficulty in managing it, says Kershaw. The literature on opposition and resistance in Nazi Germany, like much of the other literature dealing with the history of Nazism, has been subject to debate. The reader may want to consult Frank McDonough's book *Opposition and Resistance in Nazi Germany* (2001) for a concise review of recent development in the historical debate on opposition and resistance in Germany.)

A concrete case may be helpful here for illustrating the bravery, dignity, and suffering of a *Wermacht* officer who resisted the Nazi regime. Rich Cohen, author of *The Avenegers*, tells the story of some intrepid individuals, both Jewish and German, who resisted the Nazi regime. Consider the case of Anton Schmidt, a German officer. Cohen writes:

> One day, a German officer, in a long gray overcoat and knee-high boots, stepped through the ghetto gate. Germans were not allowed in the ghetto, not even high ranking officers. It was one of the ways the Nazis isolated the Jews, casting them as dangerous, diseased, inhuman; the sign on the ghetto read: "Plague! Entry forbidden!" As the officer walked down the street, crowds scattered, kids ducked into alleys. His face was stern, angular, tight-lipped. He grabbed a young man by the collar. "Take me to Abba Kovner," [a Jewish partisan leader], he said. The young man led the solider to the street outside Abba's building.
>
> "Wait here," said the kid.
>
> When Abba heard a German officer was waiting to see him, he flushed. Vitka [his comrade] suggested he go out the window, over the ghetto roofs into the city.
>
> "I must see what it's about," said Abba.
>
> He walked out of the building in shabby pants and torn clothes.
>
> "What do you want?"
>
> "Are you Abba Kovner?"
>
> "Yes."
>
> "I am Anton Schmidt," said the officer, "of the accursed German army."
>
> Schmidt was forty-two years old. He had been born in Austria and had gone to fight for Germany when the war started. . . . When Schmdit marched east, he was shocked by the slaughter, by what was happening to the Jews. Through stray conversation he found his way to the resistance. A rebel soldier told him to find Kovner.
>
> Schmdit dreamed of mass escape, of spiriting the Jews in fishing boats

across the Baltic Sea to the safety of Sweden. Like Abba, he was driven by visions of a better world. The two men—Jewish partisan and German officer—decided to work together.

When Schmidt heard of a Nazi plan to kidnap Jews from the ghetto, he told the leaders of the underground. He then filled his trucks with Jewish rebels and carried them to Belorussia. A few days later, when things quieted down, he drove them back. Other Jews hid in the basement of his building. . . . He gave the members of the underground German uniforms and transit documents. In those months, he saved the lives of many partisans. Warned of the risks he was taking, Schmidt said, "I will outlive them. They will never take me alive."

Schmidt disappeared in February 1942. Abba later learned that he had been arrested and was tortured by the Gestapo. He gave no information. In the end, he stood before a firing squad. The shirt he had been wearing was delivered to his wife. It had twenty-seven bullet holes. After the War when the Gestapo files were captured, she was given a note her husband had written a few minutes before his death. "Every man must die once," Schmidt wrote. "One can die as a hangman, or as a man dedicated to helping others. I choose to die helping other men."

Abba had lost more than a truck and a place to hide. Schmidt had been a reason to hope, to again see the world as a collection of individuals, each with the possibility to choose good over evil. "I'm Anton Schmdit," he had said, "of the accursed German army." (cited in Cohen, 2000, pp. 57–58)

Despite the moving testimonies of those who attempted to resist Nazi tyranny, some authors have stressed that passivity and cooperation were the most common responses. It has been estimated that those people who actually resisted the Nazi regime numbered less that 1 percent of the German population (McDonough, 2001, p. 63). Of course, many Germans, as mentioned above, felt coerced into a reluctant acceptance of the regime (McDonough, 2001, p. 1). The low level of resistance was somewhat limited by the repressive nature of the Nazi dictatorship. Was it wrong to passively cooperate with the Nazi dictatorship? There is no simple answer. Each of us is likely to have a different opinion.

After the fall of the Nazi dictatorship, former Nazis and soldiers upon returning to their homes cast off their Nazi selves and viewed themselves as essentially ordinary citizens eager to rebuild their country. Most Germans, however, could not return to "life as before." Instead they were faced with having to rebuild their country and identities.

In West Germany, "The expression 'Zero Hour' (*Stunde Null*) was applied retroactively to 1945, suggesting that, at that time a new era had begun" (Niven, 2002, p. 97). And in East Germany the "postwar revolution" suggested a new era had swept away the old order. In both West and East Germany beginning a new era and overcoming the Nazi past were central features of politics. (For a discussion of how overcoming the past was colored by politics see, Ian Kershaw, *The Nazi Dictatorship: Problems and Perspectives of Interpretation,* 4th ed., New York: Oxford University Press, 2000; Norman Naimark, *The Russians in Germany: A History of the Soviet Zone of Occupation, 1945–1949,* Cambridge, Mass.: Harvard University Press, 1995; and Bill Naven, *Facing the Nazi Past,* New York: Routledge, 2002.)

At a psychological level, overcoming the past involved giving meaning to the "tragedy" of World War II. Many Germans felt they were decent citizens. Many former Nazis and soldiers said they became SS men or soldiers out of necessity because Germany was surrounded by enemies and the Reich had to be protected. Or they said that they did it for positive reasons. For instance, a former senior officer of the Waffen-SS explained it like this:

> What we envisioned right along with the great majority of our people was a Reich with national sovereignty and social justice. We felt both of these goals were being reached more and more in the late 1930s. We had no cause for any kind of doubt, because our commanders were so deeply rooted not only in the German military, but also in National Socialism and the meaning it had for all of us. That's probably also a reason why the Waffen-SS accomplished such outstanding achievements during the war. . . . The Waffen-SS had nothing to do with the concentration camps, we were soldiers. . . . Their service was not considered military service like ours. The "Death's Head" division was set up at Dacahu in 1940, after the Polish campaign. But these troops were guard units which had nothing to do with the internal operation of the concentration camps. Inside, there was only a small camp command post, consisting of maybe 12 men. That was all the SS actually had

in the camps: just the commander with his staff from the general SS. . . . The nominal grouping together has the bitter disadvantage for us today that people say we were all Nazis. But we considered ourselves to be soldiers, exclusively. We wanted nothing to do with what happened in the concentration camps, for God's sake! And I would never have lent myself to anything like that! (Steinhoff, Pechel & Showalter, 1994, p. 34)

John Steiner, a sociologist and survivor of Nazi concentration camps, interviewed about 300 former members of the SS in West Germany during the years 1958 to 1978. According to Steiner (1980), many former Nazis and German soldiers took pride in having defended themselves against communism. Steiner writes: "The SS as a total institution has not accomplished what it set out to accomplish. The Allied Forces prevented them from completing their mission. Yet to this day the majority of the former SS members still adamantly claim to have served a historical mission— namely to bring about a United Europe defending itself against communist aggression and world domination" (Steiner, 1980, p. 444).

General Johannes Steinhoff, a former commander in the German air force during World War II and former Chief of Staff of the German air force and chairman of the NATO Military Committee, and Peter Pechel, a former captain in the Germany army during World War II and former correspondent for German television in Britain, interviewed more than 150 "German witnesses of World War II," many of whom were former Nazis (Steinhoff, Pechel & Showalter, 1994). The results of their interviews, like Steiner's, suggest that many former Nazis and German soldiers saw their actions in positive terms.

According to Steinhoff, Pechel, and Showalter the results from the interviews suggest that "Germany between 1939 and 1945 was not a nation of criminals" (Steinhoff, Pechel & Showalter, 1994, p. 532). Indeed, many former Nazis and German soldiers that they interviewed viewed themselves as Hitler's victims. For instance, a highly decorated German infantry officer put it like this: "I know today that I was abused. My military idealism was abused, the idealism which represented Prussian tradition" (Steinhoff, Pechel & Showalter, 1994, p. 69).

## Postwar Injustices

Besides feeling abused by Hitler and the Nazi regime, many Germans described their postwar experiences with bitterness and resentment. Many felt victimized by the Allies. According to Niven, many Germans perceived the Allied victory as a sequence of injustices that caused bitterness. One of these perceived injustices was the bombing of German cities like Hamburg and the destruction of Dresden. "One of the most beautiful cities in the world, it was razed to the ground by British and American bombers for no apparent reason other than sheer destructiveness or, at best, to plunge the retreating Germans into chaos; 35,000 people died. . . . Dresden became a symbol of arbitrary Allied violence for many Germans . . ." (Niven, 2002, p. 96).

A second perceived injustice was the fate of Germans who were expelled from their homes. Following the Nazi dictatorship's collapse in 1945, more than 13 million Germans were expelled from lands where they had lived for centuries. Tens of thousands of people died in the process. Many Germans told their children stories of these postwar expulsions.

For example, Dieter Hempel is the head of the Berlin branch of the expelees' national organization. Hempel's family was from Breslau—present day Wroclaw in Poland. "My father was a soldier at the end of World War II. He was captured by British troops somewhere in Europe, and he never again saw Breslau until 1991," said Hempel. "He lost everything in Breslau . . ." he said. In 1991, Hempel and his father visited Breslau.

"We stood in front of the house. It was still there, but there were strangers living in it," the son recalled. The experience left Hempel unsettled. "For some people there is an expectation that they should get some financial compensation from the Polish government, but that's not the position of our organization. For me, personally, the answer is more abstract. There should be some sort of recognition that what had happened to us wasn't right, it wasn't legal," he said (Hundley, 2002, p. 6).

Thirdly, there was the perceived injustice of occupation. Many Germans perceived it as the start of a campaign of arbitrary "victors' justice" (*Siegerjustiz*). The term "victors' justice" was used to mean that Germans were unjustly being accused on political grounds of having committed acts that were not in themselves criminal, but were typical acts of war, in the interest of a correct political cause.

Also, many Germans resented the Allies denazifaction procedures. "There was widespread indignation among Germans in the Soviet and Western occupation zones at internment and denazification procedures. They were viewed, as were many other Allied measures, as an attempt to attach a label of collective guilt to the Germans" (Niven, 2002, p. 96). And, according to Niven, the most keenly felt injustice was the division of Germany.

Thus, after the fall of the dictatorship, many Germans felt they had paid hard for the misdeeds committed in their name by corrupt and blind leaders. In this view, the leaders had committed the crimes, not the Germans as a whole. "As Germans we might call World War II the tragedy of our sense of duty. For generations Germans had been far more successfully educated for doing their duty than for exercising individual political and moral judgment. Hitler used and abused our sense of duty" (Steinhoff, Pechel & Showalter, 1994, p. xii).

Many former Nazis and soldiers transmitted the view that the vast majority of the German people were themselves victims of National Socialism. "It was a criminal system that committed its atrocities 'in the name of the German people'" (Steinhoff, Pechel & Showalter, 1994, p. 527). The perpetrators, according to this view, were no more than a handful of evil, criminal individuals—Hitler and his colleagues and a few others. In between, in this view, were most Germans who had followed orders.

Many former Nazis and soldiers, therefore, felt betrayed and dishonored. For instance, in response to the *Wehrmacht* exhibition mentioned above, "[t]he tenor of many soldiers' letters is that they felt dishonoured in the country for which they once fought. They accused the exhibition of 'generalized denigration'" (Niven, 2002, p. 158). In a reader's letter, one Fritz Leiterman protested: "A normal people honours its soldiers as defenders of the fatherland" (cited in Niven, 2002, p. 158). "Loyalty came across, suddenly as betrayal . . ." (Niven, 2002, p. 158).

In addition, many former Nazis and soldiers felt betrayed and accused by their own children. Many found it difficult to explain their experiences and views to their children. They felt that their children were inclined to apply their own standards to the actions of past generations.

For instance, Helmut Schmidt, who served as a German soldier for eight years, writes:

> Consequently, some of today's young Germans find it difficult to under-
> stand the blind obedience of those young Germans who had to endure the
> war either as soldiers at the front or as civilians at home. I have the impres-
> sion that former soldiers from the other side of the many fronts of World
> War II understand the behavior of their German enemies better than our
> own sons and daughters do today. Some of the latter believe us when we say
> that only very few of us were convinced Nazis, but they insist that we jus-
> tify why we were not members of the resistance. They have grown up in a
> free society. . . . They lack the experience of a totalitarian dictatorship, of a
> totalitarian state and its absolute control of information and education.
> (Steinhoff, Pechel & Showalter, 1994, pp. x–xi)

Many former Nazis and soldiers felt their children should be grateful to them for rebuilding a free nation and restoring national pride. According to Steinhoff, Pechel, and Showalter, the 150 Germans speaking in their book—each of them in a different way and based on their different personal beliefs—believed they participated in building a new Germany so that the tragedy of the past should never recur. "The war generation built this new Germany as it had fought for the old one. After the war, this generation had to ask itself: What is more important, yesterday or tomorrow? Its answer can be seen by any visitor to Germany" (Steinhoff, Pechel & Showalter, 1994, p. 532).

To rebuild a new Germany, as mentioned earlier, many former Nazis and soldiers avoided thinking about the past. By avoiding that dark period in their lives they could ban it from their consciousness, so that it did not interfere with rebuilding their lives and restoring honor to the German people. Although some former Nazis and soldiers talked about the variation among the Germans' attitudes and behavior during the war, the predominant view, as mentioned above, was that ". . . only very few of us were convinced Nazis. . . . Most soldiers under Hitler's high command were not Nazis" (Steinhoff, Pechel & Showalter, 1994, pp. x–xi). "I am convinced that the majority of Germans did behave decently during World War II— considering the all too human weaknesses that none of us can escape" (Steinhoff, Pechel & Showalter, 1994, p. xvi).

As Niven (2002) points out, this one-dimensional view implies that there was no difference between the Germans and their victims, including the survivors of concentration camps. The view implies that Nazism was something imposed on the Germans by external forces. It tends toward collective exculpatory readings. It can be interpreted as equating the Holocaust with the plight of German victims and as reducing the role of some Germans as aggressors in the war and perpetrators of the Holocaust.

The one-dimensional view that all Germans were victims is an oversimplification. Also, the one-dimensional view that all Germans were anti-Semitic Nazis is an oversimplification. And finally, the one-dimensional view that all Jews were victims is an oversimplification too. These are post hoc interpretations of history that some former Nazis and survivors have used to make sense of past events and to explain them to their children. Honoring one's dead is a basic impulse, as any human can attest. Both former survivors and Nazis felt that the losses must be remembered, the dead honored and defended. One-dimensional views are useful for honoring and preserving the past, for forming a collective identity, and for transmitting a legacy.

As discussed in Chapter 3, memories about the past are kept alive generation after generation through storytelling. Stories are an ancient means of communicating, of carrying on legacies. Stories or "legacies" transmit values, beliefs, and emotions and preserve the past. One way we preserve and simplify the past is to categorize—to organize the past by classifying events and people. Social identity theory suggests that those who feel their ethnic identity strongly will concern themselves with classifying people into groups. Once we classify people into groups—Jews, Germans—then we are likely to exaggerate the similarities within groups and to understate the variety within groups.

There is a strong tendency to see individuals within a group as more uniform than they really are (Taylor, 1981; Wilder, 1981). Mere divisions into groups can create generalizations—"all Germans were anti-Semitic Nazis," "all Jews were victims." Generalizations assume a correlation between group membership and individuals' characteristics. Research on how we think suggests that we find it easy and efficient to rely on such generalizations when we are emotionally aroused and unable to cope with variety (Esses, Haddock & Zanna, 1993; Stroessner & Mackie, 1993). Generalizations reduce ambiguities and inconsistencies.

## Transformations from One-Dimensional Views to Compassion

Voices from the interviews suggested that survivors' children and Nazis' children inherited a one-dimensional view containing generalizations that influenced their way of seeing and responding to the world. Stories about the past left a powerful imprint upon their minds and strongly affected the images and expectations they had about the individuals from the opposite group. Before attending the conference, several participants reported having nightmares.

For example, a daughter of a survivor reported, "I dreamed a car was waiting to take me to the conference. But when I got into the car, I realized I was being tricked. It was taking me to a concentration camp." Another child of a survivor said: "Since I've never been face to face with children of Nazis, I don't know if I can handle being in the same room with them in a conference." The daughter of a Nazi reported, "I dreamed I was being attacked by, not physically attacked, I mean, like —you know, people [other Germans and her family] were really angry at me for going to the conference."

Sitting face to face with descendants from the opposite group was an emotionally arousing experience for the participants. During the meeting one could observe many signs of stress in the participants' behavior: crying, trembling, raised voices, and sometimes anxious laughter. The children of survivors and Nazis were stressed because the presence of the other side evoked strong feelings. The central stressor, for many survivors' children, had to do with the essentially friendly context and their notably less than friendly feelings toward the participants on the opposite side. They were confronted with two incompatible prescriptions for action. Loyalty to their one-dimensional views conflicted with befriending the participants from the opposite group.

I suspect most readers have experienced being in a situation where just the presence of some person evoked strong feelings such as hatred, resentment, or anger. To gain a greater understanding of the feelings experienced by the conference participants, imagine someone has murdered your child. Now for the first time you meet the killer's child. More than likely the occasion will produce strong feelings. In such a situation you may respond not so much to the person, but based on what that person represents. The killer's child wants to be accepted as an individual without the taint of suspicion that, because his father killed your child, he is somehow a murderer. The killer's child may be a genuinely moral human being. However, in your mind's eye the killer's child symbolizes evil. Just the presence of the killer's child hurts your sense of fairness and you want to strike out. The killer's child senses that, resents you, and withdraws from the situation.

*Stage One: Generalizing*

Initially, during what we might call stage one of the conference, survivors' children related to Nazis' children not as individuals, but as symbols of the generalized group—"anti-Semitic Germans." Their one-dimensional views colored their beliefs about the participants from the opposite group. They related to Nazis' children as an abstract, impersonal entity. They assumed a correlation between group membership and the participants' characteristics. The emotions and generalizations contained in their one-dimensional view were obvious in their discussions. For example, a daughter of a survivor said: ". . . I don't want to show that rage toward these people, but it's right there; I can't do anything about it, the hate and distrust of all Germans. I see them all as killers of my family. . . ."

Nazis' children responded to such statements by emphasizing the variety of attitudes and behavior that existed among the Germans. For instance, a daughter of a Nazi said: "My parents never said anything bad about the Jews. In fact, my father always spoke about how the Jews were helpful to him in his business. He was just a teenager when they drafted him into the army. He was not an enthusiastic member of the Nazi party."

Survivors' children reacted with indignation to such statements. They refused to acknowledge the Nazi parents' view. There were moments when they not only refused, but confronted—indeed in some ways accused the Nazis' children sitting opposite them. For example, a son of a survivor said:

■ I don't believe your father didn't have a choice or that he liked Jews. From the stories that I heard from my parents the Germans were only too glad to destroy the Jews, take away their possessions. It wasn't just the Nazis. I was told young German children were anti-Semites who saw Jews as rats to be killed. So when I hear you say your father was just a teenager and that he liked Jews, I feel my rage. And I can't ignore those feelings, which is not to deal with my anger.

*Stage Two: Revealing*

During what we might call stage two of the conference, there was a gradual shift in the discussion. Nazis' children revealed their personal views and feelings rather than their parents' views. The Nazis' children condemned the perpetrators' actions, ideology, moral values, and conception of the victims. They said they felt enraged, guilty, ashamed, and disgraced because of the perpetrators' horrific actions. For example a daughter of a Nazi said:

■ My rage, I think, is against the same people that you [pointing to a son of a survivor] are raging against. We—it's the same, because I am enraged about the people who have done this to other people. You know, I'm enraged . . . at the inhumanity that people let themselves go into. I mean I'm enraged at these people who did this. I'm enraged that . . . my generation, we have to carry this burden of this. . . . I was enraged at my father for years, you know, I didn't know what to do with it. . . . I blamed him very much although . . . it's not just him. I mean it's just . . . I think we have the same, the same targets, in a way. That's—I'm enraged at this. I'm enraged that this could have happened. I'm enraged at the people who let it happen, who didn't say anything, you know, who just went with it, who just said yes, *Jawohl,* you know. I'm enraged at the people who did the actions, but I'm enraged also at the people who did not do anything . . . who just kind of turned away. . . . I mean I don't know— how I would have acted, but now I want to learn from this, that I do act. . . . It is my rage and I want to say . . . it made me into something. I mean I'm German, so it's like . . . I don't know how to say it, but it's guilt or this thing. I was put into this by these actions of other people.

Many Nazis' children said they were frustrated because their parents' generation would not acknowledge their guilt. Thus, they felt compelled to do penance for actions they never committed. Many Nazis' children said they felt called upon to find honest answers to old questions. For example, a daughter of a Nazi said:

■ I have, in all my years in this country, have really not met a single German who was—said, you know, I did it, and, you know, who said I did all these horrible things, but, you know, when somebody asks you would you have done the same, you say, I don't know. I mean this is the kind of honesty I've always looked for in my parents and my relatives—and never found it.

Many Nazis' children at the conference said they felt a responsibility to keep the memories of the past alive. For example, a son of a Nazi said:

■ There is no way we can heal the past. Because what happened will never be undone, and it shouldn't be undone, and it shouldn't be, and the memory should be kept alive because it is really, it's like a hole that has been burned into the soul of humanity.

Statements like the above confronted survivors' children with information that was strikingly inconsistent with the generalization "Germans are anti-Semitic." Clearly, Nazis' children's beliefs and attitudes suggested that they, as individuals, did not fit the category. In turn, this caused survivors' children to question their feelings of rage and resentment. As mentioned in Chapter 3, in Fritz Heider's terms, the feeling of resentment is a wish to produce a change in the belief-attitude of the wrongdoer that produced the unjust act. And revenge is the means of realizing this wish. Since the Nazis' children at the meeting held beliefs similar to survivors' children, this caused survivors' children to question their feelings of resentment toward the Nazis' children.

*Stage Three: Distinguishing*

During what we might call stage three of the conference, survivors' children spoke about the impact distinguishing Nazis' children from the "other Germans" had on them. Many survivors' children said it produced a conflict and was confusing. On the one hand, they wanted to punish all Germans, or at the least to vent their rage, and on the other, they felt that the Germans attending the conference were "good" people. For example, a daughter of a survivor described the confusion and conflict like this:

■ Just yesterday, before coming here, my father said, "If you ask me what I want from those German children, I would say, give me my family back. My heart would be at peace only if I knew that there would be six million German dead to equal the six million Jews. If we can't do that, then at least we should hurt them—to spit in all their faces." So, I'm just right now sitting here, you know, like I can't control it—and I feel like being physical almost, you know, it's like that kind of rage. I feel like I want to have a [PAUSE] somebody I can just like—I don't know do what with, you know—punch or something, or do something [PAUSE] and I you know, you don't dare do it here because all these people are nice, and I think there was a confusion that, that if I show, I don't want to show it that rage towards these people, but it's right there I can't do anything about it, the hate and distrust of all Germans. I see them all as killers of my family . . . .

A son of a survivor described the conflict like this:

■ I've never met children of Nazis before. I have a golden opportunity to meet you all. But that doesn't rob me of my desire and need to be very angry. I feel a great deal of rage when I look at all of you. And I'm confused . . . .

And a daughter of a survivor described the conflict like this:

■ I can sit in this room, and I don't deal with anger and rage very well—'cause it's there inside me, and I don't want to hurt anybody with my rage, but I can separate that I have rage and anger inside me for what happened to my family and how it impacted me—and I can separate that from who, who's to blame for it. I can have rage in this room but not have to blame anybody in this room. But it is, I still worry about what my rage will do to these nice people that I, that I like, and what will they — Oh God.

*Stage Four: Discussing the Here and Now*

As the meeting progressed, the participants wavered between discussing their personal conflicts, feelings, and views, and their parents' views. At one point, the daughter of a survivor while discussing her feelings about Germans in general pointed to a daughter of a Nazi and said "... you look like an SS woman to me." For the participants, this statement became a springboard for exploring their interactions in the "here and now." During what we might call stage four of the conference, there was a shift in the discussion.

The participants shifted the focus of the discussion to the "here and now." That is to say, they focused the discussion on their personal, immediate experiences and the way one participant's words or actions affected the other. Whereas before, Nazis' children did not react personally to generalizations about "the Germans," in this instance some children of Nazis focused the discussion on themselves, on their responses to being categorized and labeled. Through such exploration, each side gained some insight into the issues and concerns of the other, and the way these are affected by its own actions in the here and now. For instance, a daughter of a Nazi described her response when the daughter of a survivor said she looked like an SS woman. She interpreted the statement as an insult. With considerable personal pain, she described her response like this:

■ It hurts when somebody says that. I have so many feelings about it. I mean it's like no I cannot—I mean a lot of times, I mean I'm trying, I try to kind of say OK this is I'm a symbol for that, but no, it—it also goes through me. It happened once before when somebody did that, and [PAUSE] it's like in that moment [PAUSE] I mean I'm not seen, you know, as a person, and I think that's what hurts very much, and being put into the same [PAUSE] and it's not just being, being not seen. I think it's also it's almost, being, being called a real bad name, I mean put into—do you understand what I mean? The same category of, as some thing that, that we all know we hate. But there is nothing I can do about it. I just shut up. You know to defend myself, I put a wall around myself like a—a tank. I guess it's my own protection. But I feel attacked. It took me a long time to kind of sort that out and say OK they're—[PAUSE]—it's like their pain. But it hurts. It's not like I can just say oh OK it's just that pain and I'm just a symbol, being being a symbol for Germany it sometimes, you know, it's like you put some defense up, but then it goes through too. But nothing can be done. I put a wall around myself, you know, like a tank. It's like that—you know, and I shut up. I was hurt. That I mean I was surprised, how can—you know, this nice person, how can anybody see me this way?

*Stage Five: Sharing Their Hurts*

Immediately following this Nazis' daughter's statement, the other participants were quiet. No one acknowledged that a participant's words had a negative emotional impact on a participant from the opposite group. But the following day, during what we might call stage five of the confer ence, some survivors' children gave the impression that they were willing to understand the Nazis' children's view, rather than to accuse or to assign blame to the other side. Or justify their stake to the moral high ground.

That is to say, and I wish to stress this distinction here, when Nazis' children discussed their *own hurts* and sufferings, rather than their parents' sufferings, some survivors' children accepted the view that Nazis' children felt like victims. Some survivors' children gave the impression that they were willing to accept and give meaning to Nazis' children's hurts. The participants' here-and-now experience of seeing a daughter of a Nazi feel hurt and insulted created a new atmosphere conducive to the participants sharing their inner feelings. Participants listened to each other and tried to understand each other's hurts and sufferings. In turn, this open discussion helped the participants penetrate each other's perspective and show compassion for the other's feelings.

Survivors' children spoke about how hurt they felt by their Holocaust legacy, while Nazis' children listened attentively to survivors' children's stories, and often tried to comfort and reassure survivors' children. A daughter of a survivor described her pain to Nazis' children like this:

- The way I was brought up, everything that has happened to me has to do with the Holocaust. It's like swallowing pain, feeling pain all the time. I feel the Holocaust differently from someone who, say, watches a movie about it. It's in me. I don't trust the world. I always have the fear that I will be trampled. And then the truth is, even though it's not my experience, I've never been in the Holocaust, no one ever persecuted me directly. That's what makes it so difficult.

Another daughter of a survivor explained it like this:

- There are images, the worst images you can imagine stored in my head that can not be eliminated. I spent the first half of my life with it. Images of Germans in black boots with dogs coming to take me away, SS guards beating me, trying to kill me. And I'm trying to figure out how to escape. Images of suffocating to death, of not having enough air. I can remember when I went to the movies, I would ask my friends to sit next to the exit sign. I never told them why, but it was because I always had to sit in a room near a door or window. But, the worst image, I guess, was the one I had when my own daughter was born. I imagined she would suffocate to death in her sleep. And [participants crying the background] once I dreamed they took my daughter and me to concentration camp and I pleaded to be sent to the gas chambers, so my daughter could be saved. These are the nightmares I carry in my head.

And a son of a survivor explained it like this:

- Since the age of eight or nine I can't remember a time when the Holocaust wasn't on my mind. At times it completely consumed me. I felt I had to make up for my parents' losses. I felt an obligation to my family who was murdered and to my parents who survived. I always felt as though my life wasn't really my own, as though I was living my life for all those who were murdered too. I didn't want to disappoint my parents, to make them suffer at all. I wanted them to be proud of me. I always thought my parents had more than their share of suffering, and I was careful not to hurt them in any way. I was always aware of their experience. It's like my life's mission was to bring them happiness to make up for their suffering.

Nazis' children spoke about their pain too. They told survivors' children how the Nazi past affected their lives. For instance, a daughter of a former Nazi described it like this:

■ I feel I carry this stuff that isn't mine, and I can't move any, you know, I'm sort of buried under it. I'm paralyzed by it. I don't want to deny it but I would like to take responsibility for my own time, which I haven't been able to do because I never lived in my own time, I lived in my parents' time all my life. I'm a German, so it's like [PAUSE] it's like with that I have this, this—I don't know how to say it, but it's guilt or this thing.

Another daughter of a former Nazi explained it like this:

■ I've run from this for a long time, but one of the things for me—how to build a sense of self. That you have a sense of continuity. I always felt disconnected from the good things of German culture. I couldn't own it, because if I owned that I owned everything else too. . . . It's a sense of pride in my identity that I never really had. And that I've been looking for. And I have not been able to find that by reading Goethe and Schiller, you know, because this is not—it's not the same anymore. It's like there—there is a break, there is a bank space that I have to fill in. . . . [SNIFFS]. One of the things I feel I carried was this self-hatred.

And another daughter of a former Nazi explained it like this:

■ I have the impulse to accuse my father all the time. Accuse, accuse, accuse. Why did you do that? And I think I talked to my father when I was 14 or 15. And he kept his mouth shut. And since that time he never spoke. So this is my part of bringing him into silence in a way because of this impulse of accusing, accusing.

You know that's what it was like for us to grow up with the grown-ups around us, because you know, when you're a child, and then you find something horrible happened, and you know that some of these people might have been involved in it, and you don't know to what degree. I've wanted all my life to hear my father's story, to hear something about the why and the how. I've grown up so much feeling that my father was an animal and that I come from a people of monsters, and it's not true. German people are human beings. I was thinking how hunted I also feel, and how very frightened, how much I lived in fear my entire life.

Weeping, another daughter of a former Nazi said:

■ I have lived in fear too. I've been afraid that the children of the victims would come search for me and kill me because of my guilt. When I found out about the horrible things that were done, I fell into a deep depression. I wanted to commit suicide. No one in the family wanted to talk to me about the past. There was this silence about it.

At this point, a child of a survivor reached out to embrace the daughter of a Nazi and said: "I understand you, and I believe you're a victim too. Ultimately, I believe that you have the right to speak about your childhood, as we do. You're a victim, in my opinion, you are a victim also." Another child of a survivor said: "When I look in your eyes, I don't see hate and I don't see a murderer. I see a victim. . . ."

A daughter of a Nazi responded: "And I know I'm—I must not—I must not be afraid of you. . . ." Another daughter of a Nazi said: "When we speak together about the repercussions of hatred and what it's done in our lives . . . I could not have done that before because I could not have believed that I could be believable to children of survivors. But by hearing your stories and really taking them in, I can bring my own story out too."

A son of a survivor said: "I thank you, and I can't thank you enough, and it's so important. And the burden that we as children carried—and feelings that I have carried—it's important to know that you [Nazis' children] carry a heavy burden as well. And to be able to speak about it, recognize it, and to tell me about that is incredible."

In the relationship between Nazis' children and survivors' children, a new interaction was evident when Nazis' children and survivors' children discussed their own hurts. As they talked about their own hurts, rather than their parents' hurts, Nazis' children and survivors' children showed *compassion* for the other and tentatively restored equal moral relations. As the etymology of the word suggests, compassion involves "feeling with" the other person, sharing his or her feelings. Because compassion involves a sense of shared humanity, it promotes the experience of equality (Blum, 1980).

Compassion, this ability to feel for and understand another person's suffering is the cornerstone passion of our sense of justice. Without compassion there can be no justice, writes Solomon (1990). Compassion opposes and impedes causing others to suffer. To have compassion is to have some concern for the other's welfare (Nussbaum, 2001; Solomon, 1990). According to the philosopher Lawrence Blum and the psychologist Ervin Staub, compassion is an emotion that can be called "altruistic" in that it involves a regard for the good of the other person (Blum, 1980; Staub, 2002).

It is worth remembering that the human mind knows no neat dividing line between emotion and thought. To feel compassion is to have some thought for the other's good, to wish their suffering would end, and to do what will bring this end about. Compassion requires the attitude to do helpful actions, and to do them because we have an understanding of someone's suffering and a concern for the person's good (Blum, 1980). Compassion, above all else, moves us to act in constructive ways.

Having compassion, therefore, for someone's suffering is a motivational *transformation* that inclines us to inhibit relationship-destructive responses (such as the desire for vengeance) and to behave constructively toward others. In other words, compassion is a sedative to negative feelings such as anger, vengefulness, resentment, and indignation. As the philosopher Arthur Schopenhauer (1995, p. 175) put it, "For rain is to fire what compassion is to anger."

Compassion is the true antidote against anger, vengefulness, resentment, and indignation. Nothing removes our negative feelings toward others so easily as acquiring a measure of compassion for another person's welfare (Lama, 1999, 2000, 2002). The participants' cathartic experiences, mentioned in Chapter 4, may have been related to the emergence of compassion for the other's hurts and sufferings. Stating the obvious, letting go of negative feelings and acknowledging the position and feelings of someone else takes away much tension.

## Stage Six: Transformation

During what we might call stage six of the conference, many participants spoke about how attending the conference made a major difference in their lives. Their statements typify the type of transformation that can occur with the emergence of compassion for the other side's hurts. The first type of transformation is about the participants' feelings. And the second type of transformation is about the participants' differentiated images or categorizations. Often their statements intertwined both changes.

For example, a daughter of a survivor describes her transformation like this:

■ I think what it was, was I erased—the image of the bad Germans and I think I was able to—just—having gotten to know children of Nazis [names two specific participants] and—and having been in the conference, I just got that—negative image of Germany out of my system. I just erased it. I didn't like what it did to me before. It always made me feel uncomfortable. And I think I—deep down inside—I just knew that it was time to [get] rid of that feeling 'cause I didn't want to spend the rest of my life with it. I'd spent the first half of my life with it, and it—it—you know, cause a lot of problems. [CHILDREN CRYING IN BACKGROUND] So once I could erase—and, and get rid of those— the negative connotation of the German people, Germany, the bloodied soil, I could go forward with my life and just prove to others that you can do it too. You know, that the worst image in the world can be eliminated. You might shelve it. It'll always be part of you. But it doesn't have to gnaw away at you. And it doesn't have to haunt you the rest of your life. And for me the Holocaust, up until this meeting of coming together with Germans, really has haunted me. . . . I feel exorcized of that bad image. It feels good.

A son of a survivor describes his transformation like this:

■ And I mean a real lot of things. . . . I think the important thing I'm leaving with is the distinction that I've made in my mind—to separate the children from the parents. The fear and hatred, which is diminished. I leave here grateful to all of you to allow that transformation to help happen to me. Uhhh, when I look at you I don't see Nazis, I see people. That distinction in my mind has, that generation [of] people who were Nazis were persecutors, they should be judged and tried and dealt with appropriately. There's not question in my mind, but you did not do that. . . .

Another daughter of a survivor describes her transformation like this:

■ I've been looking for release all my life. . . . And that's what I, that's what I have found here, that's what I take away from here . . . To get through my prejudice of fear about Germany and German people, my stereotypes, to like totally defuse that crap, here, by acknowledging it and addressing it and then getting through it and over it. . . . Thank you for being a person, just an individual and not a whole phenomenon. You are not the Nazi nation, by yourself.

Another daughter of a survivor describes her transformation like this:

■ Before coming here [to the conference], I thought if my mother had a gun, you know, I was just seeing this violent possibility you know, of course played out in my mind. I though how am I going to deal with this? . . . And I think when I first wanted to come here I thought, this is fantastic; of course we should meet, of course —we're in a cycle, victim and perpetrator is in a circle; we find out the victim was a perpetrator and also a victim. It's, it's a cycle; so what's the difference? And we have to stop it. We have to stop it! And maybe the message from this place is a little light that shines and says it's possible to stop from one generation to the next. We don't have to carry the hatred; we don't have to kill each other; we don't have to live this way.

And another daughter of a survivor describes her transformation like this:

■ I can't put into words what I've experience here. It's, it's just so deep. . . . If we allow ourselves to get to know each other as individuals and then take it from there! And that's what happened to me . . . And it worked. And—one—and there's just a great sense of relief that I didn't want to attack you or [talking to a son of a Nazi]—you know— revenge. So I want to thank you for, for doing that for me and—cause it just feels like there's a big load off my shoulder too.

A daughter of a Nazi describes her transformation like this:

■ I think the German people are experiencing trauma . . . I feel after this meeting released from something—I don't know how to say this. I, I think I've tried to destroy myself you know, most of my life. I, I've wanted to be able—not knowing what to do about my heritage. I, I've been self-destructive and I've—not felt that I had a right to exist, and I've not felt that there was a place for me in the world. And coming here [the conference], really have the—I feel that I've gotten the permission to let go. And all of a sudden I realize that it's stupid! It doesn't make any sense for me to beat myself up my entire life, because it doesn't bring back your, your family. And I might as well use my pain and my legacy and do something meaningful with it .

Another daughter of a Nazi describes her transformation like this:

■ [SNIFFS] I didn't even want to speak German. [SNIFFS] I just stayed away from it . . . And I realized that I am German. I mean, you know, I can try to get—run away from it, but I am. There's no question. [SNIFFS] And I started to appreciate Germany, you know in a different way. I started to—want to speak again. I started to kind of come back in a way. And—I also would see a, I felt like I would see the, the world a little clearer about what was good that I didn't—like being German, I don't have to—it's like there are some things that are not good, but there are also good things. I started to kind of sort that; that there is a lot of good there. And—that it wasn't all bad; that there was, that I did not have to be ashamed to be German. That I am—that, that I could be, you know, it seems like I'm proud to be German. That sounds so bad.

A son of a Nazi describes his transformation like this:

■ One of the things I've learned here is that truth heals, and that lies make you sick, and—sick in your mind, and in your heart. And I think what has subsided for me is the fear. I'm not as afraid any more to ask for the truth and to speak the truth, because I know I'm not alone any more. And that happened because we all were willing to make ourselves vulnerable to each other . . . And so I hope that maybe other people will be encouraged to do, to join, the same kind of experiment in the future.

Another daughter of a Nazi describes her transformation like this:

■ I feel I have hope, and I feel that—I feel the paralysis and the fear is gone. I feel now much more capable of going to my parents and asking them questions I didn't have the courage to ask before, because the defensive that I felt within myself, or the anger that would come up, sort of got released here, and I know that if I don't come from such a place of accusation, but when I, when I'm able to also come—they, the willingness to listen, that maybe they will be more able to talk to me!

Another daughter of a Nazi describes her transformation like this:

■ I'm a German, so I must say something philosophical thing [Laughter]. But just help me with the translation. [Speaks In German] Differentiate. Differentiate. Okay. What I'm not very good but I try to become able to this ability to differentiate. Between first—between the parents and the children of Nazis or Third Reich, but also to—survivors, I mean, the background of being raised in a family of survivors and the other side. I mean, being raised in a family of you know, the other side. And also to differentiate between the people, I mean who do—who did bad, I say, and the conditions whom make them to these peoples. To differentiate—and it's important for me to see both my background and your background and my pains, I mean, not my, the pain of the group so to say, and your pain because it's not the same pain okay, but it's, it's another one.

And another daughter of a Nazi describes her transformation like this:

■ I've already talked a lot about feeling personally freed of this belief that I had to somehow harm myself to make up for the deeds of my father, but I felt I really got the permission here to really fully include myself in the human race [Laughs]. And I also feel like this has been a homecoming for me; I've never been able to really fully be German or even know what that means, and I have wanted to. I've really wanted to be German and to be able to be proud to be German. And by that I don't mean to ever forget the—the pain and the memory, and I want to witness always the pain that results from the legacy that we share here. But I want to use that pain to do something useful in the world and not to just keep beating myself up with it and to distance myself from people because of the shame.

## A New Relationship Based on Compassion

There is a hopeful note on which I can conclude this chapter. These statements suggest that despite past injustices and the tendencies toward revenge and one-dimensional views, when people experience a measure of compassion for another person's well-being, a transformation occurs. Transformation is not, as some people may believe, a mysterious and sublime process.

The fact that some participants described a set of changes in their feelings and attitudes tell us that descendants of victims when sitting face to face with descendants of victimizers can establish a new relationship. Establishing a new relationship does not mean that two truths are now equal in validity. Obviously, each side may hold the opinion that their view is the more valid one. From my standpoint, my mother's suffering was incomparable to what any German suffered. But I suspect a German mother who lost her only son may feel her suffering is equal to my mother's. Establishing a new relationship means there is a willingness to discuss differences in legacies without loss of commitment to one's own legacy. It does not mean that every legacy is equal in validity.

And establishing a new relationship does not mean there should be no assessment of guilt or responsibility. It does not mean to bury the past or to forgive. I and other children of survivors, in my opinion, do not have the proper standing to forgive what was done to our families. And since Nazis' children have not done anything wrong and are not responsible for the injustices done, there is nothing to forgive, though perhaps much to be sad about. But because we cannot alter the injustices of the past, we can start now to strive for a better future. The conference results suggest that between the sons and daughters of the Holocaust and the children of the Nazis it is possible to create a new relationship based on compassion.

# 7

# CONCLUDING REMARKS

I first found out about them when I was fourteen or fifteen or sixteen. "You see," my father said, "there was a kind German pastor who helped me. When I escaped from the German Guards and left the camp, the pastor saved my life."

I interrupted. "What was the name of the camp?"

"It was called Zwieberge. It was a subcamp of Buchenwald. It was located in a place called Langenstein, in Hartz, Germany."

He continued his narrative. "For several days, Rudolf [my father's childhood friend and a fellow inmate] and I were hiding under a straw mattress in the kapo's room in the back of the barracks. When we heard the guards stop shooting, we got out from under the mattress. We escaped from the camp. We could barely stand up. Both of us had lice and dysentery. And I had typhus. We managed to walk down a hill. I don't know how we did it.

"We knocked on the first door that we saw. A man answered the door and led us inside. His daughter took care of us. She bathed us every day. The stench must have been terrible. If it wasn't for her care, I would have died."

Then my father smiled and added with genuine lightness, like he was getting to the punch line, "I remember Rudolf and I were lying on the same bed taking turns going to the bathroom, right there on the bed. You know, we were too weak to get up, and we couldn't control it. We couldn't get up to go out anywhere." ["Go out anywhere" was my father's euphemism for going to the rest room.]

I smiled at his weak joke, then pressed him for more details. "What was the pastor's name?" I asked him. "Do you remember, Daddy?"

Speaking seriously again he said, "Yes, yes, I remember his name. His name was Pastor Seebasz. He was a really, really good man." Then he answered a question I hadn't asked.

"We found out later, after we left the pastor's house, that his daughter died. What we had was contagious. Still she washed our clothes, and she bathed us. She got it. She caught our disease by touching us."

Now he paused. It struck me that he never talked about the pastor's daughter before.

I was wordless.

My mother was listening to my father tell me this story, and must have noticed my silence and puzzlement. She said with skepticism, "You don't know, Adolf, maybe the daughter died of something else."

My father was definitive. "I know it for a fact. She died rescuing me."

For many years afterwards, I never asked my father any other questions about the pastor or his daughter. It was I who didn't want to hear more about it. I stopped probing, the questions I would logically ask: Why did the pastor and his daughter rescue you? Did you ever contact the pastor again? What was his daughter's name? Do you remember what you were feeling when you found out that she died because she contracted your disease? How do you feel about her death now?

Looking back, I see that my father's story was diametrically opposed to my assumptions about the Germans. I held strong beliefs about the Germans and the Holocaust. I held fast to an absolute and all-embracing dogma. Simply put, I was anti-German. I held all Germans accountable for the catastrophe. There was no room in it for a guiltless German. Or for a kind and decent German pastor. Or for a young German girl who sacrificed her life to save a Jewish survivor.

Belief perseverance is the tendency to retain existing beliefs even after those beliefs have been shown to be invalid. My personal history is an illustration of belief perseverance. My father's story threatened to invalidate my belief that all Germans were anti-Semitic. It threatened to undermine my view that the Germans were motivated to kill Jews because of a deep-seated hatred integral to German culture. How could I fit information about the pastor's actions and his daughter's actions with the horrifying details of the atrocities my parents had endured at the hands of the Germans? The Germans hunted Jews like animals and tortured them wantonly.

Those stories about the atrocities produced in me feelings of anger. My parents were good, decent people. I felt the atrocities were unjust because it subjected my parents and others to undeserved suffering. So I responded with moral indignation. The perception that one has been treated unjustly is widely recognized as a common, perhaps the most common, source of anger. Aristotle emphasized this link in his definition of anger:

> . . . an impulse, accompanied by pain, to a conspicuous revenge for a conscious slight directed without justification towards what concerns oneself. . . . (cited in Miller, 2001, p. 6)

My anger entitled me to take an aggressive stance against the collective group "the Germans." I believed that all members of the German community ought to be punished to compensate the victims. Avenging the injustice became a defense of restoring honor and integrity to the entire Jewish community. Revenge was the future for the Jewish community. I believed that the Germans violated the values of my group's moral community, and therefore the members of their group ought to suffer. Our Jewish hurt was the permission slip to hurt back. These "ought forces," as Heider (1958) termed them, created a mindset that guided my feelings.

Heider viewed the "ought forces" as a pervasive tendency, stemming from the more general principle of cognitive balance. In Heider's terms, justice is an *ought* force that we view as inherent in our environment, conceived as a harmonious fit between happiness and goodness and between unhappiness and wickedness.

> When they coexist, we feel the situation is as it should be, that justice reigns. On the other hand, the coexistence of happiness and wickedness is discordant. . . . Common-sense psychology tends to hold that any imbalance represents a temporary state of affairs, that the wicked may have their field day now, but that they eventually be punished and the good rewarded. . . . When we think that the wicked will be punished, our idea of 'what is' is influenced by our idea of what ought to be. (Heider, 1958, p. 235)

Thus, according to Heider, our actions are guided along certain standards called "ought." We often have the feeling that someone ought to get a punishment. These ought forces play a major role in our lives. Viewed from this perspective, perceptions of injustice arouse strong feelings of anger and punitive impulses that call out for getting even and by that re-balancing an injustice.

I was not, therefore, a dispassionate listener of my parents' Holocaust stories, tallying evidence for and against my bias about the Germans. My existing view and feelings of injustice guided my attention, my interpretation, and my understanding. Whenever I heard information that a German behaved as expected, I duly noted the fact; my existing view was confirmed. When a German behaved inconsistently with my expectation, I interpreted or explained away the behavior as due to special circumstances. The deeds of a few "good Germans," I concluded, were obviously legends about rare instances of moral behavior.

Social psychologists have noted that when people are presented information that is strikingly inconsistent with a preexisting view, they tend to salvage the view by splitting off a new category (Brewer, 1988; Hewstone, 1994; Kunda & Oleson, 1995, 1997). For example, one who believes that most women are generally passive and dependent can split off a new subtype of "aggressive feminist" to handle women who don't fit the basic view (Taylor, 1981).

Similarly, Germans who helped Jews can form a new category of the "Good Germans." This *subtyping*—forming a subcategory—helps maintain the larger view that most Germans were evil or most women are passive. The image of the subcategory "aggressive women" or "Good Germans" doesn't change the image of woman or Germans in general. My image of the demonic German was, without doubt, resistant to disconfirming information. My heart's response to the stories about the atrocities of the Holocaust imposed perceptual, cognitive, and emotional constraints on my ability to process new information. A major effect of these constraints was that they entrenched me in my own perspective on history and justice.

And these constraints, moreover, made me indifferent to how my own conduct might affect a German's conduct. I did not consider the consequences of my own actions. I ignored and radically belittled what Pastor Seebasz and his family did for my father. But it never occurred to me to ask how Pastor Seebasz might feel knowing that I, the daughter of the man his family saved, was indifferent to his sacrifice. I was indifferent, not because I had no concern for his pain or loss, but because I did not see his pain.

I did not see his pain because my family's victimization status absolved me from considering his loss, so I thought. I was not prepared to suspend my view of the demonic German or to give equal consideration to both sides. I was unable to deal with Pastor Seebasz as an equal. I could not accept that different conceptions of suffering are, or in principle are, defensible. How did Pastor Seebasz cope with his daughter's death? Was it worth losing a daughter to save a Jewish survivor? These were questions that took a long time in coming. And the route has been circuitous, involving as it does my identity, my family's history, and how I came to view it.

Social psychologists have been more successful in explaining belief perseverance in the laboratory than in discovering possibilities for overcoming it in real-world contexts. Identifying conditions for change requires a shift in empirical and theoretical attention—a shift away from speculating on the origins of sociopathology, aggression, violence, or posttraumatic symptoms, to a concern with how perceptions of injustice manifest themselves in the actual lives of people whose ancestors inflicted injustice or suffered injustice.

In this book I have provided a new framework for understanding how emotions and cognitions follow perception of an injustice. Injustices, I have pointed out, have a transcendent quality, which is one reason feelings about injustices are passed on from generation to generation. There are situations, like the Holocaust and World War II, where the evil done survives the person who has done it and can become a burden weighing on the memory of later generations.

I have presented empirical evidence suggesting that survivors' children and Nazis' children having internalized the parables of their parents, each group of children also is seeking their own justice fueled by anger, resentment, and shame. Seeking justice can turn into an escalatory, self-perpetuating dynamic. The needs and fears of individuals whose parents were involved in an injustice impose emotional and cognitive constraints on their abilities to cope with new information. A result of these constraints is that individuals may adopt a rigid belief and an unwillingness to hear the other side. And they may underestimate the possibility of change and avoid discussions altogether.

Turning from the laboratory to real-world situations has shown us the relevant points of entry at which the cognitions and emotions of individuals and the interactions between individuals can play a specific role in deciding outcomes. Thus, I have identified certain actions central to overcoming belief perseverance—including seeing justice as intergenerational, seeing justice as interpersonal, seeing justice has two sides, and seeing justice as compassion—that of necessity take place at the level of individuals and interactions between individuals.

The meeting between Nazis' children and survivors' children provided a setting in which these actions might have occurred. What would have been involved, we may ask, in carrying out these actions while overcoming belief perseverance? Specifically, what would have been involved in seeing justice as intergenerational, seeing justice as interpersonal, and seeing justice has two sides? (Later, I will discuss seeing justice as compassion.) Let me simply list some of the major conditions, desires, and attitudes that would need to be given up for these actions to occur.

Unidimensional views
Collective accountability
Adherence to one's legacy
Sense of dignity and self-worth
Moral indignation
The desire for vengeance
Resentment
Ethnic identification
Loyalty to one's ancestors
Unequal moral relations
Victimization status
The distinction between perpetrator and victim
And, ultimately, one's history and identity

What does this mean? Does it mean we should have expected the descendants of those who inflicted injustices and those who suffered injustices to carry out these actions while overcoming their beliefs? Hardly. We would, I think, be expecting too much. The demand is daunting for anyone.

The apology dynamic, offering and accepting forgiveness, is today's model for reconciliation. It, too, demands that individuals give up some of these conditions, desires, and attitudes. For example, studies on the promotion of forgiveness have hypothesized that people have to give up feelings of righteous indignation, the desire to seek revenge, and resentment to become more forgiving toward their offenders (McCullough et al, 2001). And it has been hypothesized that people have to give up ruminative thoughts about the injustices to become more forgiving too.

As noted before, McCullough et al. (2001) hypothesized that "Vengeful people ruminate on the injustices and harm they have suffered to keep themselves focused on the goals of balancing the scales, teaching the offender a lesson . . ." (McCullough et al., 2001, pp. 602–603). The more people ruminate about an injustice, the more difficulty they have in forgiving the injustice, according to McCullough (2000). Thus, according to this line of reasoning, people should give up ruminative thoughts and feelings about the injustice to become more forgiving. The inability to do so is viewed as a lack of control to suppress feelings and thoughts about the injustices.

Despite its long history in religion and philosophy, empirical research on the promotion of forgiveness has been conducted only quite recently. A variety of group, individual, and psychoeducational interventions for encouraging people to forgive has been developed and tested in recent years. Worthington, Sandage, and Berry (2000) conducted a meta-analysis of data from 12 group intervention studies. They concluded that interventions were generally effective for helping people to forgive specific individuals who have harmed them.

Most of the studies analyzed involved interventions with ad hoc groups of participants. People who might or might not have a common problem were brought together or were treated individually, and an attempt was made to teach them how better to forgive someone who hurt them. For example, in one intervention study, the participants were introductory psychology students. They were asked whether they would like to learn information and skills that might help them to forgive a specific person.

Participants wrote short descriptions of the unjust actions that they wanted to forgive. "The following are some examples: My ex got me pregnant on purpose, and then decided that it was too much responsibility. My father abuses drugs. He abandoned me and my mother when I was a child. When my father died, my 'best friend' was not there at all for me. She was very selfish and betrayed my trust in her when I needed her. My mother told me that I was not wanted in the family, and that I was an evil person" (McCullough, Worthington & Rachal, 1997, p. 12).

Researchers have raised questions about the applicability of studies like these to real-world contexts. They have questioned the generalizability of the results, since many studies on the promotion of forgiveness have targeted college students. And they have questioned the applicability of the results to severe injustices. For example, researchers Worthington et al. write:

> Severe and long-lasting harms have not been addressed via group interventions. . . . We recommend that the boundaries within which forgiveness interventions can be helpfully applied be investigated scientifically. Severity of hurts and offenses seems to greatly influence the ease with which people are able to forgive. There might be some evidence that hurts and offenses that are extremely severe result in revision of people's cognitive framework for understanding existence. Such cognitive reorganizations would undoubtedly require either a long time to repair or an extremely powerful intervention—probably beyond the capability of most interventions developed to date. (Worthington et al., 2000, pp. 236–237)

And Worthington et al. go on to note that "People from cultures such as Northern Ireland, South Africa, or Rwanda have many factors beyond the individual hurts that make extending forgiveness difficult for them. . . . Those culturally loaded issues often must be addressed" (Worthington et al., 2000, p. 242).

Finally, some researchers have noted the possibility that, in certain interpersonal situations, people who cope by forgiving might put themselves at risk for serious problems. Some research has suggested that forgiveness might be a sign of relational disturbance, as in relationships characterized by physical abuse. For example, the psychologists Katz, Street, and Arias found (1997) evidence that staying in an abusive relationship was mediated by the women's willingness to forgive the violent partners.

It is reasonable to ask, therefore, whether the promotion of forgiveness is really a good thing for all people in all situations. Since, as far I know, there are no studies that investigate the promotion of forgiveness with the descendants of an injustice, it is difficult to know whether the promotion of forgiveness is appropriate with such a population.

Our study was not set up to promote forgiveness, but rather to study the face-to-face interactions between descendants of victims and victimizers. However, the data suggested that forgiveness might be an inappropriate intervention model. During the conference, most survivors' children spoke against the notion of forgiveness. For example, a child of a survivor said: "Am I minimizing the trauma? Am I forgiving? It's certainly not in my power to forgive. And no—and it is too presumptuous even a thought about—about forgiveness." And another child of a survivor said: "I could never forgive what was done to my family. My entire extended family tree was forever eradicated. Can anyone forgive that?"

An important variable, according to research, that seems to have great import for forgiveness is the extent to which the wrongdoer makes sincere apologies or expressions of remorse. It is well established that offering an apology encourages forgiving, particularly when apologies are elaborate and include admissions of guilt (Darby & Schlenker, 1982; McCullough et al., 2000; Ohbuchi, Kameda & Agarie, 1989). Thus, today's model for the promotion of forgiveness and reconciliation often includes encouraging perpetrators to offer an apology. In some instances, entire governments like in Rwanda, Argentina, and South Africa have encouraged perpetrators to come forth and apologize for their unjust acts (Minlow, 1998).

An apology may offer a great deal of comfort to victims. And it may, in fact, be an effective strategy for healing and for promoting forgiveness between perpetrators and victims. But to my understanding, an apology is an acknowledgment of guilt. All of this points to a fundamental question: Should we expect the descendant of a perpetrator to offer an apology for an unjust act that he or she did not commit?

During the conference, most Nazis' children spoke against the notion of inherited guilt. For example, a child of a Nazi officer said: "All my life, ever since 1945, when I was 14, have I felt guilty because there was lot of talk of collective guilt. Finally now, I am not guilty. Yes, but my father's generation sure was. And I want to make that very clear. I've carried this burden. I don't want it anymore. Because I need to live my own life . . ." And another child of a Nazi said: "I think my generation was brought up to feel guilty for our parents because there was so much silence about it. We took on their guilt. But, of course, we ourselves did not do anything wrong, so we have no reason to be guilty."

Thus, many Nazis' children and survivors' children directly said that offering an apology or granting forgiveness was an inappropriate action. Their statements suggested they did not feel they had the proper standing to apologize for harms they did not inflict or to forgive harms that were not done to them. And survivors' children's statements suggested that their unwillingness to forgive had less to do with lack of control over ruminative thoughts than with principled moral action. For example, a child of a survivor said: "I think it is my duty as a human being to remind the world about the injustices that were done to my family." Similarly, a child of a Nazi said: "I think Germany, on the whole, has, even after 45 years, enormous responsibility to watch the development and to see in the country and outside the country all things similar to the beginnings of the murders of the Jews in the Third Reich."

So, it is reasonable to argue, as the philosopher Jeffrie Murphy (1988) has, that in some situations the unwillingness to forgive is a morally correct response. Murphy points out that the unwillingness to forgive may properly be regarded, in some situations, as respect for human dignity, for the demands of morality. It conveys emotionally the attitude for concern for the rules of morality. By contrast, forgiveness can convey the attitude of excusing the wrongdoing. Taken to its extreme, it can convey the attitude of moral relativism. Or it can convey the attitude of forgetting the harms that were inflicted on a victim.

The unwillingness to forgive and rumination may be pathological, as some psychologists have suggested, but in some situations they may be positive responses. Rumination and the unwillingness to forgive may have general social utility. In other words, ruminative thoughts may play an important role in the development of moral life. To ruminate means to ponder, to reflect, to engage in contemplation. By ruminating about an injustice one remembers, bears witness, and memorializes past wrongs. Rumination also can play the role of helping to establish taboos.

"Wundt describes taboo as the oldest human unwritten code of laws. Its is generally supposed that taboo is older than gods and dates back to a period before any kind of religion existed" (cited in Freud, 1950, pp. 8–9). We tend to think taboos are practices that primitive savages had, and that we civilized people have outgrown this sort of thing. But let me suggest that establishing a taboo against genocidal acts might serve a purpose in today's world, where the deliberate and systematic aggression against ethnic groups still occurs.

Social scientists have demonstrated that aggression, the desire to gain power, and the need to survive, to reproduce, and to protect are basic human instincts, which may lead to immoral acts. Sigmund Freud in his book *Totem and Taboo* writes that taboos help to inhibit immoral acts which we nevertheless desire to commit. Freud applied this viewpoint to the most universal of all taboos: the taboo that prohibits sexual relations between close blood relatives and the taboo that prohibits the practice of cannibalism. The horrors of incest and cannibalism might seem obvious to us today, but it took a long time for human beings to prohibit these acts. The taboo helped to eliminate these practices from social life. And it helped to instill in us a psychological revulsion for such acts.

Might rumination and the unwillingness to forget the injustices of a genocide serve a similar function? Might it help in establishing a taboo against harming helpless people? Milgram points out that "Of all moral principles, the one that comes closest to being universally accepted is this: one should not inflict suffering on a helpless person who is neither harmful nor threatening to oneself" (Milgram, 1974, p. 13). Still, as Milgram's experiments show, people will inflict suffering on a helpless person depending on the context.

In growing up, most of us have learned to suppress actions that go against social expectations. But the culture has failed in teaching us internal controls on destructive actions stemming from social obligations, group values, or familial legacies. Establishing a taboo against genocidal acts might help in teaching us internal controls in carrying out deliberate and systematic aggressive actions against other ethnic groups. It might create a sense of utter repugnance similar to our sense about incest and cannibalism. And this sense of repugnance could serve as an inner control.

With terrorism, continued conflict in the Middle East, and upheaval in almost every pocket of the globe, the issue of planned massacres in the name of social obligations or group values or familial legacies has taken on a new urgency, as has the need for controls against carrying out such massacres. As the social psychologist Myers notes, because of our social identifications, we conform to our group norms. We sacrifice ourselves for family, nation, religion. "We dislike outgroups. The more important our social identity and the more strongly attached we feel to a group, the more we react prejudicially to threats from another group" (Myers, 2002, p. 348).

Paradoxically, as pointed out in a document by the Pontifical Council for Justice and Peace (2002, p. 1), although globalization is growing, and countries, economies, and cultures are drawing closer together and becoming more universal and blended, ethnic violence is increasing. The violence has escalated to such a degree that, at times, barbarous acts are committed against ethnic groups. So, perhaps, establishing a taboo that prohibits genocidal acts could work toward creating a more fraternal society.

Memorializing the Holocaust is essential because later generations will find evidence of the genocidal acts inflicted on helpless people. This, in turn, may help to develop a repugnance for undeserved suffering. And it may help to elevate the plight of genocidal victims into the world's consciousness. As Holocaust survivors die, it becomes increasingly important for their testimonies to be preserved for future generations. There are many who still deny the Holocaust and many who want to try to draw discussion of the Holocaust to a conclusion. There is a generational shift within Germany toward a society with no experience in the war. As the decades go by, the injustices of the Holocaust appear to recede more and more into the past.

Memorials, memoir projects, Spielberg's Survivors of the Shoah Visual History Foundation, which has videotaped 50,000 interviews since 1994, and Fortunoff Video Archives for Holocaust Testimonies at Yale University, among other projects, are all important for memorializing the past. Similarly, Germany's memorials, war museums, and the planned Holocaust Memorial in Berlin and also the Holocaust Museum in Washington are all important for enhancing awareness and for drawing attention to the atrocities of calculated genocide.

Yet, there is one caveat. In memorializing the past, there is the tendency to overestimate a groups' unanimity. As Niven points out, this may happen because historical museums and memorials "distort . . . history to make it appear better than it really was, or play down the negative episodes" (Niven, 2002, p. 202). And from a psychological viewpoint, this may happen because of a group-serving bias. In other words, we grant members of our own group the benefit of the doubt. But when explaining acts by members of other groups, we assume the worst: "Germans were evil anti-Semites." Positive behavior by outgroups members is often dismissed. It may be seen as a "special case." For example, "Pastor Seebasz and his daughter were good, kind and selfless—not at all like other ordinary Germans." This group-serving bias, in turn, can color the way we memorialize past wrongs.

Fifty years of research in prejudice teaches us it can be dangerous to categorize an entire group's actions and attitudes. It can lead to more anger and resentment. Some of today's Germans feel a blanket moral condemnation of all Germans is unfair. Certainly, Pastor Seebasz and his family bear no historical guilt for the atrocities. Thus, they may resent, as many other Germans do, being categorized as evil anti-Semites. Some of today's Germans feel that the memorials ". . . represent the institutionalization of negative moral emotion and the raising of historical guilt to a state creed, forever blocking attempts by Germans to derive strength and orientation from a history that had more to it than National Socialism" (Niven, 2002, p. 194). If our goal, therefore, is to engage people in reflecting and contemplating the past crimes it is important to establish ". . . the most appropriate form of bridge between past [injustice] and present reflection" (Niven, 2002, p. 197).

The descendants of those who suffered injustices tend to perpetuate categorizing an entire group's actions and attitudes, the data from the conference suggested. The danger is that overestimating a group's unanimity may contribute to the escalatory dynamic of conflict interactions. The daughter of a survivor who insists that her parents' past suffering entitles her to hate all Germans and who feels all Germans are indebted to her, can it must be understood, encourage an unpleasant response. The child of a German soldier, for example, may realize that the daughter of the survivor hates him or her as a representative of the "German people," and the German child resents this, and resents "them—the Jews." And then comes the clincher. Does this spark anti-Semitism? "That question can be read either way: as a projection of resentment ('anti-Semitism is caused by Jews') . . . or as an honest diagnosis" (Joffe, 1988, pp. 226–227). Either way, it is reasonable to argue, based on years of research in prejudice, that collective accusations strike a nerve that contributes to negative relations.

Initially, the relations between Nazis' children and survivors' children in the conference were based on the assumption that the Nazis' children had a moral debt to the survivors' children. Survivors' children expressed directly a feeling of being owed something in return for the injustices their families suffered. Sitting face to face with people they considered to be on the opposite side of the victimizing barricade provoked deep emotional reactions. There were moments when survivors' children accused—indeed in some ways attacked—the Nazis' children sitting opposite them. It was hard for survivors' children to control their negative emotional reactions, the data suggested.

Ulysses chained himself to the ship's mast before coming within earshot of the Sirens. "He did so not because he feared the Sirens per se, but because he feared his own reaction to their singing. In effect, he took a precaution against himself, because he knew . . . what he would be likely to do if he heard the Sirens" (Dawes, 1988, p. 142). Since this was the first time survivors' children and Nazis' children were meeting each other, unlike Ulysess, they did not know what they would likely do in reaction to sitting face to face with people they considered "the enemy."

The good news is a cessation of reproaches and accusations occurred when some survivors' children and Nazis' children discussed their own hurts. The act of entering into and sharing their own hurts and feelings and being sensitive to and affected by the other's emotions, experiences, and especially sorrows produced a shift in their interactions. As they talked about their own hurts, rather than their parents' hurts and histories, they showed compassion for the other and, by that, restored equal moral relations.

An important implication of this finding is that compassion can lead to changes at the level of individuals—in the form of experiencing transformations in their feelings and categorizations. Compassion can inhibit negative feelings like resentment and transform the categorizations left by the inheritance of one's past. Instead of judging a whole people, one is more likely to see diversity. These individual transformations can then become vehicles for changes at the interpersonal level.

When some survivors' children gave up the unqualified right to the moral condemnation of all Germans and acknowledged that the Nazis' children at the conference could not be made guilty for the Holocaust, then normal dialogue was possible, and Nazis' children resentments deriving from being incorrectly categorized overcome. Instead of looking back with anger, resentment, and shame, some survivors' children and Nazis' children shifted toward looking forward in moral determination to prevent future genocide. In the relations between survivors' children and Nazis' children, then, a new interaction was visible. In essence, they created a legacy of responsibility for the future (Weissmark et al., 1993).

There is no simple remedy for preventing future genocides. But, we can anticipate techniques for creating a more fraternal society. In an essay, titled "Compassion," Lawrence Blum tells us that: "Characteristically . . . compassion requires the disposition to perform beneficent actions, and to perform them because the person has had a certain sort of imaginative reconstruction of someone's condition and has a concern for his good. The steps that the person takes to ameliorate the condition are guided by and prompted by that imaginative reconstruction and concern" (Blum, 1980, p. 513).

Blum points out, however, that while compassion typically prompts kindly action or a search for ways of helping where none was evident before, it also often prompts precipitous action, or makes more difficult the sort of cold, professional behavior that may be necessary. Blum points out that compassion can also be "misguided grounded in a superficial understanding of the situation" (cited in Solomon, 1990, p. 235).

But this limitation does not give too much to the cynical critics, writes Solomon (1990). "The limitations of compassion hardly undermine its virtue or the overall utility of compassionate actions. Blum rightly concludes that 'because compassion involves an active and objective interest in another's welfare, it is characteristically a spur to deeper understanding than rationality alone could ensure. A person who is compassionate by character is in principle committed to as rational and as intelligent course of action as possible.' Compassion without intelligence is no virtue, and intelligence without compassion is not justice. . . . The significance of compassion is that it forms the core of our sense of justice and provides rationality with a heart" (Solomon, 1990, p. 235).

As mentioned earlier, most of the people in Milgram's study obeyed the experimenter and continued to the highest shock level on the generator. But a few refused and took the critical step of disobeying the authority. Interestingly, if we examine the transcript closely, we can see that those who disobeyed did so out of compassion and concern for the victim's good. Here is an example of one such woman who defied the experimenter's orders to shock the learner:

She was medical technician who worked at Yale University Medical School. She had emigrated from Germany five years before and spoke with a thick German accent (Milgram, 1974, p. 85). She told the experimenter firmly but politely that she would not continue to shock the learner.

EXPERIMENTER: The experiment requires that you go on until he learned all the words correctly.

GRETCHEN: He has a heart condition, I'm sorry. He told you before.

EXPERIMENTER: The shocks may be painful but they are not dangerous.

GRETCHEN: Well, I'm sorry, I think when shocks continues like this, they are dangerous. You ask him if he wants to get out. It's his free will.

EXPERIMENTER: It is absolutely essential that we continue . . . .

GRETCHEN: I like you to ask him. We came here of our free will. If he wants to continue I'll go ahead. He told you he had a heart condition. I'm sorry, I don't want to be responsible for anything happening to him. I wouldn't like it for me either.

EXPERIMENTER: You have no other choice.

GRETCHEN: I think we here are on our own free will. I don't want to be responsible if he has a heart condition if anything happens to him. Please understand that.

The woman refuses to go further and the experiment is stopped. Ironically, the woman grew up in Hitler's Germany. When asked about the possible effect of her background, she said, "Perhaps we have seen too much pain." Milgram writes, "The woman's straightforward, courteous behavior in the experiment, . . . and total control of her own actions seems to make disobedience a simple and rational deed. Her behavior is the very embodiment of what I had initially envisioned would be true for all subjects" (Milgram, 1974, p. 85).

Several months before her death, someone from the Shoah Foundation asked my mother, "What would you like to tell the world about the pain you suffered in Auschwitz?" My mother paused for a moment and then said: "I want the world to know that no one ever again should suffer as I did."

My mother's answer surprised me. I knew she harbored hatred. It was the cocoon that nurtured her. And she never flew free of it. The pain on her face was always palpable. She lived with the ghosts of the Holocaust every day. Still, despite her pain, or maybe because of it, she focused on her desire to ameliorate other's sufferings. It was her final statement about Auschwitz. And it was an act of compassion.

Growing up, I often wondered about the meaning of my parents' sufferings. Like one might wonder about the meaning of life, I asked my mother once, "Mommy, do you think your sufferings had any special meaning?" "Do I think my sufferings had any special meaning?" my mother repeated. "Your question is, maybe, did it teach me something? You should read Viktor Frankl's story about Yehuda Bacon, an Israeli sculptor who was in Auschwitz when he was a young boy. He explains it better than I can."

So, I read the story. And this is what it said: "As a boy I thought: 'I will tell them what I saw, in the hope that people will change for the better.' But people didn't change and didn't even want to know. It was much later that I really understood the meaning of suffering. It can have a meaning if it changes oneself for the better" (cited in Frankl, 1978, p. 43). I've carried this lesson with me. And later I learned that suffering can have meaning if it changes not only one's self for the better, but also if it changes the relations between future generations for the better.

Pastor Seebasz's daughter's name was Ricarda, I discovered not long ago. She was about nineteen when she sacrificed her life to save my father's. She, who was not a survivor, had died of the survivors' illness. I'd like to take my five-year-old daughter Brittany to visit Ricarda's family. So that from the bottom of our hearts we can say, thank you. Resentment against all Germans belonged to my generation; maybe gratitude toward some Germans can belong to my daughter's.

Varying somewhat a tale of Yen Mah's, I conclude the book with a story called "The Incurable Wound."

A long time ago, there lived a child who was a good artist. After her mother died, her father remarried. Her stepmother showed preference toward her own children, and maltreated the child. The child was not allowed to play and so spent her time painting. Her pictures became famous and were sold for much money. Her stepmother now grew jealous. One night, she crept up to the child's bed and stuck a dirty nail into the child's hand, spreading feces on the nail to cause an infection.

In a few days, the child's hand became red and swollen. Though the nail was removed, pus poured from the wound. However, the child continued to paint.

Now a strange thing happened. The wound never healed, but the child's paintings became better and better. The more the pus exuded, the greater the beauty of her work. The pain in her hand seemed to imbue the child with an essence of invincibility, enabling her to prevail in every battle, overcome each adversity (Yen Mah, 1997, p. 273).

If readers examine their own lives at this point, I suspect the majority will find in their own experiences instances of unjust treatment that hurt them in deep ways. The story shows us that we can choose to respond to unjust treatment with anger, resentment, and bitterness or with the strength to come to terms with the pain. My effort to explore the relationship between Nazis' children and survivors' children was motivated by the belief that strength is achievable. The message of this book is sometimes we must use that strength to transcend our personal hurts in order to apprehend other people and their hurts. It offers the possibility of a future free from the damaging legacy of the past. This book is, I hope, evidence of that possibility.

# REFERENCES

Ainsworth, M. D. (1989). Attachment beyond infancy. *American Psychologist, 44*, 709–716.

Anderson, C. A. (1982). Inoculation and counter-explanation. Debiasing techniques in the perseverance of social theories. *Social Cognition, 1*, 126–139.

Anderson, C. A., Lepper, M. R., & Ross, L. (1980). Perseverance of social theories: The role of explanation in the persistence of discredited information. *Journal of Personality and Social Psychology, 39*, 1037–1049.

Anderson, C. A., & Sechler, E. S. (1986). Effects of explanations and counter-explanation on the development and use of social theories. *Journal of Personality and Social Psychology, 50*, 24–34.

Arendt, H. (1964). *A report on the banality of evil. Eichmann in Jerusalem.* New York: Penguin.

Arendt, H. (1978). *The Jew as pariah: Jewish identity and politics in the modern age.* (R. Feldman, Ed.). New York: Grove Press.

Aristotle. (1955). *The niomachean ethics* (J. A. K. Thomson, Trans.). Baltimore: Penguin Books.

Ashton, M. C., Paunonen, S. V., Helmes, E., & Jackson, D. N. (1998). Kin altruism, reciprocal altruism, and the Big Five personality factors. *Evolution and Human Behavior, 19*, 243–255.

Baranosky, A., Young, M., Douglas-Johnson, S., Keeler-Williams, L., & McCarrey, M. (1998). PTSD Transmission: A review of secondary traumatization in Holocaust survivor families. *Canadian Psychology, 39*, 247–256.

Barash, D. P. (1977). *Sociobiology and behavior.* New York: Elsevier.

Barocas, H. & Barocas, C. (1983). Wounds of the fathers: The next generation of Holocaust victims. *International Review of Psychoanalysis, 5*, 331–341.

Bar-On, D. (1989). *Legacy of silence: Encounters with children of the Third Reich.* Cambridge, MA: Harvard University Press.

Baumeister, R. & Leary, M. (1995). The need to belong: Desire for interpersonal attachments as fundamental human motivation. *Psychological Bulletin*, Vol. 117, No 3, 497–529.

Bettelheim, B. (1980). *Surviving and other essays*. New York: Vintage Books.

Bies, R. J. & Moag, J. S., (1986). Interactional justice: Communication criteria for fairness. In B. Sheppard (Ed.), *Research on Negotiation in Organizations* (pp. 43–55). Greenwich, CT: JAI Press.

Blass, T. (Ed.). (2000). *Obedience to authority: Current perspectives on the Milgram Paradigm*. Mahway, NJ: Lawrence Erlbaum.

Blum, L. (1980). Compassion. In A. Rorty (Ed.), *Explaining Emotions* (pp. 505–517). Los Angeles: University of California Press.

Blumenfeld, L. (2002a). *Revenge: A Story of Hope*. New York: Simon & Schuster.

Blumenfeld, L. (2002b, March 4). The apology: Letters from a terrorist. *The New Yorker*.

Bondy, R. (1981). *Elder of the Jews: Jakob Edelstein of Theresienstadt* (E. Abel, Trans.). New York: Grove Press.

Brewer, M. B. (1988). A dual process model of impression formation. In T. Srull & R. Wyer (Eds.), *Advances in social cognition*, Vol 1. Hillsdale, NJ: Erlbaum. (p. 368).

Buss, D. M. (1991). Evolutionary personaility psychology. *Annual Review of Psychology, 42*, 459–491.

Cohen, R. (2000). *The avengers: A Jewish war story*. New York: Vintage Books.

Cropanzo, R. & Greenberg, J. (1997). Progress on organizational justice: Tunneling through the maze. In C. L. Cooper (Ed.), *International Review of Industrial and Organizational Psychology* (pp. 317–372). New York: Wiley & Sons.

Danieli, Y. (1985). The treatment and prevention of long term effects and intergenerational transmition of victimization: A lesson from holocaust survivors and their children. In C. F. Figley (Ed.), *Trauma and its wake* (pp. 295–313). New York: Brunner Mazel.

Darby, B. W. & Schlenker, B. R. (1982). Children's reactions to apologies. *Journal of Personality and Social Psychology, 43*, 742–753.

Dashberg, H. (1987). Psychological distress of Holocaust survivors and offspring in Israel, forty years later: A review. *Israel Journal of Psychiatry and Related Science, 24*, 243–256.

Davies, M. E. (1997). Belief persistence after evidential discrediting: The impact of generated versus provided explanations on the likelihood of discredited outcomes. *Journal of Experimental Social Psychology, 33*, 561–578.

Dawes, R. (1988). *Rational choice in an uncertain world*. New York: Harcourt Brace Jovanovich.

De Waal, F. (1989). *Peacemaking among primates*. Cambridge, MA: Harvard University Press.

De Waal, F. (1996). *Good natured: The origins of right and wrong in humans and other animals*. Cambridge, MA: Harvard University Press.

Dershowitz, A. (2000). *The genesis of justice.* New York: Warner Books, Inc.

Dicks, H. V. (1972). *Licensed mass murder: A socio-psychological study of some S.S. killers.* New York: Basic Books.

Edwards, E. & Smith, E. E. (1996). A disconfirmation bias in the evaluation of arguments. *Journal of Personality and Social Psychology, 71,* 5–24.

Erikson, E. (1968). *Identity: Youth and crisis.* New York: W.W. Norton & Company.

Esses, V. M., Haddock, G., & Zanna, M. P. (1993). Values, sterotypes, and emotions as determinants of intergroup attitudes. In D. Mackie & D. Hamilton (Eds.), *Affect, cognition and sterotyping: Interactive processes in intergroup perception.* San Diego, CA: Academic Press.

Figley, C. (Ed.). (1985). *Trauma and its wake: The study and treatment of post-traumatic stress disorder.* New York: Brunner Mazel.

Finkelstein, N. (2000). *The Holocaust industry: Reflections on the exploitation of Jewish suffering.* New York: Verso.

Fogelman, E. (1984). (Writer and coproducer). Breaking the silence: The generation after the Holocaust. New York: Public Broadcasting Service.

Frankl, V. (1963). *Man's search for meaning: An introduction to logotherapy.* New York: Pocket Books.

Frankl, V. (1978). *The unheard cry for meaning: Psychotherapy and humanism.* New York: Pocket Books.

Freud, S. (1939). *Moses and monotheism* (K. Jones, Trans.). New York: Vintage Books.

Freud, S. (1950). Totem and taboo (J. Strachey, Trans.). New York: W.W. Norton.

Freud, S. (1961). *The future of an illusion* (J. Strachey, Trans.). New York: W.W. Norton.

Fromm, E. (1941). *Escape from freedom.* New York: Avon Books.

Fryberg, J. (1980).[67] Difficulties in separation-individuation as experienced by offspring of Nazi Holocaust survivors. *American Journal of Orthopsychiatry, 50,* 87–95.

Gaertner, S. L., Dovidio, J. F., Rus, M. C., Nier, J. A., Banker, B. S., Ward, C. M., Mottola, G. R., & Houlette, M. (1999). Reducing intergroup bias: Elements of intergroup cooperation. *Journal of Personality and Social Psychology, 76,* 388–402.

Giacomo, D. & Weissmark, M. (1986). Systemic practice. *Family Process, 25,* 483–512.

Giacomo, D. & Weissmark, M. (1987). A generative theory of the therapeutic field. *Family Process, 26,* 437–459.

Giacomo, D. & Weissmark, M. (1992a). How psychotherapy works. *The Psychiatric Times, 10,* 27–28.

Giacomo, D. & Weissmark, M. (1992b). Mechanisms of action in psychotherapy. *Journal of Psychotherapy Practice and Research, 1,* 37–48.

Goldhagen, D. J. (1997). *Hitler's willing executioners: Ordinary Germans and the Holocaust.* New York: Vintage Books.

Gottman, J., & Bakeman, R. (1979). The sequential analysis of observational data. In M. Lamb, S. Soumi, & G. Stephenson (Eds.), *Social interaction methodology.* Madison: University of Wisconsin.

Gottman, J., Notarius, C., Markman, H. Bank, S., Yoppi, B., & Rubin, M. E. (1976). Behavior exchange theory and marital decision making. *Journal of Personality and Social Psychology, 34,* 14–23.

Gove, P. (Ed.). (1981). *Webster's third new international dictionary of the English language unabridged.* Springfield, MA: G. & C. Merriam Co.

Grimsely, R. (1967). Jean-Jacques Rousseau. In *The encyclopedia of philosophy* (Vol. 7, pp. 218–225). New York: Macmillan Publishing Co., Inc., & The Free Press.

Hampshire, S. (2000). *Justice is conflict.* Princeton ,NJ: Princeton University Press.

Heider, F. (1958). *The psychology of interpersonal relations.* New York: Wiley.

Helmreich, W. (1992). *Against all odds.* New York: Simon & Schuster.

Heradstveit, D. (1979). The Arab-Israeli conflict: Psychological obstacles to peace (Vol. 28, p. 528). Oslo, Norway: Universitetsforlaget. Distributed by Columbia University Press. Reviewed by R. K. White, *Contemporary Psychology,* 1980, *25,* 11–12.

Hewstone, M. (1994). Revision and change of sterotypic beliefs: In search of the elusive subtyping model. In S. Stroebe & M. Hewstone (Eds.), *European review of social psychology* (Vol. 5, p. 368). Chichester, England: Wiley.

Hilberg, R. (1985). *The destruction of European Jews.* New York: Holmes and Meier.

Hilberg, R. (1993). *Perpetrators, victims, Bystanders: The Jewish catastrophe 1933–1945.* New York: HarperPerennial

Hirt, E. & Markman, K. (1995). Multiple explantion: A consider-an-alternative strategy for debiasing judgments. *Journal of Personality and Social Psychology,* 69, 1069–1086.

Hoess, Rudolf, (1959). *Commandant of Auschwitz. The autobiography of Rudolf Hoess* (G. Weidenfeld, Trans.). London: Weidenfeld & Nicolson.

Hogg, M. A. & Williams, K. D. (2000). From I to we: Social identity and the collective self. *Group Dynamics, 4,* 81–97.

Hundley, T. (2002, June 25). Some Germans clamor for recognition as victims. *Chicago Tribune,* p. 6.

Hunter, J. A., Stringer, M. & Watson, R. P. (1991). Intergroup violence and intergroup attributions. *British Journal of Social Psychology, 30,* 261–266.

Jacoby, S. (1983). *Wild justice.* New York: Harper & Row.

Joffe, J. (1998). "The killers were ordinary Germans, ergo the ordinary Germans were killers": The logic, the language, and the meaning of a book that conquered Germany (J. Riemer, Trans.). In Shandley, R. (Ed.), *UnWilling Germans:*

References 185

*The Goldhagen Debate* (pp. 217–227). Minneapolis: University of Minnesota Press.

Kagan, J. & Segal, J. (1968). *Psychology: An introduction* (6th ed.). Orlando, FL: Harcourt Brace Jovanovich.

Kagan, J. (1989). *Unstable ideas: Temperament, cognition and self.* Cambridge, MA: Harvard University Press.

Kaslow, F. W. (1997). A dialogue between descendants of Holocaust perpetrators and victims—session two. *Israeli Journal of Psychiatry, 34,* 44–54.

Katsenelinboigen, A. (1984). *Some new trends in systems theory.* Seaside, CA: Intersystems Publications.

Katz, J., Street, A., & Arias, I. (1997). Individual differences in self-appraisals and responses to dating violence scenarios. *Violence and Victims, 12*(3), 265–276.

Kelly, G. (1969). The language of hypothesis: Man's psychological instrument. In B. Maher (Ed.), *Clinical psychology and personalty: The selected papers of George Kelly* (pp. 147–162). New York: Wiley.

Kelman, H. & Hamilton, V. (1989). *Crimes of obedience.* New Haven, CT: Yale University Press.

Kershaw, I. (2000). *The Nazi Dictatorship: Problems & Perspectives of interpretation.* (4th. ed.). London: Arnold & copublished by Oxford University Press, Inc., New York

Kuhn, D. & Lao, J. (1996). Effects of evidence on attitudes: Is polarization the norm? *Psychological Science, 7,* 115–120.

Kunda, Z., & Oleson, K. C. (1995). Maintaining sterotypes in the face of disconfirmation: Constructing grounds for subtyping deviants. *Journal of Personality and Social Psychology, 68,* 565–579.

Krell, R. & Sherman, M. I. (1997). *Medical and psycholgocial effects of concentration camps on Holocaust survivors.* New Brunswick, NJ: Transaction.

Lama, D. (1999). *Ethics for the new millennium.* New York: Riverhead Books.

Lama, D. (2000). *The Dalai Lama's book of transformation.* London: Thorsons.

Lama, D. (2002). Understanding our fundamental nature. In R. Davidson & A. Harrignton (Eds.), *Visions of compassion* (pp. 66–80). New York: Oxford University Press.

Lebert, N. & Lebert, S. (2001). *My father's keeper: Children of Nazi leaders—An intimate history of damage and denial* (J. Evans, Trans.). London: Little, Brown & Co.

Levi, P. (1961). *Survival in Auschwitz.* (S. Woolf, Trans.) New York: MacMillian (original published in 1959).

Lifton, R. (1986). *The Nazi doctors: Medical killing and the psychology of genocide.* New York: Basic Books.

Lord, C. G., Lepper, M. R., & Preston, E. (1984). Considering the opposite: A corrective strategy for social judgment. *Journal of Personality and Social Psychology, 47,* 1231–1243.

Lord, C. G., Ross, L., & Lepper, M. (1979). Biased assimilation and attitude polarization: The effects of prior theories on subsequently considered evidence. *Journal of Personality and Social Psychology, 37,* 2098–2109.

Lupfer, M. B., Weeks, K. P., Doan, K. A., Houston, D. A. (2000). Folk conceptions of fairness and unfairness. *European Journal of Social Psychology, 30,* 399–346.

Maher, B. (2003). Psychopathology and delusions: Reflections on methods and models. In M. Lenzenweger & J. Hooley (Eds.), Principles of experimental psychopathology: Esssays in honor of Brendan A. Maher (pp. 9–28). Washington, DC: American Psychological Associaton.

Maier, C. (1988). *The unmasterable past: History, Holocaust, and German national identity.* Cambridge, MA: Harvard University Press.

Malkin, P. (1990). Eichmann in my hands. New York: Warner Books.

McCullough, M. (2000). Forgiveness as human strength: Theory, measurement, and links to well-being. *Journal of Social and Clinical Psychology, 1,* 43–55.

McCullough, M. (2001). Forgiving. In C. R. Synder (Ed.), *Coping with stress: Effective people and processes* (pp. 93–113). New York: Oxford University Press.

McCullough, M., Bellah, G., Kilpatrick, S., & Johnson, J. (2001). Vengefulness: Relationships with forgiveness, rumination, well-being, and the big five. *Personality and Social Psychology Bulletin, 27,* 601–610.

McCullough, M., Worthington, E., & Rachal, K. (1997). Interpersonal forgiving in close relationships. *Journal of Personality and Social Psychology, 73,* 321–336.

McDonough, F. (2001). *Opposition and resistance in Nazi Germany.* Cambridge: Cambridge University Press.

Mikula, G. (1986). The experience of injustice: Toward a better understanding of its phenomenology. In H. W. Bierhoff, R. L. Cohen, J. Greenberg (Eds.), *Justice in Social Relations* (pp. 103–24). New York: Plenum.

Mikula, G., Scherer, K. R., Athenstaedt, V. (1998). The role of injustice in the elicitation of different emotional reactions. *Personality Social Psychology Bulletin, 24,* 769 783.

Milgram, S. (1974). *Obedience to authority: An experimental view.* New York: Harper & Row.

Miller, D. (2001). Disrespect and the experience of injustice. *Annual Review of Psychology, 52,* 527–553.

Miller, W. I. (1993). *Humiliation and other essays on honor, social discomfort, and violence.* Ithaca, NY: Cornell University Press.

Minlow, M. (1998). *Between vengeance and forgiveness.* Boston: Beacon Press.

Mitscherlich, A. & Mitscherlich, M. (1975). *The inability to mourn.* New York: Grove Press.

Munro, G. D. & Ditto, P. H. (1997). Biased assimilation, attitude polarization, and affect in reactions to sterotype-relevant scientific information. *Personality and Social Psychology Bulletin, 23,* 636–653.

Murphy, J. & Hampton, J. (1988). *Forgiveness and mercy.* Cambridge: Cambridge University Press.

Myers, D. (2002). *Social Psychology* (7th ed.). New York: McGraw Hill.

Nadler, A., Kav-Venaki, S., & Gleitman, B. (1985). Transgenerational effects of Holocaust: Externalization of aggression in second-generation Holocaust survivors. *Journal of Consulting and Clinical Psychology, 53,* 365–369.

Niven, B. (2002). *Facing the Nazi past. United Germany and the legacy of the Third Reich.* London: Routledge.

Novick, P. (1999). *The Holocaust in American life.* Boston: Houghton Mifflin.

Nussbaum, M. (2001). *Upheavals of thought: The intelligence of emotions.* Cambridge: Cambridge University Press.

Ohbuchi, K., Kameda, M., & Agarie, N. (1989). Apology as aggression control: Its role in mediating appraisal of and response to harm. *Journal of Personality and Social Psychology, 56,* 219–227.

Panskepp, J., Siviy, S. M., & Normansell, A. L. (1985). Brain, opioids, and social emotions. In M. Reite and T. Field (Eds.), *The psychobiology of attachment and separation* (pp. 3–49). New York: Academic Press.

Piaget, J. (1952). *The origins of intelligence in children.* New York: International University Press.

Piaget, J. (1971). *Biology and knowledge: An essay on the relations between organic regulations and cognitive processes.* Chicago: University of Chicago Press.

Plato. (1980). *Laws* (L. Thomson, Trans.). New York: Basic Books.

Podietz, L., Zwerling, I., Fisher, I., Belmont, H., Eisenstein, I., Shapiro, M., & Levick, M. (1984). Engagement in families of Holocaust survivors. *Journal of Marital & Family Therapy, 10,* 43–51.

Pontifical Council for Justice and Peace. (2002). *Contribution to world conference against racism, racial discrimination, xenophobia and related intolerance* [on line], www.vatican.va/roman_curia/pontifical_councils/justpeace/documents

Posner, G. (1991). *Hitler's children.* New York: Random House.

Rakoff, V. (1966). A long-term effect of the concnetration camp experience. *Viewpoints, 1,* 17–20.

Rakoff, V., Sigal, J. J., Epstein, N. (1976). Children and families of concentration camp survivors. *Canada's Mental Health, 14,* 24–26.

Rawls, J. (1971). *A theory of justice.* Cambridge, MA: Harvard University Press.

Robinson, J, (1965). *And the crooked shall be made straight. The Eichmann trial, the Jewish catastrophe, and Hannah Arendt's narrative.* New York: The Macmillan Company.

Rosenman, S. (1984). Out of the Holocaust: Children as scarred souls and tempered redeemers. *Journal of Psychohistory, 11,* 556–567.

Rosenthal, R. & Rosnow, R. (1991). *Essentials of behavioral research: Methods and data analysis* (2nd ed.). MA: McGraw Hill.

Rouhana, N. N. & Bar-Tal, D. (1998). Psychological dynamics of intractable ethnonational conflicts: The Israeli-Palestinian Case. *American Psychologist, 53*, 761–770.

Rowland-Klein, D. & Dunlop, R. (1998). The transmission of trauma across generations: Identification with parental trauma in children of Holocaust survivors. *Australian & New Zealand Journal of Psychiatry, 32*(3), 358–369.

Ryan, A. (1984). *Quiet neighbors prosecuting Nazi war criminals in America.* San Diego, CA: Harcourt, Brace, Jovanovich.

Schindehette, S. & Seaman, D. (2002, April 15). Settling the score. *People.*

Schirovsky, P. (1988). *Born guilty: Children of Nazi families.* New York: Basic Books.

Schopenhauer, A. (1995). *On the basis of morality* (E. J. Payne, Trans.). Oxford: Bergham Books.

Segev, T. (2000). *The seventh million: The Israelis and the Holocaust* (H. Watzman, Trans.). New York: Henry Holt.

Shklar, J. (1990). *The faces of injustice.* New Haven, CT: Yale University.

Sigal, J., Silver, D., Rakoff, V., & Ellin, B. (1973). Some second generation effects of survival of the Nazi persecution. *American Journal of Orthopsychiatry, 43*, 320-327.

Sigal, J. J., Weinfeld, G. (1985). Control of agression in adult children of survivors of the Nazi persecution. *Journal of Abnormal Psychology, 94*, 556–564.

Skarlicki, D. P. & Folger, R. (1997). Retaliation for perceived unfair treatment: Examining the roles of procedural and interactional justice. *Journal of Applied Psychology. 82*, 434–443.

Solomon, R. (1990). *A passion for justice: Emotions and the origins of the social contract.* Reading, MA: Addison-Wesley.

Smith, H. J. & Tyler, T. R. (1997). Choosing the right pond. The impact of group membership on self-esteem and group-oriented behavior. *Journal of Experimental Social Psychology, 33*, 146–170.

Staub, E. (2002). Emergency helping, genocidal vioence, and the evolution of responsibility and alrtusim in children. In R. Davidson & A. Harrignton (Eds.), *Visions of compassion* (pp. 165–181). New York: Oxford University Press.

Steiner, J. (1980). The SS yesterday and today: A sociopsychological view. In J. Himsdale (Ed.), *Survivors, victims, and perpetrators: Essays on the Nazi Holocaust* (pp. 405–445). Washington: Hemisphere Publishing Co.

Steinhoff, J., Pechel, P., Showalter, D. (1994). *Voices from the Third Reich: An oral history.* New York: Da Capo Press.

Stierlin, H. (1981). The parents Nazi past and the dialogue between the generations. *Family Process, 20*, 379–390.

Stroessner, S. J. & Mackie, D. M. (1993). Affect and perceived group variability: Implications for sterotyping and prejudice. In D. M. Mackie & D. L. Hamilton (Eds), *Affect, cognition, and sterotyping: Interactive processes in group perception.* San Diego, CA: Academic Press.

Taylor, S. E. (1981). A categorization approach to sterotyping. In D. L. Hamilton (Ed.), *Cognitive processes in sterotyping and integroup behavior.* Hilsdale, NJ: Erlbaum.

Trossman, B. (1968). Adolescent children of concentration camp survivors. *Canadian Psychiatric Association Journal, 13*, 121–123.

Turner, J. C. (1981). The experimental social psychology of intergroup behavior. In J. Turner & H Giles (Eds.), *Intergroup behavior* (p. 346). Oxford, England: Blackwell.

Turner, J. C. (1987). *Rediscovering the social group. A self-categorization theory* (pp. 282, 346). New York: Basil Blackwell.

Turner, J. C. & Onorato, R. S. (1999). Social identity, personality, and the self-concept. A self-categorizing perspective. In T. R. Tyler, R. M. Kramer, and O. P. John (Eds.), *The psychology of the social self* (p. 346). Mahwah, NJ: Erlbaum.

Vallone, R. P., Ross, L., & Lepper, M. R. (1985). The hostile media phenomenon: Biased perception and perceptions of media bias in coverage of the "Beirut Massacre." *Journal of Personality and Social Psychology, 49*, 5/7- 585.

Waldman, P. (2001). Revenge without rules: On the Renaissance of an archaic motif of violence. *Studies in Conflict & Terrorism, 24*, 435–450.

Weiner, B. (1993). On sin versus sickness: A theory of perceived responsibility and social motivation. *American Psychologist, 48*(9), 957–966.

Weiss, M. & Weiss, S. (2000). Second generation to Holocaust survivors: Enhanced differentiation of trauma transmission. *American Journal of Psychotherapy, 54*(3) 372–385.

Weissmark, M. (1993, March). Interactions between children of survivors and children of Nazis. Paper presented at the Harvard Medical School Research Symposium, Cambridge, MA.

Weissmark, M. (1993, October). The analysis of group interaction between children of Holocaust survivors and children of perpetrators. Paper presented at Harvard University, the Department of Psychology, Cambridge, MA.

Weissmark, M. (1995, November). Proposal for an Institute for Social Justice [on line], www.weissmark.com/memorandium.html

Weissmark, M. (2000, October). Intergroup Relations between Descendants of Victims and Victimizers. Paper presented at the Association of American Colleges and Universities, Diversity and Learning: Identity, Community and Intellectual Development Conference.

Weissmark, M., & Giacomo, D. (1994). A therapeutic index: Measuring therapeutic actions in psychotherapy. *Journal of Consulting and Clinical Psychology, 62*(2), 315–323.

Weissmark, M., & Giacomo, D. (1995). Measuring therapeutic interactions: Clinical and research applications. *Psychiatry: Interpersonal and Biological Processes, 58,* 173–188.

Weissmark, M. & Giacomo, D. (1998). *Doing Psychotherapy Effectively.* Chicago: University of Chicago Press.

Weissmark, M., Giacomo, D. & Kuphal, I. (1993). Psychosocial themes in the lives of children of survivors and Nazis. *Journal of Narrative and Life History, 3*(4) 319–335.

Weissmark, M., Giacomo, D., & Ofosu, Yaw. (1996, October). Social injustice: Its aftermath. Paper presented at the Fifth Annual Public Psychiatry Seminar of the University of Chicago, Il.

Wilder, D. A. (1981). Perceiving persons as a group: Effect on attributions of causality and beliefs. *Social Psychology, 41,* 13–23.

Wiesel, E. (1969). (S. Rodway, Trans.). *Night.* New York: Avon.

Worthington, E., Sandage, S., & Berry, J. (2000). Group interventions to promote forgiveness: What researchers and clinicians ought to know. In M. E. McCullough, K. I. Pargament, & C. E. Thresen (Eds.), *Forgiveness: Theory, research, and practice* (pp. 228–253).

Yehuda, R., Bierer, L., Schmeidler, J., Aferiat, D., Breslau, I., & Dolan, S. (2000). Low cortisol and risk for PTSD in adult offspring of Holocaust survivors. *The American Journal of Psychiatry, 157,* 1229–1235.

Yen Mah, A. (1997). *Falling Leaves: The memoir of an unwanted Chinese daughter.* New York: Wiley & Sons.

*Television Broadcasts*

Weissmark, M. (1992, September 13). The past between them. In C. Lewis (Executive Producer), Sunday morning news with Charles Kuralt. New York: CBS. A 20-minute progam about the meeting I organized at Harvard University for the descendants of nazis and holocaust survivors.

Weissmark, M. (1993, March 16). Journey to understanding. In Dateline. New York: NBC. A 20-minute program about the meeting I organized in Germany for the descendants of Nazis and holocaust survivors.

Weissmark, M. (1995, June 29). Coming to the table. In D. Puccini (Executive Producer), PBS Channel 11's Image Union, Chicago: WTTW. A 15-minute documentary about the meeting I organized at Roosevelt University for the descendants of slaves and slave-owners.

Weissmark, M., Giacomo, D., Abdi, K., & Nour, N. (1993). Breaking the cycle. A 15-minute documentary video about the meeting I organized at Harvard University for the descendants of Nazis and of Holocaust survivors.

*Newspaper and Magazine Articles*

Interviews with me about my research appeared in:

*Psychology Today*, September–October Issue, 1995
*She Magazine England*, September–October Issue 1995
*The Chicago Tribune* Woman News Section, April 30, 1995
*Chicago Sun Times* Metro Section, May 19, 1995
*The Chicago Tribune* Tempo Section, June 2, 1995
*The New York Times* Connecticut Weekly Section, June 13, 1993
*The Psychiatric Times*, June, 1993
*Frankfurter Allgemeine Zeitung*, March 1, 1993
*MS.*, January–February, 1993
*Harvard University Gazette*, September 4, 1992
*Harvard Magazine*, November–December 1992, Volume 95, Number 21.

# INDEX